CALIFORNIA AND THE NATION
1850-1869

A Da Capo Press Reprint Series

THE AMERICAN SCENE
Comments and Commentators

GENERAL EDITOR: WALLACE D. FARNHAM
University of Illinois

CALIFORNIA AND THE NATION 1850-1869

A STUDY OF THE RELATIONS OF A FRONTIER COMMUNITY WITH THE FEDERAL GOVERNMENT

BY JOSEPH ELLISON

DA CAPO PRESS · NEW YORK · 1969

A Da Capo Press Reprint Edition

This Da Capo Press edition of *California and the Nation, 1850–1869,* is an unabridged republication of the first edition published in Berkeley, California, in 1927, as Volume XVI of the University of California Publications in History.

Library of Congress Catalog Card Number 78-87529

Published by Da Capo Press
A Division of Plenum Publishing Corporation
227 West 17th Street, New York, N.Y. 10011

Manufactured in the United States of America

UNIVERSITY OF CALIFORNIA PUBLICATIONS IN HISTORY

UNIVERSITY OF CALIFORNIA PRESS
BERKELEY, CALIFORNIA

University of California Publications in History
Volume 16, pp. xi + 1–258
Issued April 11, 1927

University of California Press
Berkeley, California

Cambridge University Press
London, England

PRINTED IN THE UNITED STATES OF AMERICA

CALIFORNIA AND THE NATION 1850-1869

A STUDY OF THE RELATIONS OF A FRONTIER COMMUNITY WITH THE FEDERAL GOVERNMENT

BY

JOSEPH ELLISON

UNIVERSITY OF CALIFORNIA PRESS
BERKELEY, CALIFORNIA
1927

TO

PROFESSOR HERBERT EUGENE BOLTON

TEACHER AND FRIEND

CONTENTS

CHAPTER IV

The Mineral Land Question in California

CHAPTER V

The Indian Question

CHAPTER VI

The Civil Fund and the Mint

CHAPTER VII

The Vigilance Committee and Federal Interference

CHAPTER VIII

Means of Communication and Transportation

PART II

CIVIL WAR ISSUES

CHAPTER IX

Sentiment for a Pacific Republic

CHAPTER X

Loyalty and Disloyalty

CHAPTER XI

Attitude of California to the Legal Tender Notes During the Civil War

PREFACE

A large part of the history of a federal country like the United States centers around the relations of the several states of the Union with the national government. Yet books on American history generally deal with either purely national affairs or purely local events. The histories by McMaster, Schouler, Von Holst, and Rhodes, while admirable in many respects, contain very little on the federal relations of a state like California, and, moreover, many of the assertions made are either only partly true or entirely wrong.

Likewise, with our so-called local histories. Much interesting and valuable information is given in the bulky standard histories of California. But these histories are, generally speaking, narratives of local events with descriptions of local personalities, usually of the more picturesque type. The two most voluminous histories of California, by Bancroft and Hittell, devote chapters to such romantic episodes as the Donner party, filibustering expeditions, discovery of gold, and the San Francisco vigilance committees. But there is practically nothing on the less exciting but nevertheless serious controversy between the state and the federal government with regard to the public lands. They devote a number of chapters to the mines and miners but they are practically silent on the very important question of the control and disposition of the mineral lands. The present study is intended to supply such omissions in the field and period chosen. And so far as I know it is practically the first attempt made in this direction.

My thanks are due to Professor Herbert Eugene Bolton, under whose guidance this work was written, for encouragement, advice, and illuminating criticism; and to Professors McCormac, Morris, and Van Nostrand for valuable suggestions.

CHAPTER I

INTRODUCTION: PRE-STATEHOOD PERIOD

American beginnings in California.—Technically California did not become a part of the United States until her formal cession by Mexico in 1848. The act that brought her into relationship with the government of the United States, however, had occurred two years earlier when Commodore Sloat hoisted the stars and stripes in Monterey. But during the years prior to these events, and serving as a prelude to the dramatic incident of July 7, 1846, there had been a gradual penetration of Americans into California, so that the territory, even before 1846, had already become a center of American civilization.

This penetration of the Americans had begun during the Spanish régime, when Yankee traders engaged in illicit commercial dealings with the sparsely settled pastoral communities along the California coast.[1] The traders were followed by the trappers and hunters of the west—the Patties, Jackson, Young, and others—who, in quest of new trapping grounds, blazed the trails of the more important routes over which later came the grand overland march of the American pioneer to the Pacific Coast. The organized overland migration to the Pacific Coast

[1] Trade relations between California and the United States began in 1795, when the first New England fur trading vessel landed at Monterey. After 1800 the New England whaling vessels also began to trade on the California coast. In 1822 the hide and tallow trade was opened up by the "Boston ships." The classic description of the hide trade is Dana's *Two Years Before the Mast.* Dana left Harvard College in 1834, at the age of nineteen, to go on a voyage to California. He stayed in California during 1835 and 1836. In his book, first published in 1840, he gives a vivid description of what he had seen in California. The best secondary authorities for the early interest of Americans in California are Cleland, *The Early Sentiment for the Annexation of California, from 1835 to 1836;* Chapman, *A History of California: The Spanish Period.*

during the forties was not an isolated movement; it was a part of the general westward movement of the American people and was impelled not merely by desire for personal gain or love of adventure but also by the prevailing spirit of national expansion. The American frontiersmen came to California imbued with the idea of "manifest destiny," and with the story of the "Texas game" still ringing in their ears.[2]

The Mexican authorities in vain attempted to stem the tide. The Americans intrenched themselves in local American colonies where they dreamed and talked of the time when California should become a part of the United States. The Bear Flag revolt was the fruition of this long nursed project. But the "California Republic" came to an early end, and California became on July 7, 1846, practically, though not technically, United States territory.

Demand for a territorial government.—The keynote to the period from 1846 to 1850 was the struggle for civil government. This was the most absorbing issue, not only in California, but also in Washington. In few other instances in United States history has civil government been ushered in with so much violent discussion. There were two reasons: the unique conditions in California and the slavery conflict in the east.

In California an effete and dilapidated system of government, adjusted to the simple wants of a pastoral people, was suddenly called upon to serve the needs of a rapidly growing, aggressive population of the conquering nation. Furthermore, the nature

---

[2] *Writings of Thomas Jefferson,* Library ed., XIII, 151; Thwaites, *Early Western Travels,* XVIII, 19; Farnheim, *Early Days of California,* 62. Davis, *Sixty Years in California,* 58. Forbes, *History of California,* 151–52; Bidwell, *California, 1841–48,* 5–6, 110–12, MS in Bancroft Library; "Correspondence of John C. Calhoun," edited by J. Franklin Jameson, in *American Historical Association Report,* 1899, II, 945–47; Wilkes, *Narrative of the United States Exploring Expedition During the Years 1838–1842,* V, 182–83; Neff, *Mormon Migration to Utah,* MS Thesis (Ph.D.), 1918, University of California Library; Thompson, *Recollections of Mexico,* 232–35; Larkin, *Documents for the History of California,* III, nos. 116, 247, MS in Bancroft Library.

of the established government was utterly repugnant to American ideas of justice. Hence, it is not at all surprising that the Americans, especially the more recent arrivals from the western states, should demand the privilege of being governed in "American fashion," and fail entirely to appreciate the argument of the military governors that, until the country was definitely ceded to the United States, the government in California must be a military one administered under the existing Mexican laws. They could not understand that Americans in California might claim no rights and privileges not also guaranteed to all the inhabitants of a conquered territory. American settlers maintained that, since for all practical purposes California was already a part of the United States, they were under the Constitution and laws of the United States, and their personal rights and privileges were the same as those guaranteed in any other portion of United States territory. As early as 1846 the California press began to advocate the immediate establishment of a civil government under the Constitution of the United States. This demand became more pronounced after the Treaty of Guadalupe Hidalgo had been signed and California definitely became United States territory.

Indeed, the situation had now become an anomaly: United States territory administered by American military officers, by means of an effete Mexican system of administration. Because of the slavery question, Congress could not organize a territorial government for New Mexico or California. From the administration in Washington came many promises but no substantial relief. The settlers were told that the military government established in California under the laws of war had, by the termination of the war, become a "government *de facto,*" to continue with the presumed consent of the people until Congress provided a territorial government for them. But the settlers could appreciate neither the promises nor the fine reasoning of the administration in Washington. They were not willing to accept the doctrine of international law, namely, that all the laws in operation in a ceded province must continue in force till superseded by the laws of the government to which the territory had been transferred. They were not even fully convinced of the sanctity of international law. Moreover, in the peculiar case of California, they argued, these principles should be disregarded. They acknowledged that the power to legislate for the territories was vested in Congress, but since that body neglected to exercise its prerogative, they believed that they were justified in acting for themselves. The right to institute a government for the protection of life, liberty, and property, they claimed, was based upon the "original and natural right of society to protect itself by law."[3]

We thus find here a struggle between two theories of right: "legal right" and "moral right," sometimes called "natural right." The first was upheld by the administration, the second, by the settlers. Much may be said in favor of the argument of the settlers. When Congress, after grappling for two sessions with the matter of government for the territories acquired from Mexico, could not, because of the slavery question, come to any agreement, then surely the settlers were justified in acting for themselves. And this they did. They organized a government and adopted a constitution for a free state, fixed the boundaries, and applied to Congress for admission into the Union.

Admission of California into the Union.—The action of California simplified the issue for the north, but it exasperated the south. For nine months the California representatives elected to Congress were kept waiting at the portals of the Capitol. The main objections raised against the state's admission to the Union were these: (1) the constitution of California was not the spon-

[3] For the controversy between the settlers and the federal authorities *see:* Buchanan, *Works,* VIII, 211–15; *H. Ex. Doc.* 17, 30 Cong., 1 Sess., 258–59, 279–80, 776–80; Burnett, *Recollections of an Old Pioneer,* 294–95, 310–17; San Francisco *California Star,* April 8, 1848. San Francisco *Alta,* Jan. 18, 25, May 12, 24, June 2, 14, 19, July 2, 19, 1849; Sacramento *Placer Times,* May 26, 1849. Hereafter "San Francisco" will be omitted from the names of the San Francisco newspapers.

taneous manifestation of her people, but had been concocted in President Taylor's office; (2) the constitution had been formed in an unprecedented, irregular way; (3) the population of California was a mere heterogenous mass of adventurers; (4) manifestations of independence had been exhibited, which, if overlooked, might lead to dangerous precedents. But the real and great objection lay in the fact that the boundaries of the state were made to extend from the Mexican border to parallel forty-two north. The south insisted upon the curtailment of the boundaries to 36° 30′.[4] Neither the north nor California would agree. California was determined not to undergo dismemberment and not to be relegated to a territorial position. Great became her dismay as one steamer after another arrived without bringing the glad tidings of admission. She voiced bitter complaints and protests which at times assumed a rebellious character.[5] It is hard to tell what might have happened had not Congress finally succeeded in terminating the memorable forensic struggle, and admitted California on her own terms.

A decade and a half of federal legislation.—The sixteen years from 1850 to 1866 may be characterized as a period of demands for federal legislation; legislation the enforcement of which required the strong arm and rich treasury of the federal government. California asked for a liberal land policy; she called for appropriations for internal improvements; she demanded protection against the Indians. The program was a costly one but California demanded its fulfillment as a right to which she believed she was fully entitled. Like all frontier communities, she considered the government to be a paternal institution whose duty it was to assist liberally in the development of the frontier

---

[4] *Cong. Globe,* 31 Cong., 1 Sess., 455, 499, App. 110, 260, 347, 392, 462, 606, 775, 961–68, 997, 1159–68, 1001–3, 1251.

[5] California Legislature, *Jours.,* 1850, 373–75, 1277–83; *Alta,* April 25, 27, June 25, Aug. 17, 1850; *Pacific News,* April 26, May 29, Aug. 27, 1850; *Courier,* July 23; *Picayune,* Sept. 14; Sacramento *Transcript,* April 20, May 4, June 27, Sept. 24, 1850.

country, and especially such a country as California; for the people there had an exalted conception of the importance of their state, whose gold, they claimed, had saved the impoverished east from bankruptcy.[6] But while California tended to exaggerate her needs and importance, the east, and particularly the strict constructionist south, underestimated them, and long controversies ensued between the state and the federal government.

[6] This opinion was expressed by the Californians in the press, at public meetings, in the legislature, and in Congress.

CHAPTER II

MEXICAN LAND GRANTS

The land question in California was of a threefold character: the adjudication upon the validity of land titles claimed under the Mexican government; the disposition of the public domain; the control and disposition of the gold fields. The first phase of this question was the most troublesome in Congress and in California. It caused considerable agitation and many clashes between the land claimants and the settlers commonly called squatters. The question of Mexican land grants emerged soon after the conquest of the territory by the United States forces and the influx of land-hungry Americans who had been accustomed to a system of land tenure different from that which prevailed in California under the former governments.

Spanish and Mexican land systems.—During the Spanish and Mexican régime the supply of land was far above the demand for it. To encourage colonization, the Spanish, and later the Mexican, government offered large tracts of land to settlers. The number of land grants made during the Spanish régime was very small. Most of the foreign land titles in California were claimed under grants from the Mexican government,[1] made under the Mexican colonization laws of August 18, 1824, and November 21, 1828.

Under the Mexican laws the grantee had to comply with many formalities. The grant had to be approved by the territorial

[1] Bancroft gives about thirty-six up to 1822. According to Hoffman's Reports of 1862, there were 27 grants; Jones, *Report on the Subject of Land Titles in California Made in Pursuance of Instructions from the Secretary of State and the Secretary of the Interior* (*Sen. Ex. Doc.* 18, 31 Cong., 1 Sess., 3–4 [589]).

assembly or by the government in Mexico. No grants of land within ten leagues of the sea could be made by the governor without the previous approval of the government in Mexico. After the approval of the grant the land was to be surveyed and the boundaries fixed. Moreover, the grantees were generally required to carry out certain conditions of occupation, such as putting up buildings and keeping some live stock on the land.[2]

But, due to the low value placed on land and the political disturbances in Mexico and in California, all the formalities were seldom complied with. Many of the grants claimed had not been approved by the territorial assembly or the national government; they were not surveyed nor were their boundaries fixed. Consequently there was a large number of land claims, varying from one to eleven leagues square, that were indefinite with respect to boundaries. Also the grantees had not always lived up to the conditions of occupation, and only the small tracts were actually occupied. These irregularities were decried by the Mexican authorities themselves, even to the extent of declaring the titles technically unsound.[3]

Complaints of American settlers.—Under these circumstances it was therefore to be expected that trouble would arise with the influx of land-hungry settlers from the western states. They had been accustomed to small holdings with fixed boundaries, and to them squatting upon uncultivated land was a perfectly respectable American practice in settling a new territory. These Americans came to California with the belief that, except for a few settlements confined to the coast, all the land in the territory was public domain, and that, as in the other territories which had been opened to settlement, they might preempt a tract of land by

[2] Halleck's *Report on the Land Titles in California, 1849* (*H. Ex. Doc.* 17, 31 Cong., 1 Sess., 120–21, 133–44 [573]).

[3] Jones, *Report* (*Sen. Ex. Doc.* 18, 31 Cong., 1 Sess., 3–5 [589]); Halleck, *Report* (*H. Ex. Doc.* 17, 31 Cong., 1 Sess., 122 [573]). In some cases a single tract of land was granted to several owners. Shinn, *Mining Camps*, 92.

squatter's rights. Hence great was their disappointment when they found thousands of acres of the best lands lying uncultivated and claimed by a small number of landowners under some inchoate loose grant of the benighted Mexican government.

Complaints against the existing land conditions were voiced by Americans even before the country was ceded to the United States. In the California *Star* of March 13, 1847, "Paisano" complained that the American settlers who had come with the intention of securing tracts of land found that wherever they turned "they were repulsed with an indignant 'this is all mine.'" To redress these wrongs "Paisano" proposed to organize a legislature which should enact a law providing that every man in the territory should be entitled to a tract of government land.[4] Sloat's promise, in his proclamation of July 7, 1846, that all "persons holding titles to real estate, or in quiet possession of lands under a color of right, shall have these titles and rights guaranteed them," was in the opinion of the settlers without any legal or moral force, for he was not authorized to make such an assurance.

The Guadalupe-Hidalgo Treaty and land titles.—The question of land titles in the ceded territories was considered in the Guadalupe-Hidalgo treaty. Articles eight and nine stipulated that "property of every kind" belonging to Mexicans in the ceded territories, "shall be inviolably respected." Article ten, which stipulated also for imperfect claims, was not ratified by the United States Senate. In the protocol it was stated that "conformably to the law of the United States, legitimate titles to every description of property, personal and real, existing in the ceded territories are those which were legitimate titles under the Mexican law in California and New Mexico up to the 13th of May, 1846."[5] In his communication to the minister of foreign

[4] California *Star,* March 13, 1847.

[5] *Sen. Ex. Doc.* 52, 30 Cong., 1 Sess., 49 (509). In this article the Mexican government stated that no grants of lands in California had been made after May 13, 1846.

relations of the Mexican government, Secretary Buchanan said that claimants who had "forfeited their grants by not complying with the conditions on which they were made" could not be recognized by the United States.[6]

Halleck's report.—To enlighten the federal government on the question of land titles, Governor Mason directed Captain Halleck to collect and examine the old archives which were scattered in the territory. In his completed report, which was forwarded to Washington on April 13, 1849, Halleck pointed out that a large number of land titles in California were "very indefinite with respect to boundaries"; that "a number of the grants of land made by the governors of California have never been confirmed by the territorial legislature," and that in some cases that body had refused to confirm them. He also stated that it had been "alleged by very respectable authority, that certain titles to land were given by Governor Pico *after* the United States had taken possession of the country, and made to bear date prior to the 7th of July, 1846."[7]

Halleck's conclusions that many of the claims were imperfect and others spurious added greatly to the distrust among the settlers with respect to the validity of Mexican land claims. Many of the settlers did not have the means to purchase lands; others were indisposed to pay exorbitant prices for lands which they believed belonged to the United States government. The most famous collision between land claimants and settlers took place in Sacramento, where a number of settlers led by James Zabriskie, a young lawyer, and Dr. Charles Robinson, later governor of Kansas, challenged the legality and genuineness of Sutter's title to lands in Sacramento. The attempt of the land

---

[6] *Sen. Ex. Doc.* 60, 30 Cong., 1 Sess., 69–70 (509).

[7] He also reported that all the mission lands in California had been secularized and made government property by a Mexican law of August 17, 1833. Halleck's *Report* is printed in *H. Ex. Doc.* 17, 31 Cong., 1 Sess., 119–33 (573). Lieutenant Halleck, later General, was well versed in civil and international law, and the author of a book on international law.

claimants to dispossess the settlers naturally led to violence and even bloodshed.[8]

The settlers complained that they did not have a fair hearing in the press. Meetings, appeals, resolutions, and memorials were their main mediums of expression. Their argument was that they were fighting in self-defense against a band of speculators who had appropriated to themselves all the public lands within the state.[9] In a memorial to Congress the settlers complained that they had emigrated with the expectation that California belonged to the United States, but on their arrival they found themselves trespassers on soil claimed by Mexican landowners, who formed a land monopoly. They urged Congress to legislate in favor of actual settlers.[10] Indeed, all who were interested in the welfare of California urged a speedy settlement of the question of Mexican land titles so that the vast tracts of tillable land might be brought under cultivation. The federal government was blamed for the "Squatter riots" in California.[11]

The Land Act of 1851.—Soon after the acquisition of California and New Mexico the Senate Committee on Public Lands reported a bill for the settlement of land titles in the ceded territories. The bill provided for a board of commissioners who were to examine the titles to land claimed in California and New Mexico, separate the claims into four classes, and report to the Secretary of the Treasury. Benton denounced the plan as

---

8 Accounts of the Sacramento squatter riots of 1850 are given in Royce. "The Squatter Riot of '50 in Sacramento," *Overland Monthly*, ser. 2, VI, 225–46 (September, 1885); Robinson, *The Kansas Conflict*, 36–65. Dr. Charles Robinson, later governor of Kansas, was one of the leaders of the squatters during this episode. His account is therefore in favor of the settlers, while Royce is hostile to them.

9 Sacramento *Placer Times*, Dec. 15, 1849; Robinson, C., *The Kansas Conflict*, 37–65; *Picayune*, Oct. 1, 1850.

10 Sacramento *Placer Times*, May 22, 1850. *Alta*, May 24, 1850. The memorial was to have been presented to Senator Walker, of Wisconsin, but by mistake it was forwarded to former Secretary Walker.

11 *Picayune*, Aug. 16, 1850. The *Picayune* was anti-squatter. In its editorials it frequently denounced the squatters as mischief makers. See editorials of October 3, 17, 1850.

equivalent in its operation to the confiscation of the landed property of the Mexican landowners in the territories, in violation of the treaty of 1848 and the law of nations. His own plan was to weed out illegal claims but not to impeach all titles in the territories.[12] Neither plan was accepted.

In 1849, Secretary of the Interior Ewing recommended the establishment of a judicial commission to examine and settle land claims in California and New Mexico. He advised recognizing as valid all claims which had been "regular and fair in their inception, but which had not been perfected." He also directed William Carey Jones to visit Mexico and California to obtain authentic information from the archives with regard to matters pertaining to Spanish and Mexican land claims in California and New Mexico.[13]

Jones submitted his report on March 9, 1850. He stated that some of the claims, good in their inception, had not been perfected on account of negligence; that in some claims the condition of occupancy had not been carried out; and that no regular surveys of grants in California had been made. His conclusions were that the grants in California were mostly "perfect titles . . . . and those which were not perfect—that is, which lack some formality, or some *evidence* of completeness, have the same *equity* as those which are perfect, and were and would have been equally respected under the government which has passed away."[14] The settlers who relied upon Halleck's report accused Jones of being prejudiced in favor of the Mexican land claimants.

Shortly after the California members took their seats in Congress, Senator Fremont introduced a bill in the Senate providing for a board of commissioners, whose decision against the United

[12] Sections of this elaborate bill are given in the *Cong. Globe,* 30 Cong., 2 Sess., 254–57, 265–67.

[13] Ewing to Jones, July 12, 1849, and Butterfield to Jones, July 5, 1849 (*H. Ex. Doc.* 17, 31 Cong., 1 Sess., 113–17 [573]).

[14] Jones, *Report* (*Sen. Ex. Doc.* 18, 31 Cong., 1 Sess., 34–35 [589]). This report is also printed in part as *Land Titles in California.*

States was to be final, but the claimant was given the right to appeal to the federal courts. Senators Gwin and Benton criticized the bill. Gwin, as the spokesman of the settlers, contended that Fremont's bill was prejudicial to the interests of the government and the American settlers. His substitute plan conferred upon the United States, also, the right to appeal from the decision of the board of commissioners to the federal courts. He intimated that some of the large claims were spurious.

Benton declared war on all plans which aimed to compel the claimants to "run the gauntlet of three different lawsuits," resulting practically in the confiscation of the property of the Spanish and Mexican landowners. "The idea of fraud," he said, "is the utmost absurdity, the utmost preposterity." His own plan provided for a recorder who was to collect the evidence of titles to lands claimed. The recorder, in conjunction with the United States District Attorney, was to summon to a hearing all claimants the validity of whose titles were in doubt. A decision in favor of the claimant was to be final except in the case of his son-in-law, Fremont. In several eloquent speeches Gwin pointed out that his own plan was in accordance with the Treaty of Guadalupe-Hidalgo, with international law, and the decisions of the United States Supreme Court.[15] Gwin's bill became a law on March 3, 1851.

The act provided for the appointment by the President, with the consent and advice of the Senate, of a board of three commissioners whose office was to continue until March 3, 1854, unless sooner discontinued by the President. To protect the interests of

---

[15] *Cong. Globe,* 31 Cong., 1 Sess., 2045–46, 2047. Gwin says in his *Memoirs,* 42, that Fremont, who was the owner of one of the largest and most valuable grants in California, was selected by the California land claimants as their spokesman; while Gwin was considered as the spokesman of the landless class. Fremont's land bill was denounced by some in California. The *Picayune* held that the bill gave too much power to the commissioners, and would open a way for the employment of sinister influences. *Picayune,* Nov. 14, 1850; Sacramento *Transcript,* Dec. 6, 1850; *Courier,* Nov. 11, 12, 1850.

the United States, the President was to appoint an agent whose duty was to attend the meetings of the board and to superintend the interests of the government. To this board, holding its sessions at times and places named by the President, every person claiming land in California under a Spanish or Mexican title was to present the same within two years; with all the documentary evidence and testimony of witnesses in support of the claim. Upon examination of the evidence presented by the claimant and the United States agent, the board was to decide upon the validity of the claim. Within thirty days after the decision was rendered, the board was to certify the same, giving the reasons on which it was founded, to the United States District Attorney. The claimant and the United States had a right to appeal to the District Court, and from its decision to the Supreme Court, within six months of the decision of the District Court. In their decisions the board of commissioners, the District Court, and the Supreme Court were to be guided by the "Treaty of Guadalupe-Hidalgo, the law of nations, the laws, usages, and customs of the government from which the claim is derived, the principles of equity, and the decisions of the Supreme Court of the United States, so far as they are applicable."

All the lands of the rejected claims were to be deemed a part of the public domain. For all claims finally confirmed, the claimant was to be entitled to a patent upon his presenting to the General Land Office an authentic certificate of the confirmation and a plat or survey of the land approved by the surveyor general of California. The patent thus issued was to be conclusive between the United States and the claimant only, but was not to affect the interests of third persons. Should any person contest the title of the claimant he might secure an injunction from the District Court preventing the issue of the patent until the final decision. In the case of town or farm lots held under a grant from a corporation or town to which lands had been granted for such purposes by the former governments, the claims were to be presented by the town authorities and the mere proof that the town was in existence on July 7, 1846, was to be prima facie evidence of the grant to the corporation, and to the individuals who held under the corporation.[16]

Policy of the first board.—The instructions to the board of commissioners stated that the object of the law of March 3, 1851, was to recognize all bona fide valid land titles and "to detect and forever put to rest, all fabricated, fraudulent, or simulated grants."[17] On January 21, 1852, the board commenced receiving petitions and notices of claimants. The work of the commissioners moved slowly, for they had to inform themselves of the intricate matters of the Mexican land grants. Moreover, the United States agent, who had to face in the counsel of the claimants the ablest talent to be had, found himself overwhelmed with work. The people of California soon became impatient and many accused the commissioners of inefficiency.

At last, in August, 1852, the board made three decisions, confirming all three claims on "broad principles of equity" which were to form a guide for future action. In the case of Cervantes, for a tract of land of two square leagues, the board overruled the objections of the United States agent that the grant lay within ten leagues of the seacoast. In the case of Reading, the board admitted that the title for a certain tract of land six leagues square was imperfect, but it held that the act of March 3, 1851, embraced also incomplete titles. Commissioner Hall held that Sloat's promise to respect all claims to real estate imposed a

[16] United States, *Statutes at Large*, IX, 631–34.

[17] The instructions were issued by the Commissioner General of the Land Office Butterfield, and approved by Secretary Stewart (*Sen. Ex. Doc.* 26, 32 Cong., 1 Sess., 2–6 [614]). They were also published in the *Alta*, Jan. 20, 22, 1852; *Herald*, Jan. 6, 1852. The *Herald* held that the instructions were stringent and not warranted by the law of March 3, 1851. Especially the provision requiring a sûrvey of the claims was considered unjust. Jan. 6, Feb. 23, 1852.

solemn obligation upon the government to live up to that promise.[18]

Public opinion was divided on the policy adopted by the board of commissioners. "Although we do not favor large landed estates, the decision of the board is just," said the Sacramento *Union*.[19] "The board decided the cases," said the *Alta*, "upon the broadest principles of equity, in the true spirit of the Treaty."[20] The settlers, on the other hand, accused the commissioners of corruption and advocated their removal. Governor Bigler recommended to the legislature that it memorialize Congress to repeal the act of 1851 and have an act passed providing a mode for deciding all claims in the United States District Court, where rules of "legal evidence are observed," and where all parties interested could come before the court.[21] A resolution to this effect was introduced in the legislature. Others laid the blame upon the law agent, who was accused of dereliction of duties and even of corruption.

The second board.—President Pierce removed the old commissioners and appointed new members. The delay caused by the change of personnel necessitated an extension of time, and by several acts the authority of the land commission was extended to March 3, 1856.[22] The second board laid down new principles. It ruled in one decision that conditions of cultivation were to be presumed to belong to all grants made by the Mexican government; and by the word *cultivation* was meant more than mere pasturage. Hence, if one used the land for mere grazing purposes he could not be considered to have perfected the conditions

---

18 The decisions of the three cases by the commissioners are found in *Pamphlets on California Lands*, I, Doc. 2, pp. 3–63.

19 Sacramento *Union*, Aug. 12, 1852.

20 *Alta*, Aug. 15, Dec. 22, 29, 30, 1852.

21 California *Sen. Jour.*, 1853, 21–22. The governor was criticized by the *Alta* and the *Herald*. They objected to his plan, contending that it would cause delay and would crowd the district court. See *Alta*, Jan. 7, 26, 1853; *Herald*, Jan. 6, 1853.

22 United States, *Statutes at Large*, X, 603.

and therefore was not entitled to equity. Out of 325 cases decided, 100 were rejected.[23]

On the whole, the general opinion was that the second board was acting fairly with both sides. Many of the settlers, however, were opposed to the whole policy of the land commission and advocated the settlement of the land question in the federal courts. The confirmation of the extensive Fremont and Bolton-Barron claims called forth condemnation of the land commission and the "landed oligarchy." At various settlers' meetings resolutions were adopted declaring that many of the large Mexican claims were fraudulent; that the land should belong to all who cultivated it; and that the rights of settlers upon uncultivated lands should be respected. They demanded that the commissioners should take better means against spurious grants, should adhere to strict ruling in adjudicating cases, and that all claims on which conditions had not been fulfilled should be considered as public domain.[24]

Policy of the federal courts.—But the settlers soon found out that the federal courts were also very liberal to the land claimants, reversing more rejections than confirmations. The United States Supreme Court declared that the act of 1851 should be administered in a "large and liberal spirit," and the tribunals were not to "exact a strict compliance with every legal technicality." The court ruled that a claimant could eject a squatter from any part of the exterior boundaries of grants even before the claim had been confirmed.[25] Justice Daniel, of the

[23] *Alta,* Dec. 14, 1853. A number of the decisions were published in newspapers like the *Alta* and the *Herald.*

[24] *Californian,* July 13, 1853, cited in the Sacramento *Union,* Aug. 19, 1853; *Alta,* July 11, 1853, Jan. 18, 28, 1854. "Announcement of a Settlers' and Miners' State Convention," *Alta,* July 20, 1855; *Alta,* June 8, 11, 22, 23, 24, 25, 26, 27, 1855; Sacramento *Union, June* 16, 29, Aug. 3, 6, 10, 1855; *Herald* June 8, 11, 17, 1855.

[25] This was due partly to the fact that the district court allowed the presentation of new testimony which the claimants used to good advantage. *Van Reynegan* v. *Bolton,* 5 Otto, 33–37; *United States* v. *Moreno,* 1 Wallace, 404; *United States* v. *Johnson,* 1 Wallace, 328–29.

United States Supreme Court, criticized the "liberal policy"' of the federal courts. He maintained that the Mexican laws and regulations with respect to the granting of lands within its territory, such as the prohibition of granting lands within ten leagues of the coast and the necessity of the sanction of the departmental assembly to give validity to a grant, were to govern the conduct of the court. And whenever any inquiries should lead to the conclusion that the claim was not valid in law, the right to the land should devolve upon the United States for the benefit of the national treasury and for the maintenance of equal privileges of all citizens, and not for the benefit of a few monopolists.[26]

Settlers' grievances.—One of the grievances of the settlers was the practice of ejectment without compensation for improvements. The settlers complained that on account of the uncertainty as to the limits of many of the large land claims, it was frequently impossible for them to know whether they were locating themselves upon public domain or lands claimed by private persons. Consequently many honest settlers, after having located themselves in good faith upon small parcels of land, and after having made valuable improvements thereon, would discover their settlements to be on lands claimed under a Spanish or Mexican grant. They therefore demanded that their locations

[26] *Arguello et al.* v. *United States,* 18 Howard, 550–53. "The decisions in all the causes above enumerated [said the justice] have, according to my apprehension, been made in violation of the acknowledged laws and authority of that government which should have controlled those decisions, and the subjects to which they relate; are subversive alike of justice and of the rights and the policy of the United States in the distribution and seating [settling?] of the public lands,—of the welfare of the people of California, by inciting and pampering a corrupt and grasping spirit of speculation and monopoly,—subversive, likewise, of rules and principles of adjudication heretofore asserted by this court in relation to claims to lands within the acquired domain of the United States. . . . I cannot consent to impair or destroy the sovereign rights and the financial interests of the United States in the public domain. I can perceive no merit, no claim whatsoever, to favor, on the part of the grasping and unscrupulous speculator and monopolist; no propriety in retarding, for his advantage or profit, the settlement and population of new States, by excluding therefrom the honest citizen of small means."

should be respected or at least that they should be compensated for their improvements.

To protect this class of settlers Gwin, in 1852, introduced a bill in the United States Senate which proposed to allow the actual settlers to retain the tracts of land covered by their improvements, not to exceed the "most minute legal subdivisions of the public lands," and to indemnify the Mexican claimants by giving them an equivalent amount of other lands from the public domain. Gwin made several eloquent speeches, pleading for the rights of the actual settler, who "has been the favorite of our legislation ever since the adoption of our Constitution." He cited authorities showing that many of the Mexican claims were imperfect or fraudulent in their inception. Jones's statement that the land claims in California were "mostly perfect titles," he held, was a "piece of imposture and deception." But the opposition—his colleague Weller among them—contended that the act would violate the letter and spirit of the Treaty of Guadalupe-Hidalgo, maintaining that the claimant was entitled to the land which had been confirmed to him. The bill was rejected.[27]

The land claimants condemned Gwin's bill as an act of confiscation. The settlers, however, commended his action. Bills were introduced in the legislature in 1853 insuring compensation to the settlers for improvements, in case of ejectment, but with no success. In his annual message of 1856 Governor Bigler advocated the passage of such an act. He could see no good reason why the landowners should object to such a law, for the improvements as a rule enhanced the value of the land.[28] In 1856 the legislature passed a law declaring that all lands in California should be considered as public domain until the legal title had passed from the government to the claimant. In case of ejectment the owner was to pay the settler for the improve-

[27] *Cong. Globe,* 32 Cong., 1 Sess., 1129–30, 2033–37, 2038.

[28] California, *Sen. Jour.,* 1854, 21–22; 1856, 39–40.

ments and growing crops.[29] The state supreme court, however, declared the act unconstitutional.[30]

The settlers also complained against the evils of floating grants and the unlimited powers of the surveyor general. It was asserted that the grantees, with the help of the surveyor general, shifted the lines of confirmed claims to absorb some valuable tracts of land on which improvements had been made by settlers, or to absorb some valuable mineral lands. "Who can lie down at night," reads the address of one of the settlers, "without fear lest morning may surprise him with some unheard of grant drifted over upon his homestead." The settlers held meetings denouncing the "mercenary" courts and the "grasping land monopolists."[31] The assembly adopted resolutions urging Congress to "prevent the issuance of a patent to claimants in all cases where the right of the claimant was imperfect, inchoate, and incomplete, at the date of the conquest of California"; also to prevent the "location of all unlocated floating grants on other than unoccupied lands"; and to make the duties of the surveyor general "fixed and certain, giving him no discretion in locating grants."[32]

The land claimants were also dissatisfied with the policy adopted under the act of 1851. In a memorial to Congress they complained that the mode of settlement of land titles under the act of 1851 was a source of injustice and hardship to the landowners and detrimental to the interests of the state. They asked for some Congressional legislation which should terminate the

29 California, *Statutes,* 1856, 54–57.

30 *Billings* v. *Hall,* 7 Cal., 1–18. Justice Terry presented a dissenting opinion, pp. 18–26.

31 See *Alta,* June 11, 1857, for the resolutions read at one of the numerous settlers' meetings. Complaints against the arbitrary behavior of the surveyor in surveying the confirmed grants were voiced throughout the decade. It was claimed that the grantees with the help of the surveyor general shifted the lines of the confirmed claim to absorb some valuable tracts of land on which improvements had been made by a settler, or to absorb some valuable mineral lands. See a sharp criticism against this practice in *Alta,* Feb. 14, 1859, and Governor Weller's annual *Message* (California, *Assembly Jour.,* 1859, p. 57).

32 California, *Assembly Jour.,* App., 1856, Doc. [17].

troublesome question of land titles without entailing further expense and labor to defend their just claims.[33]

A bill to this effect was introduced in the House, in 1856, by Herbert, of California. It provided that, upon the presentation by a land claimant in California to the General Land Office, of a certificate of confirmation issued by the board of land commissioners or by the United States courts, together with a plat or survey of the land confirmed, a patent to such lands should then be issued to the claimant without delay. The bill was denounced in California as "one of the greatest frauds ever contemplated perpetration"; a "swindle upon the people of California." Remonstrances against the passage of the bill were signed and forwarded to Washington. Denver, of California, who led the opposition to the bill, admitted that the land claimants in California had been wronged and he was in favor of having the federal government reimburse the claimants the money they had expended in prosecuting their claims. But the passage of the bill, he pointed out, would mean the issuance of patents to fraudulent claims which by mistake had been confirmed by the land commissioners, inflicting injury on the settlers who had acquired vested interests under the preemption laws. The bill was tabled.[34]

The position taken by the public in general was that, since California had been annexed with all encumbrances of land grants, it was incumbent upon the United States government to protect the property rights of the Mexican claimants, and it was wrong for the settlers, dubbed squatters, to invade vested rights. But as time went on and the commissioners confirmed several large claims, commonly believed to be spurious, the cause of the settlers became more popular. Commenting on the Bolton and Barron claim the *Alta* said:

[33] *Cong. Globe,* 34 Cong., 1 Sess., 1438.

[34] *Cong. Globe,* 34 Cong., 1 Sess., 1302. App. 709–12. The bill is given *in extenso* in Sacramento *Union,* July 9, 1856.

Time was when, if a man had a bit of dusty parchment containing an indefinite description of any tract of country which was never occupied, it was considered by some men as rank robbery to trespass upon it. Anything in the shape of a Mexican grant was esteemed sacred, and it was not thought necessary to prove its validity or have it affirmed by the rightfully constituted authority. The man who knew it to be a fraud, and knew that it could not be confirmed, if he settled upon the lands covered by it, was branded as a vagabond and thief, and the indignation of all law-loving citizens was invoked upon him.

Times change, and with the times the relative positions of men. The same parties who have for years been warring against the settlers . . . . they now fall to abusing the poor Mexicans, and swear that all Mexican grants were frauds from the beginning.[35]

Later on when the fraudulent Limantour claim was exposed, many began to question the integrity of the land commissioners and of the judges of the courts who had confirmed claims commonly believed to have been forged. They blamed the United States District Attorney for not making sufficient effort to protect the interests of the settlers, who relied upon the government to defend them against unscrupulous speculators.[36]

Attorney General Black then appointed Stanton as special counsel to assist the United States District Attorney in California in the matter of land claims. In his report to President Buchanan, Black stated that more than two-thirds of the forged land claims, valued at $150,000,000, had been exposed and defeated. In the same report Black presented a severe indictment against the California land claimants. An investigation in the archives revealed the fact that

. . . . there had been an organized system of fabricating land titles carried on for a long time in California by Mexican officials; that forgery and perjury had been reduced to a regular occupation; that the making of false grants, with the subordination of false witnesses to prove them, had become a trade and a business. Desolate islands, barren rocks, and projecting promontories, useless to individuals but of priceless value to the government, had been seized upon under these spurious titles, with a view of extorting millions from the United States, for sites necessary to defend the national

[35] *Alta,* Dec. 12, 1853.

[36] *Alta,* Sept. 11, 1859, June 2, 1860; *Bulletin,* Feb. 2, 1859. The claim of the Frenchman Limantour. *Alta,* Feb. 10, 24, Nov. 4, Dec. 6, 9, 1859; July 2, 1860.

possessions on the Pacific, and to light and guard the commerce of the coast. The richest part of San Francisco was found to be covered by no less than five different grants, every one of them forged after the conquest; Sacramento, Marysville, Stockton, and Petaluma were claimed on titles no better. . . . .

It must be remembered that the grants in most of these fraudulent cases were very skilfully got up, and were supported by the positive oaths, not merely of obscure men . . . . but also by the testimony of distinguished persons who had occupied high social and political places under the former government.[37]

In California, Black's course received both approval and condemnation. The *Alta* commended his energetic measures in "giving the subject of fraudulent manufactured grants a thorough and searching ventilation."[38] On the other hand, those who were interested in the land claims severely criticized Black. William Carey Jones denounced Black's report as a "*reckless* and mischevious *mendacity,*" offensive to the people of California by accusing so many of them of forgery and dishonesty.[39]

On the recommendation of the Attorney General, Congress passed an act for the prevention and punishment of frauds in land titles in California. To forge or assist in forging any title to lands claimed from the government was made a misdemeanor, punishable by imprisonment, hard labor, and a fine not exceeding ten thousand dollars. The bill was hurriedly passed without discussion, in order that the act might be published before knowledge of its consideration could reach California, so as to prevent the consummation of forgeries before the act went into effect.[40]

Summary and conclusions.—The question of California land titles continued to be troublesome for many years. It was even once proposed in Congress to reopen cases which had been already confirmed, but were later suspected of being fraudulent.

---

[37] *H. Ex. Doc.* 84, 36 Cong., 1 Sess., 31–32.

[38] *Alta,* June 27, 1860.

[39] Jones, *Land Titles in California,* Doc. 6, nine letters.

[40] United States, *Statutes at Large,* XI, 290–92.

This proposition raised a storm of protest among those interested.[41] By 1870, however, the acute stage of the matter had passed. According to some authorities, out of the eight hundred and thirteen claims presented to the land commission, six hundred and twelve claims were confirmed, one hundred and seventy-eight were rejected, nineteen were discontinued, and four were still pending in 1880.[42]

Undoubtedly some bad claims were confirmed[43] and some good claims were rejected. We may also concede that the policy of settling the California land grants as outlined in the act of March 3, 1851, was not very successful; it satisfied neither the settlers nor the Mexican claimants, many of whom had been impoverished by the prolonged litigation. A more satisfactory policy, perhaps, would have been the one pointed out by Henry George, namely, that the government should confirm all the small claims after a brief examination of their titles, while the large and suspicious claims should be submitted to the federal courts for a more thorough inquiry; as soon as a large claim was declared valid, the government should allow a certain portion of the grant, and compound "for the rest the grants called for by the payment of a certain sum per acre, turning it into public domain," subject to preemption.[44]

---

[41] *Pamphlets on California Lands,* I, Doc. 11, speech of Phelps of the House of Representatives before the House Committee on Private Land Claims. See also speech of Irving on the same subject (*ibid.,* II, Doc. 9).

[42] Bancroft, *California,* VI, 570, note 45. Based on the official report on the Spanish and Mexican grants in California, prepared by the Deputy State Surveyor General, Stratton, in 1880. (*In* California, *Senate and Assembly Journals,* 1881.) In the report are given the names of the grants, the confirmees, area, condition of title, and where located. The area covered by all the private grants presented to the land commission was estimated by District Attorney Black around 19,148 square miles (*H. Ex. Doc.* 84, 36 Cong., 1 Sess., 30 [1056]). According to Donaldson, the United States government had confirmed in California a total of 8,332,431,924 acres, the smallest claim being for 1.770 and the largest 133,440.780 acres. *Public Domain,* 381.

[43] A number of pamphlets were published "exposing land frauds." See Kelly, *Land Frauds of California* (in *Pamphlets on California Lands,* II, no. 10); Stuart, *Land Titles in California* (*ibid.,* no. 14); Stuart, *Open Letter* (*ibid.,* no. 15).

[44] Henry George, *Our Land and Land Policy, National and State, Addresses,* no. 7, pp. 14–17.

CHAPTER III

FEDERAL LAND GRANTS TO CALIFORNIA

Public land policy prior to 1850.—By 1850 the United States had adopted a more or less well defined land policy. It consisted in making liberal grants to the new public land states for the promotion of education and internal improvements, and in selling the remainder on liberal terms. The largest of the grants was the reservation of the sixteenth section in every township for school purposes. This grant commenced with the act of April 30, 1802, authorizing the formation of a state government in Ohio. As the influence of the west increased, it was proposed, in order to encourage settlement in the west, that two sections in each township should be reserved for school purposes. In the act of August 14, 1848, for the organization of the territory of Oregon, the sixteenth and thirty-sixth sections in each township were reserved for school purposes.[1]

Congress also donated to all new states five hundred thousand acres for internal improvements, two townships for universities,[2] four sections[3] for public buildings, and five[4] or three per cent of the net proceeds of the sale of the public lands within the state. The school land grant, together with a saline reservation, the four sections of land for public buildings, and the five per cent fund, were given on condition that the states would not tax the lands sold by the United States for a period of five years after the date of the sale.

---

[1] United States, *Statutes at Large,* IX, 330.

[2] Some of the states received more than two sections.

[3] This grant varied from two to eight sections.

[4] Although commonly known as the five per cent fund, it varied from two to five per cent.

The other phase of the disposition of public lands was the policy of dealing with the settlers. The manner of disposing of the public lands to settlers underwent a change. Up to 1800, the government looked upon the public domain as a source of revenue with which to discharge the national debt, and not so much from the point of view of settlement. Hence the policy was to sell the land only in large quantities of six hundred and forty acres at two dollars the acre as the minimum price.[5] In 1800 was inaugurated the system of selling small tracts of public lands on credit at two dollars an acre. The credit system led to speculation and resulted in financial disaster. It was then displaced by a policy of selling land for cash at one dollar and twenty-five cents an acre. The next step in favor of the bona fide settlers was the enactment of the general preemption law of 1841, giving citizens the right to settle on surveyed lands, offered or not offered for sale, and to purchase their holdings, not over one hundred and sixty acres, at the minimum price of one dollar and twenty-five cents an acre.

A liberal land policy for California.—This, in brief, was the federal land policy prior to 1850. By the cession of California to the United States, all the lands which had not been granted by the former governments to individuals or towns became a part of the public domain. That California would receive as much as the most favored state or territory in this respect was almost a foregone conclusion. In their messages to Congress Presidents Polk and Taylor recommended a liberal policy with regard to the public lands in California[6] and a bill was introduced in Congress, but no action was taken upon it.

There was, however, a strong sentiment in California that the whole public domain within her limits should belong to her. The question came up at the constitutional convention in 1849 when

[5] Donaldson, *Public Domain*, 200.

[6] *Message*, Dec., 1848. Richardson, *Messages*, IV, 643; *Message*, Dec., 1849. Richardson, *Messages*, V, 20.

McCarver, from Sacramento, submitted a resolution declaring that the public domain within the boundaries of California, "in right and justice, belongs to the people of California." McCarver pointed out that, if the federal government should retain the public lands in California, half a century would elapse before the state could derive any revenue from them. The resolution was rejected partly for the reason that it was a matter for action of the legislature and not for the convention, and partly because it was believed that the adoption of such a resolution might cause objection in Congress and thereby strengthen the opposition to the admission of the state into the Union.[7]

Although the resolution was rejected a number of delegates expressed themselves in favor of its sentiment. Some who discountenanced any claim to the lands as a matter of right, admitted that it would be advisable to ask Congress to relinquish to California all the public lands in view of the fact that she had no appropriation for the support of the government. The convention also adopted an ordinance in which the state, in return for its pledge not to interfere with the primary disposal of the vacant lands within its borders, asked for large land grants: one section for every quarter-township of the public lands; seventy-two sections for the support of a university; 500,000 acres in addition to the 500,000 acres granted to every new state under the act of 1841; four sections for a seat of government; all salt springs within the state; and five per cent of the net proceeds of the sale of the public lands within the state.[8]

Shortly after California was admitted into the Union Senator Fremont introduced into Congress a few bills for land donations to California. But the session closed without passing any land

7 Browne, *Debates*, 316, 465. Indeed Senator Soulé, of Louisiana, used McCarver's resolution as an argument against the admission of California, pointing out the radical tendencies among the people in California (*Cong. Globe*, 31 Cong., 1 Sess., App. 960 *et seq.*).

8 The ordinance is given in full in Browne, *Debates*, 467. The people of California believed that their state was entitled to more lands, because of its peculiar conditions.

laws for California and without making to her any of the customary land grants made to each new state upon its admission into the Union. By the general act of September 4, 1841,[9] however, California received her 500,000 acres for internal improvements, and by the act of September 28, 1850,[10] granting to all the public land states the swamp and overflowed lands within their limits, California became the owner of several millions of acres of some of the best lands within her boundaries.

Early in the second session of the thirty-first Congress, Gwin introduced a bill in the Senate "to provide for the survey of the public lands in California; the granting of donation privileges therein and for other purposes." Many, especially the southern Senators, objected to the third section of the bill, which proposed to donate a tract of land, three hundred and twenty acres, to any citizen of the United States (and to those who had declared their intention of becoming such) who on the 30th of May, 1848, inhabited and cultivated a tract of land in California not rightfully claimd by others and who should continue to inhabit and cultivate it for three consecutive years.

The opposition contended that such a liberal policy in dealing with the public lands would squander away the whole public domain and would tend to hold out inducements to immigration into California that would drain the eastern states of their laboring population. "When have we ever acted thus towards any other people of this country?" exclaimed Dawson of Georgia. He complained that "Whenever California comes up, everybody lets her have her way and nobody seems to oppose her." The opposition admitted that the Oregon law extending the time to January, 1851, was even more liberal than the California bill, but the two cases, they said, were unlike, for in Oregon, where the country was sparsely settled and where the land itself held

9 United States, *Statutes at Large,* V, 455. By the eighth section of this act, a grant of 500,000 acres was made to the new states which had been admitted, and to the new states which should hereafter be admitted.

10 United States, *Statutes at Large,* IX, 519–20.

out small inducements for immigration, there was some justification for offering bounties to increase immigration. None of these inducements were needed for California.[11] The result was that another session closed without legislation for the California public lands, with the exception of an appropriation providing for their survey.

California resented the neglect of Congress to legislate for the public domain within her boundaries. It was complained that this policy of Congress retarded the growth of the state. Were the lands rapidly surveyed and the people of California allowed to acquire titles to land, an immense impetus would be given toward the settlement of the country, building of permanent improvements, etc., thereby increasing the taxable property of the state. In newspaper editorials, at party state conventions, in the messages of the governor and resolutions of the legislature, Congress was urged to donate the public lands in limited quantities to actual settlers.[12] The arguments in favor of this policy given in a senate memorial to Congress were: the reduced proportion of arable lands belonging to the public domain within the state on account of the extensive Mexican land grants; the heavy cost of immigration to California; the great expense to be incurred in the preparation and settlement of a farm; and the need of a large sturdy yeomanry as the best means of self-defense in case of war with a foreign power, for, on account of the inadequate facilities for communication, California would have to depend upon her own man power. Give a man sufficient land to support himself and his family, pleaded the memorial, and "he will be found fighting beneath your banner in the day of battle."[13]

---

[11] *Cong. Globe,* 31 Cong., 2 Sess., 153, 744–47.

[12] *Courier,* Sept. 17, 1850; *Alta,* Feb. 13, March 1, April 19, Aug. 6, Nov. 22, Dec. 15, 1851; *Herald,* Feb. 10, 1852; *Evening Picayune,* Mar. 24, 1851, Jan. 27, 1852, April 16, 1852; Davis, *Political Conventions in California,* 13, 19, 24–25, 28; California, *Sen. Jour.,* 1852, 77–78; Jan. 5, 1853, 22.

[13] California, *Sen. Jour.,* 1852, 575–84.

The Act of March 3, 1853.—California finally succeeded in having Congress pass a bill which provided for the introduction of the whole land machinery for the disposition of the public domain in the state. The act of March 3, 1853, provided for surveys and land offices, and opened the unreserved agricultural public lands, surveyed, and unsurveyed, to preemption according to the act of September 4, 1841. It also provided for several grants of land to the state, such as the sixteenth and thirty-sixth sections of each township for the purpose of public schools, two entire townships for the use of a seminary of learning, and ten entire sections of land for the purpose of erecting public buildings.[14] There was opposition to the grant of two sections in every township for school purposes, but the California Senators argued that their state was entitled to the same amount of land for educational purposes as their neighboring territory, Oregon. Moreover, in view of the character of the country, California would in the end receive in her two sections of land less value than the other states received in their one section.[15]

California was not fully satisfied with the land act of 1853. Governor Bigler urged the legislature to memorialize Congress to grant the public lands in limited quantities to actual settlers. He could see no reason why the government should require from the settler in California one dollar and twenty-five cents an acre, while in Oregon public land was given to the settlers free of charge. He held that the immigrants to California encountered the same hardships as those who immigrated into Oregon.[16]

State ownership of the public lands.—Neither did the land grants to the state entirely satisfy the state authorities. A movement was set on foot in 1853, 1854, 1855, to urge Congress to

[14] *Cong. Globe*, 32 Cong., 1 Sess., 1771, gives the bill in entirety; United States, *Statutes at Large*, X, 244–48.

[15] *Cong. Globe*, 32 Cong., 1 Sess., 1772, 1784, 2235. California was the first *state* to receive two sections; United States, *Statutes at Large*, X, 244–48.

[16] California, *Sen. Jour.*, 1854, 22.

relinquish the public lands within California to the state. The arguments of the advocates of this policy, as expressed in Governor Bigler's messages, in the debates of the legislature, and in the press were as follows: California had gone through a peaceful revolution, had organized an independent sovereign state, and had come into the Union with the ownership of her public lands as an attribute of sovereignty, just as in the case of Texas. To be sure the constitutional convention adopted an ordinance disclaiming all rights to the public lands, but the convention had no right to pass such an ordinance, and this ordinance was of no effect, because it had not been voted upon by the people. Neither did the legislature assent to the stipulation in the act of admission that the state should not interfere with the primary disposal of the public lands.

A special committee was appointed in the senate to inquire into the expediency of reporting a memorial to Congress, asking it to concede to the state of California all the public lands within her limits. On April 4, 1853, the committee submitted a report and a memorial to Congress. In the report the committee stated that some of them believed that "the public lands within the State are, without further action, the property of the State." They were therefore against drawing up a memorial that would concede to the federal government the right to these lands. The committee, however, agreed on a memorial which asked Congress to acknowledge California's right to all the public lands within her limits, or to relinquish these lands as a matter of expediency.

The argument given in the memorial for the claim of the state to the public lands is as follows:

> The rights of sovereignty and eminent domain possessed by each State, carry with them the right to all the lands, bays, lakes, rivers, water courses, and other property of the State not belonging to individuals, unless the State have yielded up that sovereign right, in whole or in part, to another. The people of California, left without government, formed a government of their own. . . . . Thus organized, and possessed of all the powers of a sovereign State, they asked and were received into the Union on an equality with their sister States. . . . .

The right of the United States to the public domain within a State, did not exist in the early history of our Confederacy. It has been created since by compacts and agreements between the Federal Government and several of the new States. This State has never been a party to any such compact, nor does the constitution of the State authorize the compact to be made on behalf of the State. . . . . As the United States does not derive this right either from the Constitution or from compact with the State, it follows that she does not possess it. The sovereignty, the jurisdiction, and the right to public property within the State, reside in this State as fully as it does in the State of Texas, or in any of the original thirteen.

As the United States had done many acts tending to show that she claims right to the public lands of this State, inconsistent with the sovereign dignity of the State, it becomes necessary for the State to assert her rights, and to ask, in distinct terms, an acknowledgment of them on the part of the General Government. If this acknowledgment should be withheld from us, then, without acknowledging any right in the United States to the public lands in California, we ask that her claim to them be conceded to the State.

The memorial gave several reasons why the public lands should be relinquished to the state. First, a political reason: the ownership of the public lands by the federal government would increase the patronage of the government within California to such an extent that, in view of the remoteness of the state from Washington, there would be danger of abuse of this power, threatening the safety and institutions of the state. Second, an economic reason: should the general government retain the public lands they would prove to be a burden instead of a source of revenue, while at the same time the progress of the state would be retarded.[17]

In his annual message of 1855, Governor Bigler discussed this question at considerable length and urged the legislature to memorialize Congress to relinquish the public lands to the state.[18] The question was discussed at great length in the assembly,

[17] California, *Sen. Jour.*, 1853, App., Doc. 55. The report was accepted and laid on the table, and it was ordered that two thousand copies be printed (*ibid.*, 295).

[18] California, *Sen. Jour.*, 1855, 34–36. The governor as well as the senate committee followed here the ultra states' rights doctrines. Their arguments rested upon the assumption that the states are absolute sovereignties and that sovereignty necessarily includes the ownership of the public domain; and finally that the general government claimed the public lands by virtue of its sovereignty, not by acquisition and deeds of cession.

where Speaker Stow and Assemblyman Ryland made elaborate speeches for the state ownership of the public lands. On the other hand, Assemblyman Graves contended that Texas was an independent state when she entered the Union, while California never had been independent. The United States government had acquired California from Mexico and it had never divested itself from the lands within the territory.[19]

The right of the state to the public lands was a moot question from time to time throughout the decade. As late as 1859 Judge Ralston continued to assert the claim of the state upon legal and constitutional grounds.[20] But the majority of the people were not in favor of this doctrine, fearing that it might lead to an open conflict between the state and the federal government. The legislature frequently passed resolutions asking for additional grants of land to the state. A resolution adopted in 1859 asked Congress to grant to California ten million acres of arable land by which donation the state would be enabled to aid in the construction of a transcontinental railroad. The legislature also passed joint resolutions urging Congress to donate the public lands to settlers.[21]

"The five per cent fund."—The act of March 3, 1853, made liberal land grants to the state but did not settle the public land question in California. In the first place there was the question of the "five per cent fund." This fund was granted by Congress to the public land states from the net proceeds derived by the federal government from the sales of the public

19 The speech is reported verbatim in the Sacramento *Union,* Feb. 16, 1855; also see *Daily State Journal,* Nov. 2, 1854.

20 Judge Ralston's lengthy communication on this subject was printed in the Sacramento *Union,* April 27, 1859. See also Sacramento *Union,* March 8, 1855, Feb. 21, 1857. It was also discussed whether the state had a right to tax the United States lands. See California, *Sen. Jour.,* 1859, 243. It was claimed that one of the issues of the new party, the "Pacific party," was the relinquishment of the public lands to the state. See *Alta,* Feb. 19, 1855.

21 California, *Statutes,* 1858, 350–51; 1859, 394–95; 1860, 417. *Placer Times and Transcript,* June 30, 1854; *Alta,* Feb. 27, 1855; Sacramento *Union,* Feb. 8, 10, 1855.

lands within their boundaries, on condition that the states should not tax the federal lands within their limits. It was generally granted to the states at the time of their admission into the Union. But neither the act of September 9, 1850, nor the act of March 3, 1853, mentioned the five per cent fund. California considered the omission an unfair discrimination against her. Governor Weller and Superintendent of Public Instruction Moulder remonstrated against this discrimination, and the legislature adopted a resolution asking Congress for this fund[22] but it was not until 1906 that California secured this donation.

The 500,000 acre grant.—In their extreme desire to secure the greatest amount of the best lands, the state authorities construed the land grant acts very liberally. This frequently led to a conflict between state and federal authorities. First, we shall consider the controversy concerning the 500,000 acre grant.

The act of September 4, 1841, provided that the selections of the 500,000 acres should be made in such manner as the legislature of each state might direct, but they were to be located in parcels of not less than 320 acres in any one location and upon surveyed lands.[23] Yet, notwithstanding this provision, the state legislature passed an act in 1852 authorizing the governor to issue and sell school land warrants of 160 acres upon any vacant and unappropriated lands belonging to the United States within the state of California.[24]

The Commissioner of the General Land Office protested against the provisions of the state act of May 3, 1852,[25] and

---

[22] California, *Assembly Jour.*, 1858, 302–6; California, *Statutes*, 1858, 353. The constitutional convention, taking for granted that Congress would allow to California the "five per cent fund," devoted this money, in advance, to school purposes.

[23] The grant was made for the purpose of internal improvements, within the states, such as roads, bridges, canals. These improvements, it was believed, would facilitate the transportation of the United States mail and munitions of war. United States, *Statutes at Large*, V, 455. In spite of this original intention of the framers of the act, the constitution of California diverted these lands to the school fund.

[24] California, *Statutes*, 1852, 41–43.

[25] The opinion of the Commissioner of the General Land Office is in California, *Sen. Jour.*, 1854, App., Doc. 1, pp. 11–15.

Attorney General McConnell advised the state authorities that warrants could not be legally issued for school lands located upon unsurveyed public lands, nor for quantities less than three hundred and twenty acres.[26] But Governor Bigler and Superintendent of Public Instruction Hubbs contended, in view of the fact that only a small portion of the public lands in California had been surveyed, that a strict adherence to the law of Congress would delay the state in its selections for many years, during which time the best lands would be preempted by settlers. They recommended that the legislature memorialize Congress to confirm by a special act the California state law of May 3, 1852.[27] The resolution of the legislature, passed in accordance with this recommendation, urged Congress to confirm the act of May 3, 1852, for it would be a great injustice to deprive of their land those who, under the law of the state, had purchased unsurveyed lands[28] and had located upon them.

In spite of the protests of the federal officials, the sale of the school land warrants continued and most of the locations were made upon unsurveyed lands. The Commissioner of the General Land Office declared that they could not hold good against any preemptors.[29] There began a conflict between the government preemptors and those who had purchased the lands from the state. The state claimants denounced the "encroachment" of the settlers but the United States preemptor contended that the act of September 4, 1841, did not permit any right of selecting

---

[26] California, *Assembly Jour.*, 1854 App., Doc. 4.

[27] California, *Assembly Jour.*, 1854, App., Doc. 5.

[28] California, *Statutes*, 1854, 220–21. According to the records in the office of the surveyor general of California, there were in 1860, 159,520 acres located on unsurveyed lands (16 California, *Reports*, 332 note).

[29] The legislature memorialized Congress again in 1857 on this subject (California, *Statutes*, 1857, 372–73). In 1858, the legislature passed an act repealing the act of May 3, 1852, and provided that the locations should be made in conformity to the laws and regulations of the United States. It provided that the sale of the unsold portion of the five hundred thousand acres should be located by a state agent on surveyed lands only (California, *Statutes*, 1858, 248–51).

unsurveyed lands, while the act of March 3, 1853, expressly conferred the right to preempt unsurveyed lands.

Up to 1864 the California supreme court sustained the claims of the state purchasers. In the case of *Doll* v. *Meador* decided in 1860, the court held that the act of September 4, 1841,

> [did] not require the State to postpone the selections until the survey of the United States. It is only with reference to the old States . . . . that the clause determining the time of the selections applies. As to the new States, the interest in the 500,000 acres vests upon their admission into the Union.[30]

But in the case of *Terry* v. *Megerle,* decided in 1864, the court reversed its former opinion, holding that the

> State has no more right to select and locate lands before the survey has been made than she has to locate in tracts of a hundred and sixty acres each. . . . . The mode, the time, the quantity of the selection and location are fixed by the act.[31]

There the case stood up to July, 1866.

School land grant.—Difficulties between state and federal authorities arose also concerning the school land grant. The seventh provision of the act of March 3, 1853, provided that sections sixteen and thirty-six were granted to the state for school purposes and were not subject to the preemption laws. It also provided that

> where any settlement . . . . shall be made upon the sixteenth and thirty-sixth sections, before the same shall be surveyed, or when such selections may be reserved for public uses, or taken by private claims, other land shall be selected by the proper authorities of the state in lieu thereof . . . . subject to the approval of the Secretary of the Interior.[32]

The state authorities held that according to this act, when the sixteenth and thirty-sixth sections were covered by a private grant or had been taken for public use, they had the right to

---

[30] *Doll* v. *Meador,* 16 California, *Reports,* 332. The decision was delivered by Chief Justice Field. This was reaffirmed in *Van Valkenburg* v. *McCloud,* decided in 1863 (21 California, 335–38).

[31] *Terry* v. *Megerle,* 24 California, 624. It is noticed that the personnel of the court had completely changed by 1864.

[32] United States, *Statutes at Large,* X, 246–47.

select other lands in lieu thereof. And since there was no provision in the grant restricting the selections to surveyed lands only, they claimed the right to make selections on unsurveyed as well as surveyed lands. They also believed that it was the intention of those who had passed the law to include the mineral lands in the grant to benefit all districts in the state.[33] The state legislature passed several acts authorizing the sale and location of the school section lands upon any vacant lands belonging to the United States.[34]

On the other hand, the federal authorities held that the grant contemplated only such townships as could be legally surveyed and divided into sections. Hence, since the mineral lands were excluded from survey, there could be no selections upon them. They also held that the selections must be made on surveyed lands only, and that the state was not entitled to indemnity for sections sixteen and thirty-six when a "township falls *wholly* within the limits of a private claim," because in such a township there was no public land and there could not be any land for school purposes.[35]

The California authorities claimed that the decision of the Commissioner of the General Land Office was contrary to the policy manifested in a number of acts of Congress and that it was in conflict with the decisions of the state supreme court. On April 22, 1861, the legislature passed an act authorizing the selection of other lands "in lieu of those sixteenth and thirty-sixth sections already sold by the General Government to the preemptors, or which may be reserved or covered by private claims or grants." The selections were to be made on unsurveyed as well as surveyed lands.[36]

[33] California, *Statutes*, 1857, 375; 1858, 351–52.

[34] California, *Statutes*, 1858, 318–21.

[35] For the correspondence between the Commissioner of the General Land Office, Mr. Hendricks, and Mr. Moulder, the Superintendent of Public Instruction for the State of California, on some of these questions see California, *Sen. Jour.*, 1860, App., Doc. 9, which is the annual report of the state superintendent of public instruction.

[36] California, *Statutes*, 1861, 218–21.

Up to April 1, 1864, the state had sold several hundred thousand acres, many of them located on unsurveyed lands. But the Commissioner of the General Land Office refused to recognize these selections. The state authorities were told that they would not be allowed to make selections on unsurveyed lands and that the interests of preemptors in good faith would be protected against the state.[37] And thus not an acre of these lands had been patented by the United States Land Office by 1863.[38] The state authorities considered the position taken by the federal officials as illegal and injurious to the interests of California. Before we consider the settlement of this matter we must review briefly another phase of the public land controversy, namely, the dispute over swamp and overflowed lands.

Dispute about the swamp lands.—The act of September 28, 1850, which granted to the public land states all the swamp and overflowed lands within their boundaries, came into Congress as a "meek innocent looking stranger." The supporters of the measure argued that these swamp lands were of "no earthly value" while undrained, and that they rendered the contiguous country exceedingly unhealthful, shortening the lives of the pioneers in the new states. Since the government of the United States would not engage in a system of drainage, it would be right to donate these lands to the states that would drain them.[39]

[37] *Annual Report* of the surveyor general of California for 1862 (California, *Sen. and Assembly Jours.*, 1863, App. 7).

[38] *Annual Report* of the surveyor general of California for 1863 (California, *Sen. and Assembly Jours.*, 1864, App. I, Doc. 3, p. 5).

[39] *Cong. Globe.*, 30 Cong., 2 Sess., 238, 594; 31 Cong., 1 Sess., 75, 232, 1191, 1432. Efforts to induce Congress to cede to the Mississippi Valley states the marshy lands within their limits were made by Thomas H. Benton ever since 1826. March 2, 1849, was passed an act ceding to Louisiana all the lands subject to overflow within her limits (Donaldson, *Public Domain*, 218, 219–21; Horace Greeley, *Recollections of a Busy Life*, 230–31). At the time the grant was made the General Land Office estimated the amount of swamp lands around twenty-one million acres. But up to 1894, there were listed about 85,500,000 acres. Florida alone received some 22,500,000 acres. Gross frauds were perpetrated in connection with these swamp lands. (*Annual Message* of President Cleveland, Dec. 3, 1894; Richardson, *Messages*, IX, 542.)

The act provided that the Secretary of the Interior should make out an accurate list and plats of the swamp and overflowed lands, the greater part of which was wet and unfit for cultivation, and transmit the same to the governors of the respective states. At the request of each governor he was to issue a patent to the state vesting in it the fee simple to these lands. The proceeds of these lands were to be "applied exclusively, as far as necessary, to the purpose of reclaiming them" by means of levees and drains.[40]

In a circular letter of November, 1850, Commissioner Butterfield instructed the United States Surveyors General in the different states to include under the grant lands which were subject to destructive overflow at the planting, growing, and harvesting season, taking the average season as the rule of determination. The states were to have the option of either adopting the field notes of the United States as the basis of the selection, or making the selection through their own officials. In the latter case the states were required to furnish affidavits of the county surveyors, and other "respectable" persons, that the lands selected were swamp and of the character specified in the act of September 28, 1850.[41]

California appreciated this grant, which entitled her to several millions of acres of fertile land bordering upon the bays and rivers. Governor Bigler, among many others, at first advocated that these lands should be granted in limited quantities to settlers on the condition that the grantees should drain them within a stated time. But in his message of 1855 he recommended the sale of these lands at a fixed price, the fund from this source to be used for the reclamation of the lands of the

---

[40] Act of September 28, 1850, United States, *Statutes at Large*, IX, 519–20.

[41] A digest of the circular is given in the *Report* of the California surveyor general for 1858 (California, *Sen. Jour.*, 1859, App., Doc. 3, pp. 5–7).

state. He did not believe that individual enterprise would be successful in reclaiming the lands.[42]

As to the method of selecting these lands, Governor Bigler recommended the passage of an act authorizing testimony in regard to overflowed lands to be presented to the United States Surveyor General. He held that the method of following the field notes of the United States surveyor would be unsatisfactory to the state, for the government authorities might base their selection upon the surveyor's field notes only. On this basis of selection California would be deprived of many acres of land to which she was entitled under the act, for the reason that, if the surveys were made in dry seasons, lands ordinarily swampy would be classed as dry.[43] The legislature passed an act providing for the disposal of the swamp land.[44]

When the Commissioner of the General Land Office was informed that the county surveyors in California were returning to the state authorities land as swamp and overflowed not shown to be such by the returns of the United States surveyor, he wrote a letter to Governor Johnson advising him that, in order to avoid conflicting interests and future litigation, the state authorities should inform the Land Office of any selections before their disposal to settlers. He also pointed out that the act of Congress was designed to grant to the states only those lands which in

[42] California Legislature, *Jours.*, 1851, 28–29. For the years 1850 and 1851 the journals of both houses are bound in one volume (California, *Sen. Jour.*, 1852, 15). The Commissioner of the General Land Office claimed that immediately after the federal surveying system had been organized in California he instructed the United States Surveyor General for that state to request the state authorities to indicate the method of selection which they preferred in adjusting this grant. But the state authorities did not seem to indicate any method of selection. Letter of the Commissioner General of the Land Office to Mandeville, United States Surveyor General in California, Sept. 19, 1859 (California, *Sen. Jour.*, 1860, App., Doc. 3, pp. 15–16).

[43] California, *Sen. Jour.*, 1854, 362–63, 1855, 33–34.

[44] California, *Statutes*, 1855, 189–91. This act authorized the sale of the swamp lands upon the survey by the county surveyor. The surveys were not confined to those townships which had been already surveyed by the federal surveyors. And no affidavits as to the character of these lands were required.

their natural condition were unfit for cultivation of any staple crop, hay as well as grain.[45]

The state authorities, of course, interpreted differently the word *cultivation.* They denied that lands where the water receded during a few months in the year sufficiently to make possible the growth of a crop of grass, could be classified as fit for cultivation. If a spontaneous crop of grass was to be considered a crop, then the state of California would be deprived of the benefit of the act of Congress. The state surveyor general pointed out that the United States deputy surveyor, whose work was done by contract and during the driest part of the year, reported as dry all land over which he could stretch his chain, and his report, "unsupported by any testimony, any certificate, any affidavit, is considered the last proof of the character of the soil. Yet two months after his survey, it may be, a boat would be necessary to pass over his lines." On the other hand, claims laid by the state to this kind of land had to be supported by affidavits of residents in that locality who were fairly familiar with the nature of the land. He also pointed out that many tracts of land which were swampy at the time the grant was made, had been made fit for cultivation by means of drains by the time they were surveyed by the United States surveyors, and so were returned as high land.[46]

Difficulties arose when a portion of the land sold by the state as swamp land was later offered for sale by the federal authorities. The purchasers from the state appealed to the state authorities for protection. The legislature passed an act instructing the state surveyor general to transmit without delay to the Commissioner of the Land Office all evidence showing that the

[45] Hendricks to Johnson, May 9, 1856 (California, *Sen. Jour.*, 1857, 69–70).

[46] *Annual Report* of Surveyor General Brewster for 1856. California, *Sen. Jour.*, 1857, App., Doc. 5, pp. 12–14; *Report* for 1857, California, *Sen. Jour.*, 1858, App., Doc. 7, pp. 13–15; *Annual Report* of Surveyor General Higley for 1858, California, *Sen. Jour.*, App., Doc. 3, pp. 18–20.

lands which had been sold by the state as swamp and overflowed were such in their nature; and to request him to withdraw such lands from market.[47] The state surveyor general addressed circulars to the United States land offices in California asking them to withdraw from sale certain swamp lands. But the registrars of San Francisco and Marysville districts replied that without orders from Washington they were not authorized to withdraw from sale any land advertised by the proclamation of the President.[48]

Governor Weller addressed a letter to the Secretary of the Interior calling his attention to the fact that certain lands which were advertised for sale by the federal government had been sold by the state as swamp land, and unless the government agreed to withdraw them from sale, the purchasers from the state would suffer.[49] Upon the receipt of the governor's communication Secretary Thompson instructed the Commissioner of the General Land Office to withdraw from sale lands sold by the state as swamp land if they were shown by the field notes of the official survey to be of such a character. He also authorized the United States Surveyor General to receive testimony as to the swampy character of certain lands sold by the state, and should the evidence confirm the claim of the state, these lands were to be withdrawn from sale. But he did not feel himself authorized to except from sale all lands sold by the state, when the government records contained no evidence that these lands came under the grant of 1850.[50]

---

[47] California, *Statutes*, 1858, 58–59. The legislature also passed a resolution instructing the California delegation in Congress to urge the passage of a law authorizing the state to segregate, at its own cost, the swamp and overflowed lands, from the public domain. The state was to furnish to the Land Office maps of these lands and reliable testimony. See also *ibid.*, 354–55.

[48] *Annual Report* of Surveyor General Higley for 1858 (California, *Sen. Jour.*, 1859, App., Doc. 3, pp. 8, 20).

[49] California, *Assembly Jour.*, 1859, 286–87; California, *Statutes*, 1859, 385.

[50] The correspondence between the governor and the Washington authorities will be found in California, *Assembly Jour.*, 1859, 287–89.

State Surveyor General Higley believed that the General Land Office could be made to understand the situation in California if a competent person were sent to Washington to explain the peculiar nature of the California seasons, the topography of the country, the extent and locality of the swampy land, and other similar matters. On his own account he visited Washington to effect some arrangement with the Commissioner General of the Land Office. But the only thing he accomplished was to get the consent of the Land Office to permit the agents of the state to accompany the government deputies in their surveys of land adjacent to the swamps, and the right to combat their decisions.

Higley believed that the General Land Office required too much from California by demanding that the affiant should take an oath that he was not interested in the subject. He contended that every citizen of the state was naturally interested in this question. Moreover, the only ones who were competent to testify in this matter were those who had resided in the neighborhood of the swamp lands and were naturally personally interested in these lands; otherwise they would not have lived there. In view of this remonstrance, the Commissioner finally agreed to have a note attached to the affidavit stating what the interest of the affiant was, and to leave to the Land Office the decision upon the weight of the evidence.[51]

Thus in 1862, about a decade after the several land grants had been made to California, the federal and state authorities

[51] *Annual Report* of surveyor general for 1859 (California, *Assembly Jour.*, 1860, App., Doc. 3, pp. 18–19). As a further attempt to bring about an adjustment of the swamp land question, as well as to provide a systematic policy of managing these lands, the legislature created in 1861 a board of swamp land commissioners. The board was to take charge of the segregation and reclamation of these lands within the borders of the state. The county surveyors were instructed to segregate the swamp lands within their respective counties, making complete maps of the swamp lands segregated. These maps, together with affidavits proving the character of the lands, were to be forwarded to the surveyor general. One of the copies of the general map compiled by the surveyor general, with a schedule of the swamp and overflowed lands claimed, and the affidavits, was to be transmitted to the governor, and by him to the Land Office at Washington (California, *Statutes*, 1861, 355–61).

were still wrangling about the construction of the grant acts. The state had sold several hundred thousand acres of unsurveyed lands but not an acre of these lands had been patented by the United States Land Office up to 1863. Moreover, the state had sold forty-three thousand acres as swamp and overflowed lands which were claimed by the United States and were advertised for sale in the President's proclamation.[52]

In view of these difficulties the legislature adopted a resolution appointing W. H. Parks as a committee to visit the Secretary of the Interior and the Commissioner of the General Land Office for the purpose of settling all matters of controversy in relation to the lands claimed by the state under the general acts of Congress. In case this effort should prove unsuccessful the whole matter was to be referred to the California members in Congress, who were to urge congressional action in behalf of the state.[53]

Parks had several conferences with the Commissioner of the General Land Office. He told him that California had proved up a large part of the swamp and overflowed lands and had sold part of them on credit until she could give a title to them. Now, in accordance with the act of Congress making this grant, the state was obliged to reclaim the swamp and overflowed lands. But until the titles to the lands sold were secured, and the money collected, it would be unable, for want of funds, to proceed with the work of reclamation. He therefore requested that the patents be issued as soon as possible. He also asked the Commissioner to change the instructions with regard to proving the swampy character of the lands, claiming that in the case of California it would be difficult to prove that the lands were swampy and subject to overflow at the time the grant was made,

[52] *Annual Report* of the surveyor general of California for 1863, California, *Sen. and Assembly Jours.*, 1864, App. I, Doc. 3, p. 5; *ibid.*, for 1862. California, *Sen. and Assembly Jours.*, 1863, App., Doc. 3, p. 10.

[53] *Report* of Parks, California, *Sen. and Assembly Jours.*, 1863, App., Doc. 14.

because at that time a large part of these lands had not been seen by any white man.

In regard to the school township grant, Parks contended that the comparison, made by the federal authorities, of a township wholly within a Mexican grant to a township covered by a lake, where in neither case could there be any public lands for schools, was not a good one, for in the latter case there would be no inhabitants and consequently no need for public schools. He also maintained that the state had a right to select other lands in lieu of sections sixteen and thirty-six when these happened to fall upon mineral lands, for the act of 1853, making this grant, contained no reservation and the mineral districts were in need of educational facilities just as well as other districts.

But all the requests of the state commissioner were refused by Commissioner Edmunds. He replied that by the term "overflow" was meant a class of lands *"made unfit thereby for cultivation without necessary levees and drains."* Hence a casual overflow would not include the land within the meaning of the grant. He claimed that he was not authorized to depart from the procedure as laid down in the act of December 13, 1859, requiring the state to prove what was swamp and overflowed at the time the grant was made. He ruled that the state had no right to any swamp lands unil they were reported as such by the United States Surveyor General.[54] The mission was fruitless. On April 24, 1863, the legislature adopted a concurrent resolution requesting the California delegation in Congress to procure the passage of an act which should confirm to the state any portion of the public lands selected by it in part satisfaction of the several grants made to the state by several acts of Congress, and which had been sold by the state in good faith to private purchasers. The state promised to pay a dollar and twenty-five cents for every acre selected if, upon final investigation and decision, it should turn out that the state was not entitled to some of these

[54] *Report* of Parks, California, *Sen. and Assembly Jours.*, 1863, 38–44.

selections.[55] The state surveyor general also prepared a bill designed to adjust the whole matter and forwarded it to the state delegation in Congress. The delegation had several conferences with the Commissioner of the Land Office, trying to convince him that the claims of California were just, but all to no effect.[56]

Final settlement.—State Surveyor General Houghton then went to Washington. He had several long conferences with Commissioner Edmunds and succeeded in gaining his promise to cooperate with the members from California in urging Congress to pass a law satisfactory to the interests of the state.[57] On May 29, Senator Conness of California introduced a bill to quiet land titles in his state. After a hurried consideration in the Committee of the Whole it passed the Senate. But it met with strong opposition in the House from Julian of Indiana, chairman of the Committee on Public Lands. He contended that the bill was in the interests of land speculators and was subversive to the interests of the government preemptors in California. He had the clerk of the House read several letters which he had received from settlers in California who stated that, encouraged by the decisions of the Land Office with regard to the invalidity of many of the locations made by land speculators under the authority of the state, they had in good faith settled on these lands and made valuable improvements under the general preemption laws. Should Congress confirm these locations, then all the settlers would be ejected. Julian charged California with bad faith toward the national government. After resorting to logrolling and private interviews with the members of the House,

[55] California, *Statutes*, 1863, 798–99.

[56] *Report* of the surveyor general of California from November 1, 1865, to November 1, 1867 (California, *Sen. and Assembly Jours.*, 1867–1868, App. I, Doc. 3, p. 13); Coy, *Development of the Humboldt Bay Region*, MS Thesis (Ph.D.), University of California.

[57] *Annual Report* of the surveyor general of California for 1865–1867 (California, *Sen. and Assembly Jours.*, 1867–1868, App. I, Doc. 3, p. 17).

the California members were finally successful in having the bill passed also in the House.[58] It was approved July 23, 1866.

The act confirmed to the state of California, in part satisfaction of the several grants made to the state by Congress, all its selections upon the unsurveyed portions of the public domain which had been sold under the state laws in good faith, excepting those illegal selections on which existed adverse rights acquired by settlers under the preemption and homestead rights prior to the passage of the act; it also confirmed to the state any lands which had been reserved for military purposes, or for Indian use, mineral lands, and lands held by or claimed under a valid Mexican or Spanish grant. The state was not to secure a greater quantity of land than it was entitled to under the grants. In case the surveys made by the state did not agree with those made by the United States, the state locating agent was to file a certificate of correction in the United States Land Office. The holder of the state title was to prove up his purchase and claim, and if all was in accordance with the provisions of the act, the Commissioner General was to certify over to the state the land embraced therein.

The fourth section of the act instructed the Commissioner General to certify over to the state, within one year after the passage of the act, all of the swamp and overflowed lands represented as such upon the approved plats of townships made by the United States. Should California claim as swamp any land which was not represented as such upon the maps of the United States surveyor, the character of these lands, on September 28, 1850, should be determined by testimony to be taken before the

[58] *Cong. Globe,* 39 Cong., 1 Sess., 2866, 2957, 3080, 3564–67. Julian was always fighting against that which he considered wrong. He was a champion of freedom and justice. He was one of the leaders of the early Free Soilers. He advocated the homestead policy; fought against land monopolies; was always championing the rights and interests of the true settlers. In his opposition to the bill he was actuated by his aversion to land monopolies, and to despoliation of the public domain.

United States Surveyor General. The sixth section of the act recognized the right of the state to select for school purposes other lands in lieu of sections sixteen and thirty-six which "were settled upon prior to the survey, reserved for public uses, covered by Spanish and Mexican grants, when the final survey of such grants shall have been made."[59]

The settlement outlined in this act conceded to California many of the points she contended for, but there still remained a number of matters to be adjusted between the state and federal authorities. There was the question whether or not the act of March 3, 1853, granted to the state the sixteenth and thirty-sixth sections in mineral districts. The state authorities contended that since the act did not mention any reservation with regard to the mineral lands, while all the other acts making land grants to the state expressly reserved to the United States such lands, the natural inference was that Congress did not intend to exclude mineral lands from this grant, and that the title of the state became vested in these lands at the time the grant was made. In support of this position were cited the cases of *Higgins* v. *Houghton*, and *Sherman* v. *Buick*, in which the supreme court of California decided that the act of Congress granting to California the sixteenth and thirty-sixth sections in each township did not except the mineral lands from the operation of the act.[60]

On March 28, 1874, the state passed an act for the disposition of the sixteenth and thirty-sixth sections belonging to the state, which were known to be mineral in character.[61] The United States Land Office, however, maintained that the mineral lands were not included in the school land grant, for it was the uniform policy of the federal government to exclude the mineral lands from all land grants. Moreover, the act of July 23, 1866,

---

[59] United States, *Statutes at Large*, XIV, 218–21.

[60] *Annual Reports* of the surveyor general of California for 1870–1871, 5–6; 1871–1873, 7; 1879–1880, 9–10 (25 California, 252–62; 45 California, 656–69).

[61] California, *Statutes*, 1873–1874, 766–68.

expressly reserved the mineral lands to the government and the amendatory act of July 9, 1870, providing for the disposal of placer mining lands, made no reference to the sixteenth and thirty-sixth sections. In 1880 the question came up before the United States Supreme Court in the case of *Mining Company* v. *Consolidated Mining Company*. In view of the fact that the case involved an issue of great importance to the state of California and to the federal government, the Court permitted the counsel for the state of California to participate in the argument. The decision of the Court was that the grant of the sixteenth and thirty-sixth sections of public lands to California did not include the mineral lands, thus upholding the contention of the Land Office that it was the uniform policy of the government to exclude the mineral lands from all land grants, and declaring that it was not the intention of Congress, when the act of March 3, 1853, was passed, to depart from that policy.[62]

The Commissioner of the General Land Office also refused to allow indemnity lands for the sixteenth and thirty-sixth sections to be chosen within mineral districts, in spite of the protest of the state authorities that such a policy would deprive the mining counties of the school fund. Bills were then introduced in Congress to allow the state of California to select other lands for mineral school lands. One bill was passed in the Senate several times, but it failed in the House.[63]

Another subject of frequent controversy between the state and federal authorities was the practice of overlisting lieu lands. This was due partly to the irregular and loose way in which the business between the state and the General Land Office was carried on. On the charge that there were listed to California 140,000 acres of land in excess of the number she was entitled to under the law, the Secretary of the Interior issued an order

[62] XII *Otto*, 167–76.

[63] The state is now entitled to select other unappropriated lands in lieu of the mineral lands.

in 1880 that no further applications for land under the various grants be received from the state of California. When the state surveyor general compared his ledger of all the lieu school lands with the maps and records of the General Land Office, he found that the state of California had received 70,000 acres more than she was entitled to.[64] A few decades later we hear again of a controversy between the state and federal government with regard to overlisting some 50,000 acres of land. As a result of the adjustment, the state relinquished to the federal government 32,997.97 acres of land and paid into the federal treasury $22,760.36.[65]

The five per cent claim.—The five per cent claim, also, was responsible for considerable controversy. In 1878 Captain John Mullan was appointed agent and counselor for the state to prosecute the claim against the federal government. Upon his arrival in Washington Mullan addressed himself to Congress. Bills were introduced in both houses of Congress asking for the five per cent grant to California. The main argument of the sponsors of these bills was that California, having been admitted into the Union on an equal footing with the other states and having duly surrendered to the federal government the right to tax certain lands, was now in equity entitled to the five per cent claim like all the other states. But the chairman of the House Committee on Public Lands was not favorably disposed to the bill. He held that California had accepted admission into the Union without such a grant. At almost every session of Congress bills asking for this grant were introduced in both houses. A number of committee reports were made, generally favorable,[66] yet the bills were defeated. The defeat usually occurred in the House. It

[64] *Annual Report* of the surveyor general of California, Aug. 1, 1880–Aug. 1, 1882, 6–7.

[65] *Annual Report* of the surveyor general of California, 1919, 10–11.

[66] *Senate Report* 193, 47 Cong., 1 Sess.; *Senate Report* 125, 55 Cong., 1 Sess.; *House Report* 707, 45 Cong., 2 Sess.; *House Report* 345, 47 Cong., 1 Sess.; *House Report* 1602, 53 Cong., 3 Sess.

was not until 1906 that the persistent efforts of California were crowned with success, for which probably the San Francisco earthquake and fire of that year were partly responsible. When "this great State is still under the shadow of an overwhelming catastrophe," pleaded Blondell of Wyoming in the House, it is an "appropriate time to do this act of justice to the people of California." The act of June 27, 1906, granted to the state of California five per cent of the proceeds of cash sales of the public lands in California which had been sold since the admission of the state into the Union. The money was to be devoted to school purposes in California. The aggregate payment on this account up to 1907 was $989,658.78,[67] and by 1915 the state's income from this source had reached over a million dollars.

Conclusion.—After studying the California public land question it seems safe to assert that the action of the state authorities in this matter deserves little credit, to say the least about it. In the reports and messages of the state authorities, issued after the passage of the act of July, 1866, it was frequently admitted that the difficulties in this matter were due to the legislatures of the state "which in some instances authorized improper and illegal selections of these lands."[68] Referring to the same subject in his annual message for 1867, Governor Low said:

> For the confused state of our land matters, the State is largely responsible, consequent upon the passage of acts authorizing sales of lands in manner and form contrary to the rules and regulations laid down by the Land Department. Indeed it would seem that former Legislatures had endeavored, by the various acts relative to the sale of land, to devise and carry into execution, plans "how not to do it."[69]

In each case of the several important grants, the state had, by legislative enactment, actually overriden some of the pro-

---

[67] United States, *Statutes at Large,* XXXIV, 518.

[68] California, *Sen. and Assembly Jours.,* 1909, App. I, p. 21. *Annual Report* of the surveyor general of California for 1865–1867, 5.

[69] California, *Sen. Jour.,* 1867–1868, 35. See also his annual message of 1865, *in* California, *Sen. Jour.,* 1865, 44.

visions of the acts making the donations, and had authorized illegal selections. For instance, the act of Congress of September 4, 1841, made the grant of five hundred thousand acres to new states for the express purpose of internal improvements which were calculated to benefit the federal and the state governments. California's state constitution, however, diverted this grant to the school fund—truly a worthy cause—but contrary to the provision of the grant. Moreover, the act provided that the selections should be made on surveyed lands in parcels of not less than three hundred and twenty acres in one location; yet the state authorities, under an act of the legislature, sold school land warrants in quantities varying from one hundred and sixty to six hundred and forty acres, to be located on unsurveyed as well as surveyed lands.

Likewise with the school township grant. There is nothing in the provisions of the act of March 3, 1853, to indicate that the sixteenth and the thirty-sixth sections might be located on unsurveyed lands. Yet the state authorized the selection upon unsurveyed lands.

Then the question of the swamp and overflowed land grant. The most acrimonious criticisms of the policy of the state in relation to the swamp land question were made by later governors and by several investigating committees of the legislature. They pointed out that the state had disregarded the condition of the grant that the proceeds from the sale of these lands should be applied exclusively to a system of reclamation, and had squandered the meager proceeds without devising a real policy of reclamation. In this respect California was not an exception. It was the same story in many other states. "Never a shake of ague," says Horace Greeley, "has any pioneer been spared by reason of all the drainage done under the specious act."[70]

[70] See *Annual Message* of Governor Stanford of January, 1863, *in* California, *Sen. Jour.*, 1863, 40; *Annual Message* of Governor Low, Dec., 1867, *in* California, *Sen. Jour.*, 1867–1868, 35–36; *Annual Message* of Governor Haight, Dec. 8, 1869, *in* California, *Sen. Jour.*, 1869–1870, 42–43; also his

The conclusions arrived at by the several investigating committees were that "the grossest frauds have been committed in swamp land matters in the state." "That, through the connivance of parties, surveyors were appointed who segregated lands as swamp, which were not so in fact. The corruption existing in the land department of the General Government has aided this system of fraud." From a mass of evidence examined by the committees, it was shown that much of the land surveyed as swamp was really high and dry,[71] or, to use once more Horace Greeley's apt expression, "lands that had not muck enough on the surface to accommodate a single fair-sized frog."

The saddest part of the story is that California derived little benefit from these enormous grants:[72] for she squandered away the lands thus acquired.

Annual Message of Dec., 1871, *in* California, *Sen. Jour.*, 1871–1872, 39–40; "Report of the Joint Committee to inquire into and report upon the condition of the Public and State Lands lying within the Limits of the State," *in* California, *Sen. and Assembly Jours.*, 1871–1872, App. II, Doc. 6; "Report of the Special Committee on Resolutions of Mr. Barker of Nevada Concerning Land Monopoly, etc." (California, *Sen. and Assembly Jours.*, 1871–1872, App., Doc. 7); "Report of the Swamp Land Investigating Committee" (*Sen. and Assembly Jours.*, 1873–1874, App., Doc. 5).

[71] Reports of the Committees cited above.

[72] In addition to some minor grants, such as seventy-two sections for a seminary of learning, ten sections for public buildings, and 150,000 acres for an agricultural college, California received 500,000 acres for internal improvements; the swamp and overflowed lands, about 2,042,214.99 acres patented up to 1907; sections sixteen and thirty-six amounting to some 5,610,702 acres, and in 1867 California and Oregon received 2,765,677.10 acres for railroads, thus making an aggregate of some ten million acres.

CHAPTER IV

THE MINERAL LAND QUESTION IN CALIFORNIA

Mineral land policy prior to 1848.—Prior to the discovery of gold in California the United States government had had experience with the regulation of mineral lands that contained only the base metals. The early policy of the government was to reserve the mineral lands, subject to lease by miners. For a few years the miners paid the rent with some regularity, but after 1834 the expense of collecting the rent exceeded the amount collected. Hence in his message to Congress of December 2, 1845, President Polk recommended abolishing the leasing system and offering the mineral lands for sale. He pointed out that the leasing system had not only proved a burden upon the national treasury, but had also led to a wasteful manner of working the mines, and had given rise to much "friction between the United States and individual citizens."[1] Accordingly, by the acts of Congress of July 11, 1846, and March 1 and 3, 1847, the mineral lands containing lead, copper, and other base metals were put on the market.[2]

Attempts to legislate for the California mines.—When gold was discovered in California[3] the government did not know how

[1] Richardson, *Messages*, IV, 410, 454, 504. According to the official records the rent received for the years 1841, 1842, 1843, and 1844 amounted to $6354.74, while the expenses of the system during this period amounted to $26,111.11.

[2] United States, *Statutes at Large*, IX, 37, 146–47, 179.

[3] Marshall's discovery of gold in Sacramento Valley was on January 24, 1848. But long before 1848 gold had been found in California near the Colorado River, near present San Diego County, around Los Angeles, and near Monterey. The mineralogist, James D. Dana, of the Wilkes expedition in 1841, mentioned in his book on mineralogy that gold had been found in Sacramento Valley. In his letter to Secretary Buchanan, Thomas O.

to meet the situation. The plans suggested by the government agents in California differed greatly. Colonel Mason recommended either the granting of licenses to work small tracts of land, about one hundred yards square, at a rental ranging from $100.00 to $1000.00 per annum; or, the selling of the lands in tracts of twenty or forty acres at public auction to the highest bidder.[4] On the other hand, Thomas Butler King, in his report to the President, strongly opposed the sale of the mineral lands. He believed that capitalists, by means of paid secret prospectors, would find out the best lands, overbid the poor miners, and thus monopolize the best locations. The resulting inequality in the distribution of wealth would produce discontent among the poor miners and it would be doubtful whether any law opposed to the interests of the great masses could be enforced. Even the employment of troops would be ineffectual, for the soldiers would desert and anarchy would result. King's plan was to regard the mineral lands as the common treasure of the American people, and any American citizen, by paying to the commissioner of mines an ounce of gold, or sixteen dollars, should be entitled to receive a license to dig anywhere in California for one year. The money collected from these licenses was to be devoted to educational purposes, to the construction of roads and bridges in the mineral districts, and to the discharge of the indemnity to Mexico.[5]

Shortly after Mason's report was received in Washington, President Polk recommended that Congress either preserve the mineral lands of the Pacific Coast for the use of the United States government, or sell them in small quantities at a fixed minimum price which would secure a large return of money to

---

Larkin wrote on May 4, 1846, that there was no doubt that gold, silver, and other minerals would be found in California. *Report of Browne upon the Mineral Resources of the States and Territories West of the Rocky Mountains,* November 24, 1866, in *H. Ex. Doc.* 29, 39 Cong., 2 Sess., 13–14 (1289).

[4] *H. Ex. Doc.* 17, 31 Cong., 1 Sess., 532–33 (573).

[5] *H. Ex. Doc.,* 59, 31, Cong., 1 Sess., (577).

the national treasury and at the same time "lead to the development of their wealth by individual proprietors and purchasers."[6]

In accordance with these recommendations, the Senate Committee on Public Lands reported a bill providing for the division of the mineral lands into lots of about two acres each, to be offered for sale at public auction at a price not less than one dollar and twenty-five cents an acre. Senator Benton was opposed to any plan which aimed to secure revenue from the mineral lands, especially from the placers which contained only one crop of gold. His bill provided that the agents grant permits for working the mines without seeking any revenue therefrom. His policy, he claimed, would preserve order among the miners, while the plan of the Committee would place the miners in opposition to the law.[7] Neither plan was adopted.

President Taylor and his Secretary of the Interior, Ewing, took considerable interest in the mineral land question. Secretary Ewing recommended that the quartz mines, which require large capital for their successful working, should be sold, and the placer mines leased on favorable terms in order that many industrious citizens could work them and pay the rental out of the proceeds. He did not think that the government would experience difficulties in collecting the rent. In his annual message of December 4, 1849, President Taylor recommended that the gold fields be divided into small tracts "and be disposed of by sale or lease."[8]

In the absence of any legislation the military officials in California, who had charge of all government property in the territory, adopted the *laissez faire* policy with regard to the gold fields. Colonel Mason believed that the miners ought to pay some rent to the government for the privilege of digging in

---

[6] Richardson, *Messages*, IV, 643.

[7] *Cong. Globe*, 30 Cong., 2 Sess., 257–59. Benton held that the gold mines are a curse and not a blessing to a nation, for they demoralize a people.

[8] Richardson, *Messages*, V, 20; *Cong. Globe*, 31 Cong., 1 Sess., App. 22–23.

government lands, but since he had no instructions to that effect, nor sufficient soldiers to enforce such rules in such an extensive territory, he decided not to interfere. General Smith at first intended to expel all foreigners from the gold fields. He admitted that legally all gold diggers were trespassers, but since Congress always made distinctions in favor of early settlers by granting preemption, he felt justified in allowing American citizens to work in the mines. He wrote to the consul at Panama asking him to inform the other consuls on the South American coast that the laws of the United States forbidding trespassing on the public lands would be enforced by him against all foreigners in California.[9] Under cover of this proclamation many American miners undertook to drive out the South American and Mexican miners. But General Riley declared that neither American citizens nor foreigners had any right to dig gold in California on government land; and until Congress should legislate in this matter, he would not permit any class of miners to monopolize the gold fields.[10]

Attitude of California toward the mineral land question.—The question of the regulation of the gold fields aroused much interest in California. Discussion on the subject at the constitutional convention of 1849 indicates that the general sentiment of the delegates, particularly from the mining districts, was in favor either of free mining, or of government regulation for the benefit of the state. One resolution requested Congress to allow the free use of the mineral lands to all American citizens. Another resolution recommended that Congress should, by legislative enactment, throw open the placer mines to all persons on the payment of five dollars a month for a permit to dig. The income from this source was to be turned over to the state of California. Some favored the entire relinquishment of the mines to the state.[11]

---

[9] *H. Ex. Doc.*, 17, 31 Cong., 1 Sess., 704, 707, 708, 710 (573).

[10] *Ibid.*, 788–89 (573); Sacramento *Placer Times*, July 9, 1849.

[11] Browne, *Debates*, 430–31, 461, 462, 463–64.

The first legislature took considerable interest in the mining question. In the assembly two reports were submitted by a select committee advocating that the privilege of working the mines should be restricted to American citizens and to foreigners who had legally declared their intention to become citizens. The argument was that California had been acquired at the expense of the American nation, hence the benefits from this acquisition should accrue to Americans only. It was also argued that most of the foreign miners were adventurers, peons of low character, who might jeopardize the morals of the young Americans; and in time of war a large foreign population in California would prove a positive danger to the safety of the state. On the question of the disposition of the mineral lands the committee could not agree. The majority was not opposed to leasing or even selling the mineral lands in small tracts. But the minority report opposed both leasing and selling, believing that either system would result in the monopoly of all the best placers by capitalists. The policy advocated in the minority report was to let the American citizens work the mines freely without a tax other than enough to secure them some protection.[12] The adoption of the minority report by the assembly indicates that the policy then advocated was commonly favored in California, especially among the mining communities.

Fremont's bill.—Shortly after the California delegation took their seats in Congress, Fremont introduced a bill in the Senate to make temporary provision for the working of the gold mines in California. Its leading principles were the rejection of all thought of making the minerals in California a source of revenue for the federal government, and the prevention of the monopoly of mineral lands by capitalists. The bill provided for a number of agents in the mining districts, whose duties were to grant permits to American citizens, to visit the mines, and to settle disputes. Each miner was to have a lot thirty feet square to be

[12] California, *Legislature Jours.*, 1850, 802–16.

worked by manual labor on a placer, or a lot two hundred and ten feet square to be worked by machinery in the rocks. The fees for the permits were to be one dollar a month for a placer and twenty-five dollars a month for a mine. A certain per cent of the proceeds from the sale of the permits was to go for internal improvements in the state of California. No person might have two permits at the same time; but to encourage prospecting the first discoverer was to have double the quantity of land without paying any fee. The agents, together with a jury of six disinterested miners in the neighborhood, were to settle all disputes equitably.

The bill elicited considerable discussion in the Committee of the Whole. Seward moved to amend the bill, extending the privilege of mining gold to persons who should legally declare their intention of becoming citizens. Such a policy, he said, would induce immigration to California. The California Senators agreed to the amendment after it was modified to include only Europeans. Ewing's principal objection to the bill was the absence of any provision insuring the national government a revenue from the mines to cover the expenses of the acquisition of the territory. His amendment provided that the miner should deliver the gold collected to the United States district agent each week and be compensated therefor in United States coin at the rate of sixteen dollars an ounce, which was the current rate in California. Anyone refusing to comply with this law should forfeit his permit and location. Benton and the California Senators opposed the amendment, contending that the government's experience with the lead mines in Illinois and Missouri was conclusive against any idea of deriving revenue from the California mineral lands. The amendment was rejected.

Felch, on the other hand, opposed Fremont's bill on the ground that it proposed a leasing system, which had been found impracticable in a decentralized government like the United States. He also claimed that it was derogatory to the rights of the states because it withheld from state taxation great quantities of land. His subsitute plan provided that the national government sanction a policy of the freedom of the mines unhindered by any agents and permits. This was the policy that was actually pursued, without legislative provision, up to 1866. It was believed in the Senate, however, that some machinery was needed for the preservation of order in the mines. After being amended, Fremont's bill passed the Senate, but its friends did not succeed in getting it taken up in the House, where it was laid over to the next session.[13]

In an "Address to the People of California," Fremont defended his plan, maintaining that, in view of the novelty and difficulty of the subject, his policy was the most practicable and the most liberal to the miners.[14] But the majority of the people of California were against government regulation of the mineral lands. "The bill is odious and impracticable," said the *Picayune*.[15] The *Courier* was opposed to rents or fees, except on the quartz mines.[16] The Sacramento *Transcript* held that on account of distance Congress was not competent to legislate wisely for the gold mines.[17] "There is but one method left for the disposal of the California mineral lands," said the *Herald*, "and that is the cession of those lands to the state of California, for the state will know better than the federal government how to administer the mines."[18]

California's opposition to Fillmore's recommendation.—In spite of the determined opposition of California to the sale of the gold fields, President Fillmore and his Secretary of the Interior, Stuart, recommended to Congress that these lands be

[13] For the bill and debates see *Cong. Globe*, 31 Cong., 1 Sess., 1815, 1869, 2018, 2029–30, App. II, 1362 *et seq.*

[14] The "address" was printed in the *Alta*, December 24, 1850, and the *Pacific News*, December 24, 1850.

[15] *Picayune*, November 14, 1850; *Pacific News*, December 6, 1850.

[16] *Courier*, November 12, 1850; January 31, 1851.

[17] Sacramento *Transcript*, December 6, 1850.

[18] *Herald*, January 30, 1851.

divided into small tracts to be sold "under such restrictions, as to quantity and time, as will insure the best price, and guard most effectually against combinations of capitalists to obtain monopolies." They admitted that the leasing system would be more profitable to the government, and would afford the best security against monopolies; but such a system, they believed, would create feuds between the government and the lessees, making it difficult to collect the rents.[19]

President Fillmore's recommendation was criticized in California as undemocratic and in the interest of the capitalists. "The suggestion of President Fillmore," said the *Pacific News*, "shows that the authorities in Washington do not understand the situation in California. The adoption of such a policy would inevitably result in monopoly, and in such a case the land would be either kept for speculation and not be mined, or the laboring people would be forced to pay a high price for it." The *Herald* pointed out that the miners had no desire to own the title in fee simple, for as soon as the "lead" gave out they moved to another place. "The mineral lands," said the *Alta*, "are best as they are now, and they can never become a source of revenue for the government."[20] In the assembly a joint resolution was adopted declaring that the policy of selling the mineral lands would be in conflict with the true interests of the state and nation, for the richest mineral lands would fall into the hands of speculators, resulting in the stoppage of immigration and the retardation of the progress of California. It warned the government that the miners, grown up in a spirit of independence, had become accustomed to consider the mineral lands as a common heritage and would not brook any interference.[21] The Whig

[19] *H. Ex. Doc.*, 31 Cong., 2 Sess., 11, 27–28 (595).

[20] *Alta*, March 1, 1851; *Pacific News*, January 28, February 21, February 28, 1851; *Picayune*, September 18, 1851; Sacramento *Transcript*, January 31, 1851; *Herald*, January 5, 25, 30, 1851.

[21] California Legislature, *Jours.*, 1851, 1021. The resolution and long preamble were printed in the *Pacific News*, January 29, 1851.

state convention adopted a resolution favoring the retention of the mineral lands by the government, "for the benefit of the miners, to be worked by them, free from any tax or toll whatever."[22] In their messages to the legislature Governors McDougal and Bigler deprecated the policy of leasing or selling the mineral lands.[23]

While the majority of the people of California opposed the leasing or selling of the gold fields, there was, however, no unanimity of opinion on any other policy. A convention of miners and settlers was held in Sacramento but the opinions voiced there were too dissimilar to lead to a well digested plan for the regulation of the mineral lands. Some held that the rules and regulations adopted by the miners were working satisfactorily; others held that some definite legislation was needed to unify the mining regulations. But the question was who should legislate, Congress or the state legislature, and it was contended that for want of necessary experience Congress could not legislate properly for the mineral lands, hence it should relinquish them to the state.[24]

The determined opposition of California to their earlier plan, convinced President Fillmore and Secretary Stuart that the mineral land question "is a subject surrounded by great difficulties." They now recommended that Congress leave the gold fields open to the industry of all American citizens, "until further experience shall have developed the best policy to be ultimately adopted in regard to them." "It is safer to suffer the inconvenience that now exists, for a short period," said the President, "than by premature legislation to fasten on the country a system founded in error, which may place the whole

---

22 Davis, *Political Conventions in California*, 13.

23 California, *Sen. Jour.*, 1852, 17, 78–79.

24 *Alta*, March 1, August 5, 13, 1851; *Herald*, June 6, 1851. *Picayune*, September 18, October 11, 1851; *Pacific News*, March 6, 1851; Sacramento *Union*, January 26, 1852.

subject beyond the future control of Congress.''[25] The policy of *laissez faire* recommended by President Fillmore was favored in California, especially among the miners.[26]

The policy of ''non-interference'' was practically followed until the passage of the acts of July, 1866, and July, 1870. During this period, however, the mineral land question continued to be a vital issue in state politics. In the first place, there was the feeling of uncertainty and fear that speculators might influence Congress to take up again the proposition to sell the mineral lands. Hence it was deemed necessary, at the party conventions and in annual messages of the governors, to reiterate that public opinion in California was opposed to leasing or selling the mineral lands.[27]

Foreign miners' tax.—Then there was the vexatious question of the foreign miners. The American miners, who considered the gold fields to be the property of the American people, looked with jealousy on the continual influx of Asiatics and Latin Americans into the mines. To check the influx of undesirable foreign miners and to insure a large revenue to the state, the first legislature passed an act prohibiting non-American citizens from digging gold in California without a foreign miners' license. The license fee was twenty dollars a month.[28]

The foreign miners protested and evaded the law. The American miners and their sympathizers criticized the evading foreign miners as ungrateful people, intruders upon American soil. But the merchants, whose interests suffered by the exodus of a large number of customers, denounced the act as impolitic, unjust, and illegal. The *Picayune* questioned the right of the

[25] Richardson, *Messages,* V, 127; *H. Ex. Doc.* 2, 32 Cong., 1 Sess., 501 (635).

[26] California, *Assembly Jour.,* 1853, App. Doc. 35, p. 4.

[27] California, *Sen. Jour.,* 1853, 23; 1854, 23; 1855, 41–42; Davis, *Political Conventions in California,* 13, 20, 36.

[28] California Legislature, *Jours.,* 1850, 217, 493–97; California, *Statutes,* 1850, 221–23.

state to legislate and control property belonging to the United States. It pointed out that the foreign miners' act was in violation of commercial treaties between the United States and Mexico, wherein it was provided that the citizens of both countries should not be subjected to any other charges, or contributions of taxes, save such as were paid by the citizens of the states in which they resided. The act therefore violated Article six of the United States Constitution, which declares that the treaties made by the United States "shall be the Supreme Law of the Land."[29]

In the case of the *People* v. *Naglee* the California supreme court upheld the constitutionality of the law. It held that the state had the power to require the payment by foreigners of a license fee for the privilege of mining within the state; and that the act did not violate the Constitution of the United States, for the power of taxation was one of those powers retained by the state and it could not be taken away from it by a treaty between the United States and a foreign government.[30]

The opposition to the foreign miners' tax, and the difficulties encountered in collecting the license fee, led to the repeal of the act in 1851.[31] But the American miners held public meetings protesting against allowing Asiatics and Latin Americans to dig freely in the mines. They petitioned the legislature to enact a law prohibiting the importation of Asiatics and preventing those

---

[29] *Pacific News,* October 10, 1850; *Picayune,* August 14, 1850. Inflammatory bills were posted on the trees and in the mines. One of them read: "Note to foreigners: It is time to unite, Frenchmen, Chileans, Peruvians, Mexicans, there is the highest necessity for putting an end to the vexations caused by the Americans in California. . . . " (California Legislature, *Jours.,* 1851, 660; *Pacific News,* May 28, 1850.)

[30] *People* v. *Naglee,* 1 California, 232–55.

[31] California, *Statutes,* 1851, 424. Instead of a monthly revenue of several hundred thousand dollars, as it had been estimated by the legislature of 1850, the total amount received from this source up to December 15, was only $29,731.16.

in California from entering the gold fields, and threatened to take the law into their own hands.[32]

In 1852 the legislature passed a new foreign miners' bill.[33] Because the license fee was only three dollars a month, there was less opposition to the new act. Many protest meetings were held, however, denying the right of the state legislature to pass such laws. "Where and when did the federal government authorize California to legislate for the mines?" asked the *Alta*.[34] The French miners felt themselves slighted when they saw how exacting the collectors were with the Latin nations, while the English, Irish, and Germans were seldom required to pay the tax. They protested against the foreign miners' tax and appealed to the French government for protection. The San Francisco *Echo du Pacifique* asserted that to tax French miners was illegal because the state had no right to levy a tax on mineral lands which were government property, and also because the act violated a consular convention signed in 1853 by representatives of the American and French governments wherein it was provided that the French people in the United States should not be compelled to pay taxes, excepting those which were equally imposed on all citizens. The *Echo* advised the French miners to take the case to the Supreme Court of the United States.[35]

---

[32] Meetings were held at Auburn, Horse Shoe Bar, Michigan Flat, and various other places. (*Alta*, July 1, 16, 1852; Sacramento *Placer Times and Transcript*, May 9, 1852.)

[33] California, *Statutes*, 1852, 84–87. The fee was raised to four dollars a month at the next session, and the act was further amended in 1855 (*ibid.*, 1853, 62–65; 1855, 216–17). The receipts for 1854 were $100,557.92, and for 1855, $123,323.28 (Fankhauser, *Financial History of California*, 160).

[34] *Alta*, May 12, 1852, June 24, 1853; California, *Assembly Jour.*, 1853, App., Doc. 28, pp. 1–21; California, *Sen. Jour.*, 1855, App., Doc. 19, pp. 1–13.

[35] *Bulletin*, June 23, 1860. The reason for the partiality was partly due to the clannishness of the French and their lesser readiness to become citizens. See Malloy, *Treaties, Conventions, International Acts* . . . . , I, 531.

Mines and state taxes.—There were also the questions of quartz mining, state taxes, and the settlement of the state. The southern agricultural counties complained that their ranches were taxed to their full market value, while the mining claims, yielding thousands of dollars to their owners, were not paying any taxes. They pointed out that the six southern counties, with a population of 6,367 souls, paid more taxes than the twelve mining counties with a population of 119,917 souls. Yet the mining counties had forty-four representatives in the legislature while the six southern counties had only twelve. To escape the heavy taxation the southern counties advocated a revision of the constitution in matters of taxation, or the division of the state.[36] Others complained that the growing quartz mine industry, which required the investment of considerable amounts of capital, was being retarded for the want of titles in fee.[37]

The great stumbling block in the way of equalization of taxes and the investment of capital in quartz mining was the ownership of the mineral lands by the federal government. Various plans were proposed. The committee on mines and mining interests in the assembly advocated the continuation of the policy of non-interference in the placer mines until the time when capital would have to be applied. But it favored granting to the owners of quartz mines a title for a certain period during which time the grantee could "transfer or work his claim at pleasure." Meanwhile the state should be authorized to levy and collect taxes on the assessed value of the property of the quartz miners.

[36] California, *Assembly Jour.*, 1852, 12–13. Governor McDougal pointed out in his annual message that the six southern counties with a population of 6,367 souls had paid into the state treasury for the fiscal year ending July 1, 1851, the sum of $41,705.26; while the twelve mining counties, with a population of 119,917 souls, had paid during the same period only $21,253.66. The amount of capitation taxes assessed in the twelve mining counties was $51,495.00, and the amount returned as delinquent $47,915.00; while the amount assessed in the agricultural counties was $7,205.00 and the amount returned as delinquent $3,291.50.

[37] *Alta*, January 28, December 8, 1852.

It was also proposed to induce the federal government to grant the mines to the state.[38]

A committee composed of one member from each of the mining counties within the state was appointed in the assembly to report as to the expediency of calling a miners' state convention to consider a policy with reference to the mines. The majority report of the committee, presented March 19, 1853, was opposed to a miners' state convention fearing that it might result in a recommendation to Congress "for the adoption of some system by which miners would be required to procure a fee simple title to their claims, that they may be subject to additional taxation." The miners contended that the mining occupation was full of hardships and it would be difficult to assess mining claims fairly; that a fee simple title would not keep the miner a single day longer when he found it impracticable to work his claim.[39] The miners of California, said the Sacramento *Union*, should be as free as the air, and any project of legislating for the mineral lands by the state or federal government, would be impracticable and impossible to enforce the law. "A fee simple title," said the *State Journal*, "would produce confusion and hardship." "The policy of the state and nation should be 'hands off'," said the Placerville *Herald*.[40] Thus the miners frustrated an attempt of the agricultural and commercial interests to devise a policy for the taxation of the mines.

State ownership of the minerals.—There had always prevailed an opinion in California that by right the gold fields

---

38 California, *Assembly Jour.*, 1852, 829–35. Also see report of the Senate special committee (California, *Sen. Jour.*, 1852, 584–88).

39 California, *Assembly Jour.*, 1853, App., Doc. 35.

40 For a discussion of the mineral question during this period see *Alta*, March 16, May 20, 1853; Sacramento *State Journal*, February 17, 1853; Sacramento *Union*, January 28, 1856, December 12, 1857, January 22, 1858, February 12, 18, 22, 25, 1859. In the opinion of the *Alta* the state's taxable property would be increased by $200,000.00 if the mines were granted to the miners.

belonged to the state and not to the federal government. This doctrine gained considerable popularity when the state supreme court held in the case of *Hicks* v. *Bell* that "the mines of gold and silver on the public lands are as much the property of this State, by virtue of her sovereignty, as are similar mines in the lands of private citizens." This principle was reiterated two years later in the case of *Stoaks* v. *Barrett*.[41] The *Placer Times and Transcript* congratulated the people of California upon the "acquisition of so splendid a heritage." "Why should we entrust these matters," it said, "to those who are removed from us thousands of miles, and who do not possess the necessary knowledge nor sympathy to manage the mines efficiently."[42]

In the senate Dosh introduced a bill which assumed for the state, by virtue of its sovereignty, the ownership of all the mines. In his minority report on the bill Dosh contended that under the Spanish and Mexican law, the minerals in all lands, public and private, were reserved to the sovereignty. The right to the mines in these lands became vested in the "sovereignty which superseded that of Mexico," that is the state of California. This conclusion was based upon the following argument: For many years prior to the conquest by the United States, the department of California had a "regularly organized government"; this system of laws, with some modifications, continued in force until the time when the state government was put into full operation. "*The first recognition of California by Congress, was as an independent sovereignty,*" a state; and by reason of that independent sovereignty, the right of eminent domain "which had been transferred to the government of the United States by

---

[41] *Hicks* v. *Bell,* 3 California, 227; *Stoakes* v. *Barrett,* 5 California, 39. But in *Moore* v. *Smaw,* and *Fremont* v. *Flower* (17 California, 223), the supreme court of California refused to sustain the doctrine advanced in the above cases.

[42] *Placer Times and Transcript,* August 14, 1853. The *Alta* of August 12, 1853, and the Sacramento *Union* of August 17, 1853, expressed themselves against the doctrine of state ownership of the mines.

the treaty of Guadalupe Hidalgo, by the Act admitting California into the Union, passed to the sovereignty of this State.''[43]

The majority of the committee reported adversely to the passage of the bill, maintaining that the mineral lands belonged to the federal government. The placer miners feared that the doctrine of state ownership of the mines was fraught with great danger to the mining interest, ''that it would not be a great while until those lands would be wrested from the miners and placed in the hands of monopolists.'' All they asked was ''*to be let alone.*'' They claimed that the federal government which was the rightful owner of the mines had ''solemnly declared'' that these lands should not be surveyed and sold, but should be open to the free use and enjoyment of all American citizens under the mining laws adopted by the miners themselves.[44]

Miners' rules and regulations.—These miners' rules and regulations,[45] which seemed to suit the interests of the miners so well, were based upon the European and Mexican mining laws adjusted to the needs and experiences of the new environment. By 1860 they had been formulated into a miners' code resting on equitable principles and democratic in character. The main purposes were to determine the size of the claims and to prescribe

---

[43] California, *Sen. Jour.*, 1857, 275–81. The same opinion was expressed by J. W. Denver of California in his speech in Congress on the California land claims (*Cong. Globe,* 34 Cong., 1 Sess., 1842). There was also considerable controversy between the state and federal authorities with regard to the question whether or not the mineral lands were included in the township grant of 1853. The federal authorities contended that the grant contemplated only such townships as could be legally surveyed and divided into sections. But since the mineral lands were excluded from survey by an act of Congress, there could be no such selections from them. The California authorities, on the other hand, maintained that the Act of 1853 contained no reservation with regard to the mineral lands, and the mining districts were in need of educational facilities just as well as other districts. See California, *Sen. and Assembly Jours.*, 1863, 38–44.

[44] California, *Sen. Jour.*, 1857, 274–75.

[45] Good accounts of the miners' rules and regulations are given in Yale, *Legal Titles to Mining Claims and Water Rights,* chaps. 7, 8; Shinn, *Mining Camps,* chaps. 2, 10, 13, 21, 23. See also Browne's *Report* in *H. Ex. Doc.* 29, 39 Cong., 2 Sess., 226–64 (1289).

the methods of recording, working, and holding them. The size varied according to the richness of the placers, ranging from ten to one hundred and fifty feet square. In general, a reasonable amount of work had to be done in order to establish and hold a claim to a placer mine. The purpose of limiting the size of the claims and defining the condition of holding them was to guard the mines from being monopolized. Here we notice the common aversion of the frontier democracy to monopoly. The promulgation of the rules and the settlement of disputes were also handled in a typical frontier democratic fashion. The rules were generally framed and amended at a public mass meeting conducted in an informal manner. The disputes were arbitrated by a board of miners selected by the disputants from the neighboring mining camps or by a miners' jury previously appointed at a miners' meeting. The decision of this board was final.

The state legislature, after some consideration, declared by statute that in "actions respecting 'Mining Claims' proof shall be admitted of the customs, usages, or regulations established and in force at the bar, or diggings, embracing such claim; and such customs, usages, or regulations, when not in conflict with the Constitution and Laws of this State, shall govern the decision of the action."[46] Thus the legislature declared the miners' laws to be binding in matters relating to mining claims. The "let alone" policy of the federal government was interpreted by the miners as a tacit approval by the federal government of their mining code.

Revival of the mining question in Washington.—After Fillmore's recommendation of 1851, the mining question slept in Congress. In his annual report of 1858, Secretary of the Interior Thompson revived it, pointing out the need of adopting some definite policy with regard to the mineral lands.[47] California immediately protested against "Congressional tinkering" with

[46] California, *Statutes*, 1851, 149.

[47] *H. Ex. Doc.* 2, 35 Cong., 2 Sess., 77 (997).

the mines. Congressman Scott asserted that the government had no right to dispose of the California gold fields and that it could never enforce such a policy, for California would "resist to the last any such encroachment on the part of the federal government." The *Alta* and the *Bulletin* warned the government not to attempt to prescribe mining regulations, or to expect to realize any revenue from the mines. "A revolution, and nothing short of it," they threatened, "would in all probability be the result of any improper interference on the part of the General Government, with the rights of that large and deserving class of our population" and if persisted in "would result in the loss of California to the Federal Union."[48]

The California Senators now introduced a bill to legalize the existing state of affairs which the government had tacitly sanctioned, and thus remove the technical charge that the miners were trespassers on the public lands. The bill brought forth a long discussion. Senator Latham reminded the Senate that the California supreme court had decided that the right to the mines existed in the state. But the opposition contended that such a law would be equivalent to a virtual cession of the mineral lands to the state of California, or to private individuals, without any remuneration to the federal government. The bill was rejected.[49]

Effect of the Civil War on the mining question.—On the outbreak of the Civil War the mining question was again revived. The costliness of the war and the depleted condition of the national treasury convinced the federal authorities that it would be no more than just to make the valuable gold and silver mines contribute some revenue to the government. Secretary of the Interior Caleb B. Smith and Commissioner of the General Land

[48] *Cong. Globe,* 35 Cong., 2 Sess., 1487; *Alta,* January 14, 1859; *Bulletin,* November 24, 26, 1858.

[49] For the bill and debate see *Cong. Globe,* 36 Cong., 1 Sess., 1754, 1771, 1777, 1795.

Office Edmunds called the attention of Congress to the advisability of taxing the mines. "When multiplied demands upon the treasury weigh upon it with unprecedented pressure," argued Commissioner Edmunds, "it could not be deemed unreasonable, after the hundreds of millions of dollars allowed to be taken free of cost, if the government should hereafter subject the product of such mines to a moderate seignorage."[50]

California immediately protested against the taxing plan, maintaining that it would be a "tax on labor and enterprize"; a policy that would be inexpedient from an economic as well as from a political point of view, for it would discourage the production of the precious metals—the sinews of war. The legislature adopted a resolution opposing the passage of any law taxing the gold and silver mines. In his annual message of January, 1863, Governor Stanford criticized the plan to tax the mines. He believed that it would be better to dispose of the land in small tracts, thus enabling the state to tax the mines.[51]

But Commissioner Edmunds and Secretary of the Interior Usher urged the abandonment of the policy of non-interference. Commissioner Edmunds pointed out that the auriferous regions in British Columbia, by proper control and management, had been made a source of revenue to the British government, while the mines of the precious metals in the United States had been left open to the people of all nations without the payment of any tax whatever. Thus during the sixteen years of free mining, $100,000,000 had been extracted from the mines, "without a dollar's revenue to the national exchequer." At a time when the "nation is weighed down with financial obligations," he argued, the mining industry should contribute its share to sustain the government. His plan was to require the placer miner to secure a license to work his mine by the payment of a small sum. If found profitable, the claimant might continue to work

---

[50] *H. Ex. Doc.* 1, 37 Cong., 2 Sess., 445, 489 (1126).

[51] California, *Sen. Jour.*, 1863, 41–42; California, *Statutes*, 1862, 601.

it by the payment of a reasonable amount per foot and a certain percentage of the product secured.[52]

The next year Secretary of the Interior Harland and Secretary of the Treasury McCulloch urged again the discontinuance of the policy of non-interference. Secretary McCulloch denounced any system of leasing the mines as impracticable, un-American, and unconstitutional. His advice was to sell the mineral lands and "substitute an absolute title in fee for the indefinite possessory rights or claims now asserted by the miners." Such a system, he held, would give a character of permanency to the mining district.[53] Commissioner Edmunds, however, maintained that it would be inexpedient to sell the mineral lands. He pointed out that without expensive investigation the government could not fix the minimum price, which should bear an equitable ratio between the various locations. And if the explorations should be left to individuals, then the lucky miner who should discover a rich deposit would keep the fact secret until he became the possessor of it. In view of the many difficulties and the system of mining rights which had grown up in the mining regions, Commissioner Edmunds believed that no wise policy could be devised until the whole question had been more carefully investigated by the government.[54]

There was, however, a prevailing belief in Washington that the time had come to abandon the policy of non-interference. On July 9, 1865, Julian, chairman of the House Committee on Public Lands, reported a bill providing for the sale of the gold and silver mines in small tracts, at a minimum price adjusted according to the size and value of the deposit. It limited the quantity which one individual could buy to forty acres, and it prohibited combinations among the different bidders. In an elaborate speech Julian denounced the non-interference policy

52 *H. Ex. Doc.*, 1, 38 Cong., 2 Sess., 5–6, 39–42 (1220).

53 *H. Ex. Doc.*, 1, 39 Cong., 1 Sess., pp. III–IV (1248); *H. Ex. Doc.*, 1, 39 Cong., 1 Sess., 31–32 (1254).

54 *H. Ex. Doc.*, 1, 39 Cong., 1 Sess., 38–43 (1248).

as "financial profligacy," "legislative madness." "How long," he exclaimed, "will the people thus sport with their resources and bear with the public servants who are thus recreant to the public good?" Moreover, the sale of these lands, he argued, would benefit the mining districts also, for under the system of tenancy at will, permanent settlements were impossible since the population was nomadic, thus preventing the establishment of homes and organized public life. "It is a conspiracy against the establishment and sacredness of the American Home!" he exclaimed. The bill was recommitted.[55] To gain more information on the subject, several members of Congress visited the mineral regions of the Pacific Coast.[56]

Attitude of California.—Public opinion in California was divided on the mineral land question. The quartz miners, the agricultural, and the commercial interests, generally favored a policy which should confer titles in fee to the miners. Such a policy, it was argued, would induce people to settle down and make improvements on their claims, and would result in the equalization of taxation. But the placer miners were opposed to any change, fearing that any system devised by Congress would be inimical to the interests of the miners. "The mining interest of the Pacific States and Territories is destined to receive too much affectionate attention at Washington this Winter," said the Sacramento *Union.* The *Union* argued that the nomadic character of the mining population was due not to the want of titles in fee simple but to the very nature of the miners' trade, and no government title could keep the miners after a deposit had become unprofitable.[57]

---

[55] See *Cong. Globe,* 38 Cong., 2 Sess., 684–87.

[56] California, *Assembly Jour.,* 1865–1866, 58.

[57] Sacramento *Union,* January 6, 1866. Resolutions against selling or taxing the mineral lands were adopted at the state Democratic convention (Davis, *Political Conventions in California,* 209, 224, 229). But also see *Bulletin,* January 19, June 29, July 6, 31, 1866.

In an elaborate memorial drawn up at the miners' state convention of January, 1866, and forwarded to Washington, it was pointed out that the policy of selling the mineral lands would revolutionize the whole mining system under which the mines had been developed to the benefit of the state and the nation. But in view of the existing situation, argued the memorialists, the next wisest policy would be to extend the preemption system over the mineral lands and to donate to their possessors the claims which they held under the miners' regulations.[58]

Passage of the Act of 1866.—The settlement of the mineral land question came in the first session of the thirty-ninth Congress. On May 28, 1866, Conness of California, chairman of the Senate Committee on Mines and Mining, reported a bill favorable to the mining interests of the Pacific Coast. After a long discussion the bill passed the Senate. When it came to the House, Julian succeeded in having it referred to his Committee on Public Lands. This meant the defeat of the bill, for Julian insisted on the measure which he had introduced and reported. Finding their plan thwarted in the House, Senators Conness and Stewart called up a House bill entitled an "Act granting the Right of Way to Ditch and Canal Owners over the Public Lands, and for Other Purposes," and skilfully managed to carry a motion to strike out the whole of the House bill except the enacting clause and insert the mining bill which had been passed in the Senate. In spite of Julian's opposition the friends of the measure managed to push it through the House, and it became a law.[59]

---

58 The memorial was published in the Sacramento *Union,* January 31, 1866.

59 For the several bills and debates see *H. Rep.*, 66, 39 Cong., 1 Sess. (1272). *Cong. Globe,* 39 Cong., 1 Sess., 1844, 2965; *H. Rep.*, 105, 39 Cong., 1 Sess. (1240); *Cong. Globe,* 39 Cong., 1 Sess., 3225–37, 3451–54, 3951–52, 4054. A full account of the history of the passage of the bill was given by a correspondent in Washington, published in the *Alta* on May 17, 1867. A different view of the same subject is given by Julian in his *Political Recollections,* 286–92. "The clumsy and next to incomprehensible bill," he says, "thus became a law, and by legislative methods as indefensible as the measure itself."

This great act of July 26, 1866, legalized the miners' rules and regulations which were not in conflict with the laws of the United States and made it possible to acquire a title in fee simple to the precious-metal bearing lands. The first section reads:

> The mineral lands of the public domain, both surveyed and unsurveyed, are hereby declared to be free and open to exploration and occupation by all citizens of the United States, and those who have declared their intention to become citizens, subject to such regulations as may be prescribed by law, and subject also to the local customs or rules of miners in the several mining districts, so far as the same may not be in conflict with the laws of the United States.

It also provided that miners, who had occupied and improved or who should hereafter occupy and improve a mine according to the local regulations, might receive a patent at the cost of five dollars per acre. As a preventive against monopolies it was provided that "no location hereafter shall exceed two hundred feet in length along the vein for each locator, with an additional claim for discovery to the discoverer of the lode," and no person was to make more than one location on the same load. The maximum for an association of persons was three thousand feet.[60]

The new policy was generally well received in California.

> The passage of the bill [said the San Francisco *Bulletin*] whatever defects it may develop when more critically developed and enforced, marks a change in the public land policy equal in importance to the adoption of the preemption and homestead systems. . . . . Eastern and European capital will flow to California and Nevada in large sums under the new system. . . . . The new law will furthermore secure equality of taxation. . . . . California may well rejoice at its passage.[61]

The *Placer Herald*, a mining paper, hailed the new policy as the dawn of a new era for California. "It is the fairest and most practicable proposition that has yet been considered in Congress," said the Sacramento *Union*. "It is a great stride toward the final adjustment of a dangerous question, and a vast improvement upon the measures broached at Washington at various

[60] United States, *Statutes at Large*, XVI, 251–52.

[61] *Bulletin*, July 31, 1866.

periods during the past three years.'' According to the *Bulletin* not a single newspaper was opposed to the act.[62] In his message of 1866, Governor Low said: ''The apprehension of miners in regard to unwise and unfriendly legislation by Congress touching the mineral lands has been allayed by the passage of just and generous laws which guarantee the actual possession to those on whom the prosperity of the State so largely depends.''[63]

The act of July 26, 1866, pertained only to vein mines. No provision was made for the acquisition of title to placer mines. The committee in Congress believed that, since the placers were becoming exhausted, there was no need to legislate for them. The act of July 9, 1870, remedied this omission, and ordered the sale of placer mines at two dollars and fifty cents an acre. It limited the extent of one location by an individual or an association to one hundred and sixty acres. In other respects the placer locations were to conform to local rules and regulations. The act of May 10, 1872,[64] ''to promote the development of the mining resources of the United States,'' in general reaffirmed the policy outlined in the former two acts, especially with regard to exploration and purchase of the mineral lands.

Summary.—The question of the control and disposition of the mineral lands was an agitating subject in the state, and to some extent in Washington, for about eighteen years. During this period the general government made several attempts to legislate for the mines, but it lacked the necessary information as well as courage to work out a definite policy. As a result the administration floundered from one plan to another: at one time it suggested the system of leasing; at another, selling the lands in small parcels; and when California protested against both systems it recommended ''non-interference.'' It was of course much easier to follow the policy of ''masterly inactivity''

---

62 Sacramento *Union,* June 23, 1866; *Bulletin,* August 8, 1866.

63 California, *Sen. Jour.,* 1867–1868, 53.

64 United States, *Statutes at Large,* XVI, 217–18; XVII, 91–96.

than to brave the opposition of California. And thus, in spite of some protest against the failure of the government to assert its rights to the mines, the federal treasury derived no revenue from the hundreds of millions of dollars worth of gold extracted during this period from the Pacific Coast mines by people from all parts of the globe.[65] It was the exhaustion of the placer mines and the heavy cost of the Civil War that finally brought the government to adopt a policy that enabled it to derive some revenue from the mines.

The passage of the several mining acts marked the end of the policy of reserving the gold and silver mines to the government. Thus came to a close another chapter in the history of the relations of California with the national government. The controversy about the control and disposition of the gold and silver mines on the Pacific Coast demonstrates the influence and effect of public opinion, in a state or particular section of the country, upon the policies of the federal government.

---

[65] In his report of 1866, Browne estimated the total production of gold in California up to 1865 at about $900,000,000. The gold exportation from San Francisco during these years was as follows: 1849, $4,921,250; 1850, $27,676,346; 1851, $42,582,695; 1852, $46,588,434; 1853, $57,330,034; 1854, $51,328,653; 1855, $45,182,631; 1856, $48,880,543; 1857, $48,976,697; 1858, $47,548,025; 1859, $47,649,462; 1860, $42,203,345; 1861, $40,639,080; 1862, $42,561,761; 1863, $46,071,920; 1864, $55,707,201; 1865, $44,984,546. Total, $740,832,623. To this he added $200,000,000, the amount carried away during this sixteen years unmanifested. *Report upon the Resources of the States and Territories West of the Rocky Mountains* (*H. Ex. Doc.* 29, 39 Cong., 2 Sess., 50 [1289]).

CHAPTER V

THE INDIAN QUESTION

California, like many other frontier communities in the United States, had her Indian[1] question which proved exceedingly troublesome to the state and to the national government. In many respects the problem was more acute in California than elsewhere. Unlike most frontier communities, where the advance of the white man was gradual and in a more or less straight line, in California the adventurous white settlers and miners in a short time penetrated the whole territory and partly destroyed the Indian's means of subsistence, which had never been too plentiful. The Indian, though he had but a vague idea of his right to the soil, resented this intrusion. "This is our country," said an Indian chief to Sub-agent Johnston, "why do the Americans come here? They are good and brave, but they come upon the land of my people. What do they intend to do?"[2] Actuated by the fear of starvation and frequently provoked by reckless whites, the Indians often resorted to stealing and to robbing the frontier settlements.

---

[1] The California Indians stood low in the scale of civilization. The valley Indians were mild, but those living north from the headwaters of the Sacramento to the Oregon border, and around the Gila and Colorado region were warlike and thievishly inclined. The number of Indians in California in the fifties of the nineteenth century is variously estimated from 75,000 to 500,000. Probably a hundred thousand would be nearer the mark. Even this number, according to Kroeber, was an eighth of the whole of the Indian population in America north of Mexico. See Kroeber's article on the Indians of California, *in* Eldredge, *History of California,* V, 125; *Sen. Ex. Doc.* 4, 33 Cong., Special Sess., 62, 68, 242, 261 (688).

[2] *Sen. Ex. Doc.* 4, 33 Cong., Special Sess., 65 (688).

Early Indian disturbances.—Reports of Indian depredations and calls for military aid were not infrequent occurrences even during the period of military occupation. Colonel Mason and General Riley, finding themselves powerless to prevent disturbances on such an extended frontier, adopted the policy of issuing arms and ammunition to the Americans who were exposed to Indian attacks, and told them to fight the Indians themselves.[3] General Riley recommended that the army on the coast be increased and that forts be built. He also suggested the advisability of placing the Indians in districts over which the United States government should retain exclusive jurisdiction, or that the government relinquish to California the control of the Indians.[4] In 1850 three federal commissioners were appointed to negotiate treaties with the Indians in California.

Policy of the state authorities.—Collisions between Indians and whites were becoming more frequent. The settlers on the borderland called for military protection but Governor Burnett advised each district to defend itself against the Indians. On two occasions he deviated from his policy and ordered out a portion of the state militia against the Indians. These two expeditions were unsuccessful from a military point of view and they involved the state in a debt of $149,199.91.[5]

The frequent calls for aid induced Governor Burnett to recommend to the legislature the adoption of some effective measures against the Indians. He believed that this "war of extermination will continue to be waged between the races until the Indian race becomes extinct," and that it was beyond the wisdom of man to avert the "inevitable destiny of this race."[6]

---

[3] *H. Ex. Doc.* 17, 31 Cong., 1 Sess., 556, 557, 642, 645, 682, 936 (573). In August, 1848, there were about six hundred and sixty officers and men in California. But the whole army of the United States in 1849–50 aggregated 12,927 members. Bancroft, *California,* VII, 450; *H. Ex. Doc.* 17, 31 Cong., 1 Sess., 943 (573).

[4] *Sen. Ex. Doc.* 52, 31 Cong., 1 Sess., 43, 56–57, 74 (561).

[5] California, *Sen. Jour.*, 1851, 16–18, 603–5, 734–35.

[6] California, *Sen. Jour.*, 1851, 14–15.

His successor, Governor McDougal, was even more alarmed. He recommended the adoption of an energetic policy as the only expedient way to avert a protracted struggle. He was confident that ultimately the federal government would take over the duty, but for the present he believed California must rely upon her own arm for protection.[7]

A few days later he addressed letters to General Smith, commander of the United States forces on the Pacific Coast, and to the Indian commissioners, stating that a general Indian war threatened California. The former he asked to send military aid; the latter he requested to repair to the scene of hostilities as soon as possible and attempt to reestablish friendly relations with the Indians.[8] He also instructed Colonel Johnson of the state militia to proceed to the Mariposa district, investigate the situation, and take the measures necessary to deal "judiciously" with it. He emphasized strongly that the great object should be to effect a peace with the least bloodshed and at the least expense.[9]

To protect the mining districts, the legislature passed an act authorizing the treasurer of the state "to negotiate a loan upon the faith and credit of the State for the purpose of defraying the expenses which have been or may be incurred in suppressing Indian hostilities in this State, in the absence of adequate provision being made by the General Government."[10] The state authorities were confident that the general government would, as

---

[7] *Ibid.*, 601–2. Governor McDougal came to California in 1849, from Indiana.

[8] California, *Sen. Jour.*, 1851, 670–71, 676, 677.

[9] *Ibid.*, 672–75; *Assembly Jour.*, 1470.

California, *Sen. Jour.*, 1851, 734–35 (*Report* of the adjutant general).

[10] California, *Statutes*, 1851, 520–21. The act of March 7, 1851, prescribing the amount of compensation to officers and men allowed to each major $15 a day; to each captain, $12 a day; to each lieutenant, $10 a day; to each sergeant, $7 a day; to each private, $5 a day, etc. (California *Statutes*, 1851, 489–91).

in the case of many other states, assume the war debt, a "debt legitimately due by the General Government."[11]

On March 1, 1851, Governor McDougal sent a letter to President Fillmore informing him that the rapid settlement of the country had suddenly brought into contact two races of widely different character, resulting in bitter conflict along the entire frontier of the state. He stated that there were about 100,000 Indian warriors, "all animated by a spirit of bitter hostility, and whom pacific and forebearing policy encourages into renewed acts of outrage." The only course left to the state, he thought, was to coerce them into submission. To accomplish this object a strong military force was needed. But unfortunately, he complained, the general government had neglected California; the military force assigned to that state was entirely inadequate; and it was stationed on the coast where there was little need for troops. Moreover, observation and experience had convinced him that the "regular troops of the United States were unfit for a desultory Indian war, to be carried on among the fastness of our mountains." He asserted that a temporary force of rangers selected from the experienced frontiersmen and mountaineers, of whom there were a large number in California, might settle the difficulties in a much shorter time than government troops. But the heavily burdened state could not undertake it without the aid of the national government. He therefore requested that the executive of California be authorized to call out from time to time, as exigencies might require, portions of the militia, who were to be equipped, provisioned, and compensated by the national government.

> It may seem to your Excellency that this is an extraordinary suggestion, [he said] but you will remember that we occupy an extraordinary situation—very far removed from the seat of the General Government, with conditions peculiar to California, and necessities that admit of neither question nor delay.

---

[11] California, *Assembly Jour.*, 1851, 853–54, 1368.

Protection by our people is regarded as their constitutional right; it is about the only benefit they can derive from their relation to the Federal Government, while their burthens are not light ones.

It is not to be disguised that there is a feeling, and that a growing one, of dissatisfaction here with the General Government. They are aware and feel that they have been taxed, but not protected.[12]

Attitude of the federal authorities.—The federal authorities entertained different views. In his communication to Washington, General Smith contended that the Indian disturbances were due to the intrusion and reckless behavior of the whites who "have determined that there shall be a war." He was opposed to the use of state militia by the general government on the grounds of economy, efficiency, and expedience. He pointed out that the pay of a private during the latest expedition undertaken by California was equal to the salary of any officer in the army except his own. He also believed that frontiersmen were not the proper class of people to use for the restoration of order on the frontier.[13]

Guided by information from "reliable sources," and by the general experience with respect to relations between frontier communities and the Indians within their borders, Secretary of War Conrad replied to Governor McDougal that the information received by the War Department showed that the Indians in California were not so warlike as the governor believed and that the hostile attitude of the Indian was largely due to the aggressive behavior of the whites, particularly the adventurous miners. He did not think that a perpetual war between the two races was inevitable; these disturbances were merely a transitory inconvenience experienced by many frontier communities.

As to the question of sending military aid, the Secretary stated that the force in California was as large as could be spared from other places. Moreover, since it was the opinion of

[12] McDougal to President Fillmore, March 1, 1851 (*H. Ex. Doc.* 2, 32 Cong., 1 Sess., 138–40 [634]).

[13] General Smith to General Jones, March 13, 1851 (*ibid.*, 137–38).

the governor that regular troops were unfit for Indian warfare, it would be useless to send more troops. In regard to the proposition of authorizing the governor to call out the militia at the expense of the national government, the Secretary stated that the President did not consider himself authorized to adopt such a plan, for the act of 1795 empowered the executive to call out the militia only when the United States "shall be invaded, or be in imminent danger of invasion from any foreign nation or Indian tribe," and it was doubtful whether the situation in California was serious enough to be called an invasion. Moreover, the use of militia for Indian warfare was inexpedient for two reasons: in the first place, it was too expensive, especially in California, where the pay stipulated to be paid to volunteers (who had been recently organized) was "exorbitant and beyond anything ever known in this country." In the second place, there was

> reason to fear, if that plan were adopted, that in a population like that of California, where there are so many ardent young men, the love of adventure with some and the high pay with others, would operate as inducements to perpetual collisions with the Indians. . . . . Independently of its experience in other parts of the country, it has been informed that a partial and temporary adoption of the plan recommended by your Excellency has already produced these results in California. The President deems it his duty to make these suggestions, not doubting that your Excellency will do all in your power, to prevent abuses as injurious to the State, as they are revolting to humanity.[14]

Meanwhile reports of Indian attacks, of white men literally flayed alive, became more frequent. The press, particularly the mountain journals, was full of hostile expressions against the Indians. It was asserted that "any patching up of paper treaties" with the Indians, was "mere moonshine." The proper way to deal with the Indians was to keep an effective force of mounted men in the field until the savages were completely subdued. The legislature was urged to remonstrate against the

[14] Secretary of War Conrad to Governor McDougal, April 30, 1851 (*H. Ex. Doc.* 2, 32 Cong., 1 Sess., 139–43).

neglect of the federal government to protect the California frontier.[15]

The Indian commissioners issued an address on January 13, 1851, appealing to the people of California, especially the frontier settlers and miners, to abstain from their belligerent attitude and "pursue a course of conduct marked by mildness, moderation and forbearance." The commissioners pointed out that in the absence of a farther western territory, to which the Indians could be removed, the only way to solve the racial problem in California would be either to exterminate or to domesticate the red man, and justice demanded the latter policy.[16]

The commissioners visited the state capitol to consult with the governor and members of the legislature concerning the Indian disturbances. Most of the Indian attacks, the commissioners held, were induced by cruel acts of unprincipled whites, while the politicians who did not approve the "address" were simply seeking to make political capital of the Indian disturbances by posing as the only friends of the immigrants and miners. They also condemned Governor McDougal for his belligerency and disapproved of his order calling out two hundred volunteers for a punitive expedition against the Indians, at the rate of five and ten dollars a day, thus piling up "another pretty little claim" for "Uncle Sam." This belligerent policy, they claimed, put unnecessary difficulties in their way.[17]

The commissioners were convinced that the proper way to deal with the Indians was to hold out "an olive branch rather than a sword." They believed that nothing could induce the

---

[15] *Herald,* March 14, 1851; *Alta,* Jan. 6, 21, 31, Feb. 14, 1851. The *Alta* was less hysterical; it inveighed against the circulation of exciting stories in the press; it openly asserted that the white adventurers were greatly to be blamed for the disturbances. The *Alta* was also opposed to the use of prejudiced frontiersmen as volunteers against the Indians, claiming that such means would only embarrass the Indian commissioners and prevent a speedy settlement of the troublesome question.

[16] This address was published in the *Alta,* Jan. 14, 1851.

[17] *Sen. Ex. Doc.* 4, 33 Cong., Special Sess., 53, 56–58, 59, 249 (688).

Indians, when their stomachs were full, to attack the whites. Hence they adopted the general policy of removing the Indians to special tracts of land set apart for them within the state and supplying them with enough provisions to last for some time. Eighteen treaties were made with the Indians, reserving for them some seven per cent of the total area of the state. The commissioners maintained that in the end these would be the cheapest treaties ever made by the United States government, for it was cheaper to feed the Indians a year than to fight them a week, especially when the expeditions were conducted by the state of California.[18]

The treaties were violently attacked in California. Many in the southern counties were afraid that they would be deprived of the Indian's cheap and easily procurable labor. The settlers and miners grudged the tempting mining and agricultural tracts embraced within the reservations, while the frontiersmen were opposed to the whole policy of settling hordes of savages in the heart of the state. "The Indian must go!" was their slogan. The press fulminated against the reservation policy which ceded to the Indians "the best mineral and agricultural lands" to the detriment of the white miners and farmers. It warned the government that the miners were determined to disregard the treaties, and "if necessary to take possession of the reserved land by force." It was asserted that the savages needed first a severe lesson that would impress them with the power of the white man.[19]

The commissioners attempted to "disabuse the public mind" in regard to the supposed extent and great mineral and agricultural wealth of the land reserved to the Indians. They pointed

[18] The Commissioners to Lea, May 1, 1851 (*Sen. Ex. Doc.* 4, 33 Cong., Special Sess., 54–56, 76, 128–30 [688]). About 11,700 square miles or 7,488,000 acres. Ellison, "Indian Policy in California, 1846–1860," in *Mississippi Valley Historical Review*, IX, 57 (June, 1922).

[19] Los Angeles *Star*, March 13, August 14, 1852; *in* Hayes, *Collection*, XXXVIII, 18, 19; *Herald*, August 2, 1851; *Alta*, July 26, 1851; Sacramento *Placer Times and Transcript*, September 24, 1851.

out that their purpose was to withdraw the Indians from the mountain fastnesses and settle them upon land rich enough to furnish means of livelihood. The interests of the whites, however, had not been overlooked; it was the policy, whenever possible, to exclude the Indians from the mining districts.[20] Such papers as the *Alta* and the *Picayune* championed the policy of the commissioners as the most humane and economical; they also denied that the reservations contained some of the best mineral and agricultural lands.[21]

But the efforts of the commissioners and their supporters to influence public opinion in favor of their policy were in vain. Both Governor McDougal and his successor, Governor Bigler, were openly opposed to the reservation system on the ground that large tracts of mineral and agricultural land were reserved to the Indians; also that the policy of settling numerous tribes of savages within the heart of the state would be productive of conflicts between the whites and the reds, involving the state and nation in great expense and inconvenience. Governor Bigler recommended that the legislature should transmit to the United States Senate a vigorous protest against the reservation system, urging the rejection of the treaties.[22]

In both houses of the legislature were drawn up reports and resolutions condemning the Indian treaties. It was asserted in these reports that the policy of assigning to a "few tribes of ignorant barbarians" a considerable portion of the richest mineral and agricultural lands would not benefit the Indians, who were not accustomed to a sedate life, but would cause the ejectment of a number of worthy American citizens who had preempted parts of these lands. It would also affect the prosperity of the state by withdrawing large portions of taxable

---

[20] *Alta,* Sept. 9, 1851. Letter of Barbour to the people, Sept. 13, Oct. 10, 1851, a communication from Wozencraft; McKee to Commissioner Mix, Oct. 28, 1851 (*Sen. Ex. Doc.* 4, 33 Cong., Special Sess., 213 [688]).

[21] *Picayune,* Sept. 13, 1851; *Alta,* May 31, July 26, Sept. 12, 1851.

[22] California, *Sen. Jour.,* 1852, 21, 79, 44–46.

property. Moreover, the reservation policy was contrary to the practices of the Mexican republic, which never admitted the right of the Indian to the soil; and contrary to the policy of the United States government of removing the Indians outside of the limits of the state, thereby preventing collisions between the two races. It was also pointed out that the inclusion of the neophytes of the missions would withdraw from the farms and vineyards of the southern districts a large part of the laboring force, and thereby strike a blow at the agricultural interests of the south. The resolutions in both houses of the legislature recommended that the California Senators be instructed to urge the rejection of the treaties in the Senate and to insist that the former policy of removing the Indian beyond the state should be also applied in California.[23]

An eloquent plea in behalf of the reservation system was made by Senator Warner in his minority report. He pointed out that the general government could not remove the Indians to Oregon, Utah, or New Mexico; nor could they be removed to the sterile regions of the Sierras. In view of these peculiar conditions, the commissioners had to devise the new policy of appropriating portions of land within the state where the Indians could be settled and "escape that certain destruction which awaits them on every other side."

> Will it be said that the land is not broad enough for them and us? or that while our doors are open to the stranger from the uttermost part of the earth we have not spare room for the residence of the once sole inhabitants of our magnificent empire? . . . . Has the love of gold blotted from our minds all feelings of compassion or justice?

The rejection of the treaties, Warner held, would be considered by the Indians as a breach of faith, and never again would they place reliance in any agents of the federal government. If the

[23] California, *Sen. Jour.*, 1852, 597–604.

treaties were unfair to the whites, they should be amended, not rejected.[24]

In newspaper columns and at public meetings the commissioners defended the reservation policy. Commissioner McKee addressed the legislature, pointing out that the lands reserved for the Indians were the least valuable. He warned the legislature that should the treaties be rejected the Indians would lose all confidence in the white man and a war of extermination would follow along a frontier of sixteen hundred miles. McKee also had an ineffectual conference with the assembly committee on Indian affairs and the resolution was adopted by a vote of thirty-five to six.[25]

While the treaties were still pending in the United States Senate, there were frequent conflicts between the whites and the Indians. General Hitchcock rebuked the miners who were intruding upon the reservations set apart for the Indians, maintaining that until the treaties were rejected they must be respected. He appealed to Governor McDougal to intervene in the matter in order to prevent further disturbances.[26] Also, Commissioner McKee complained to the governor of ''alarming difficulties'' between the whites and the Indians. He stated that the whites, relying on the opposition of the legislature to the treaties, disregarded the agreements and adopted summary measures in dealing with the Indians, killing in cold blood between thirty or forty Indians. ''The wanton sacrifice of human life,'' he said, ''brought lasting disgrace upon the American name.'' McKee requested the governor to bring some of the white culprits to punishment and to issue a proclamation ''calling upon all who have the true interests of California at heart, to frown upon such

24 California, *Sen. Jour.*, 1852, 602–4.

25 *Herald*, March 23, 1852. *See also* their communications to Washington in *Sen. Ex. Doc.* 4, 33 Cong., Special Sess., 207–8, 221, 248, 309–10, 333 (688); California, *Assembly Jour.*, 1852, 396–97.

26 *Alta*, Oct. 6, 1851.

attempts to imbrue the frontier in blood, by exciting in the Indians the spirit of revenge and retaliation.''[27]

The state authorities and the frontiersmen had a different conception of the relative rights of the two races; they were ready to underestimate the misconduct of the whites and exaggerate the cruelties of the Indians. In his reply Governor Bigler called the attention of the commissioners to a memorial submitted to the governor by the ''respectable gentlemen'' representing the northern counties in the legislature, where it was stated that within a few months the Indians had murdered about two hundred and fifty persons in the northern counties and had destroyed about $240,000 worth of property. These disturbances, asserted the memorialists, emanated ''from the known character of the Indians, a mischievous disposition and a desire for plunder.'' Unless the state or national government should send the proper military aid, the frontiersmen would either have to unite and exterminate the Indians, or withdraw from the border regions.[28] Governor Bigler maintained that McKee's attitude implied an ''imputation on the character of American citizens,'' and that as a public magistrate chosen by American citizens, he could not yield his approbation to any ''imputations upon their intelligence or patriotism.'' He was confident that a thorough investigation of the circumstances would fully acquit the American citizens of the charge of murdering ''defenceless Indians in cold blood.''[29]

McKee replied in the same tone. He asserted that he entertained as much regard for the character and honor of the Amer-

---

[27] McKee to Bigler, April 5, 1852. California, *Sen. Jour.*, 1852, 712–14. McKee also addressed a letter to General Hitchcock, informing him of the lawless behavior of the frontiersmen, which produced results that ''are sickening to the mind, as well as disgraceful to our State and national character.'' He asked the general to establish several military posts on the frontier for the mutual protection of the Indians and the whites (*ibid.*, 716–17).

[28] The memorial to Governor Bigler is found in California, *Sen. Jour.*, 1852, 703–4.

[29] California, *Sen. Jour.*, 1852, 714–16.

ican citizens as did the governor, but his regard "for *the dear people*" must not interfere with his sense of justice. He was unwilling to admit that special credit should be given to statements of members of the legislature, for the "accidental elevation of a man to a political station, especially in our frontier States, does not necessarily change his moral perception or sensibilities."[30]

In response to the appeal of the northern counties for military aid, Governor Bigler addressed a letter to General Hitchcock complaining that the neglect of the general government to provide adequate protection for the citizens of California was responsible for the loss of many lives, and should the government refuse to provide the necessary military protection, then results would ensue "which every true friend of the government must deplore." For there is a line of reciprocal duty upon which the mutual relations of a government and a people depends. He suggested to General Hitchcock that volunteer forces could be immediately enrolled if the general was authorized to state that the national government would assume the expense of such a force.[31]

General Hitchcock replied that he was doing his best to afford every protection possible under the circumstances, but because of the nature of the settlements, and the inadequate supply of troops, his earnest efforts could not always prevent disturbances. The reluctance of the War Department to station more troops on the coast was due to the belief that on account of the temptations

---

[30] McKee to Bigler, April 12, 1852 (*ibid.*, 717–21); *Sen. Ex. Doc.* 4, 33 Cong., Special Sess., 314–18 (688).

[31] Bigler to Hitchcock, April 8, 1852 (California, *Sen. Jour.*, 1852, 705–6). These views of the governor undoubtedly expressed the opinion of a majority of the people of California. Dissatisfaction with the military protection extended by the federal government was quite general even on the coast. It is a very sad spectacle, said the *Alta* of July 28, 1851, when the national government cannot afford proper protection for its people on the Pacific Coast. The San Francisco *Herald* asserted that the federal government entirely neglected to protect California, while at the same time it was collecting large amounts in taxes. All these things, it declared, rankle in the breasts of our people.

to desert it would be useless to send them. In regard to calling out the militia of the state, he told the governor that such a force could be recognized only when called into service by the President of the United States.[32]

Here again we see the differences in the point of view of the state and the federal authorities. The federal authorities did not think the situation serious enough for calling out the militia. The federal authorities had, in general, little sympathy with the idea of employing volunteers for punitive expeditions against the Indians. They believed that the "prime movers" for the Indian wars in California "were not without *substantial pecuniary reasons* for their patriotism," and that if it were not for these people the frontier would remain quiet.

Rejection of the treaties.—The Department of Indian Affairs received the California Indian treaties during the last months of 1851 and the early part of 1852. But being aware of the opposition to the treaties in California, the Department decided to delay their transmission to the Senate until it could obtain more information which would better enable it to judge correctly as to their merits and as to whether it should recommend their adoption, amendment, or rejection. Beale, superintendent of Indian affairs in California, was instructed to make a full report on the merits of the treaties.

Beale expressed himself in favor of the treaties. He pointed out that there was no place to which the Indians could be removed; the territory east of the Sierras was mostly a barren desert; Oregon had enough Indians of her own; to remove them to the south would place them directly in the line of the immigration routes, and would also be a violation of the treaty stipulations with Mexico, wherein the United States government promised not to colonize Indians on the Mexican border.[33] Com-

---

[32] Hitchcock to Bigler, April 10, 1852 (California, *Sen. Jour.*, 1852, 706–9).

[33] Beale to Lea, May 11, 1852 (*ibid.*, 326–30); *California Treaties 1851–1852*, 6–10.

missioner Lea was in favor of the treaties, though he admitted the novelty of some of their stipulations, especially the stipulation for the permanent settlement of tribes *"within the limits of a State on lands not previously owned by them."*[34]

But the California members in Congress opened war upon the treaties even before they were presented for discussion. "Where are the treaties?" asked Senator Gwin, "Why are they not transmitted to us. . . . . The people of California are up in arms against these treaties." In the House, McCorkle denounced the commissioners and the treaties. Commissioner Lea had a conference with the California members in Congress, but the latter were determined to do all within their power to have the treaties rejected in the Senate.[35]

On June 1, 1852, President Fillmore transmitted to the Senate the eighteen treaties. The California Senators immediately opened fire on them. They asserted that it would be impossible for the federal government to retain the Indians in undisturbed possession of the lands, for a whole army of the United States could not keep the white miners from intruding upon the reservations.[36] There was also a prevailing opinion in the Senate that, since the Indians had no usufructuary or other rights in the soil under the Mexican government, the United States government, as the successor to that sovereign power, succeeded to its rights in the soil and was under no obligation to treat with the Indians for the extension of their titles. All the treaties were rejected.[37]

Increase of military forces for California.—Even before the rejection of the treaties President Fillmore recommended that Congress increase the army so as to enable the War Department

[34] Lea to Secretary Stuart, May 14, 1852; *California Treaties 1851–1852*, 4–6.

[35] *Cong. Globe,* 32 Cong., 1 Sess., 890, 1121–22, App., 1082.

[36] *Cong. Globe,* 32 Cong., 1 Sess., 2173; 32 Cong., 2 Sess., 1085.

[37] It was stated by McCorkle that the treaties were rejected unanimously (*Cong. Globe,* 32 Cong., 1 Sess., 1082; 32 Cong., 2 Sess., 1085).

to augment the military force on the Pacific Coast for the protection of the frontier settlements.[38] Senator Gwin introduced a bill empowering the commanding officer of the United States forces on the Pacific Coast to make a requisition upon the governors of California and Oregon for volunteers to suppress Indian hostilities. The volunteers were to be armed at the expense of the United States government and to be paid three times as much as the regular officers and soldiers serving on the Pacific Coast. Commenting on his bill, Gwin pointed out that for an extensive country like California, with a long frontier of sparsely settled communities, the normal military force was a mere mockery, scarcely able to "protect their own scalps from the tomahawk of the Indians." He advocated the use of volunteers. "We have in our State," he said, "the picked men of the nation, and they only wish the Government to call for their services, and pay for them."[39]

When Gwin's bill was killed, his colleague, Weller, introduced a resolution calling for the organization of an additional regiment of mounted men and the establishment of military posts in California. Weller asserted that there were at least seventy-five thousand Indians in California, who only needed a "master spirit to confederate the tribes in a bloody and desolating war." He held that the extermination of the Indians was inevitable. He then gave voice to the usual frontier complaint against the inadequacy of military defense.

> It is not to be expected that a Government too weak to defend, or so unmindful of its duty as to refuse adequate protection, can command the respect or affection of its people. . . . . Recall your tax collectors, your hordes of Federal officers, and California would soon take care of herself. But if you tax us; if you claim our allegiance to the Federal Government; if we are to contribute towards its support, you must protect us. There must be a reciprocity in this matter. That some disaffection exists amongst the people, growing out of these causes, is certain; that unless the cause is removed this will increase is equally certain.[40]

---

[38] *H. Ex. Doc.* 2, 32 Cong., 1 Sess., 19 (634).

[39] *Cong. Globe,* 32 Cong., 1 Sess., 470–71.

[40] *Cong. Globe,* 32 Cong., 1 Sess., 1587.

Conciliation of the Indians.—With the rejection of the treaties the Indian situation became even worse than before. Many of the Indians had already been removed from their mountain homes and settled upon reservations, which in consequence of the rejection of the treaties they now had to leave. But by this time the whites had spread over their former hunting grounds, thus destroying their only source of subsistence. It was therefore feared that hunger and disgust with the whites would arouse the Indian to greater hostilities than before. Hence, to appease the Indians, Senator Weller offered an amendment to the Indian appropriation bill, proposing to appropriate the sum of $100,000 "for the purpose of purchasing supplies and presents to be distributed to the Indians of the State of California." The southern Senators objected to the whole paternalistic policy of feeding Indians from the federal treasury. Moreover, it was pointed out that at California prices the sum of $100,000, to be distributed among an Indian population of 75,000 souls, would be but a "drop in the bucket." Weller protested. He warned his fellow-Senators that if no provision for the Indians in California were made, his state would be involved in a prolonged war. "Who is to pay the expenses of the war?" he asked. He warned the Senate that

> if they are determined that the State of California shall not only feed these Indians, but that she shall be compelled to fight them with her own troops and at her own expense, and in the meantime you are taxing the very necessaries of life which they consume, the very bread which they eat, the time will come when there will be a spirit of disaffection upon the shores of the Pacific.[41]

Walker, of Wisconsin, deprecated the threats of secession. And Dawson, of Georgia, protested against the charge of illiberality to California. He asserted that no territory or state was ever more protected than was California.[42] The amendment was finally adopted. One hundred thousand dollars were appro-

41 *Cong. Globe,* 32 Cong., 1 Sess., 2172–75.

42 *Cong. Globe,* 32 Cong., 1 Sess., 2177.

priated for the "preservation of peace with the Indians who had been dispossessed of their lands in California."[43]

Military reservations.—Meanwhile Superintendent Beale began to experiment with a new plan. He congregated about a thousand Indians on a small reservation and put them to work, thus making the colony self-supporting. Satisfied with the success of his experiment, he wrote to the Indian Commissioner at Washington recommending the establishment of a number of small reservations on which the California Indians were to be collected. The tracts of land set aside for this purpose were to be regarded as military reservations, each one to be garrisoned by a military post. The Indians were not to receive the fee simple title to these lands. To make these little colonies self-supporting, the Indians were to be instructed by government agents in the art of productive labor. To enable him to carry out this policy he asked for an appropriation of $500,000.[44]

Commissioner Lea approved of this policy, and a law was passed in March, 1853, authorizing the establishment of five military reservations in California, New Mexico, and Utah. Each reservation was to contain not more than 25,000 acres.[45] In his report of December 5, 1853, Secretary of the Interior McClelland called the attention of Congress to the difficulty of finding suitable locations for military reservations in the northern part of California. He recommended the purchase of tracts of land from private persons, and suggested the advisability of requesting the state of California to grant to the federal government the right of exclusive jurisdiction over the reservations.[46]

When the subject came up for discussion in the Senate, several members voiced their dissatisfaction with the whole reservation system. Gwin thought it was not right to force upon the

---

[43] *Cong. Globe,* 32 Cong., 1 Sess., 2181.

[44] Beale to Lea, Nov. 22, 1852 (*Sen. Ex. Doc.* 4, 33 Cong., Special Sess., 374, 379–80 [688]).

[45] United States, *Statutes at Large,* X, 699.

[46] *H. Ex. Doc.* 1, 33 Cong., 1 Sess., 62 (710).

people of California a policy which they opposed. He also questioned the power of the federal government to reserve large tracts of land for Indian settlement within the limits of a state, and he doubted whether California would ever consent to cede jurisdiction. Weller maintained that it would be unfair to withhold from the people of California an area of 125,000 acres of arable land. He did not think the federal government could exercise exclusive jurisdiction over the reservations without the consent of the state. Others held that it was not necessary that the government should have exclusive jurisdiction, for the Indian who should commit an offense against the laws of the state could just as well be tried in the state courts.[47] The act finally passed provided for three reservations, but on the advice of the Indian Department a bill was passed at the next session providing for two additional reservations, each one not to exceed 25,000 acres.[48]

In California the new Indian policy was praised by some as the one most humane and economical. Many, however, were opposed to the whole reservation system. In his annual message of January 4, 1854, Governor Bigler urged the legislature to insist that there ''shall be no departure from the Indian policy which has so long received the sanction of the Government of the United States.''[49] In spite of occasional adverse criticism the new Indian policy was followed for some time.

The Indian war debt.—We have already seen that the failure of the federal government to supply the desired military aid for the protection of the frontier caused the state authorities to resort to the use of volunteers. Now volunteer service is always expensive, but it was especially costly in California because of the peculiar social and economic conditions. To cover the indebtedness which the state had incurred in suppressing Indian

[47] *Cong. Globe,* 33 Cong., 1 Sess., 1028–29, 1042–43.

[48] Act of July 31, 1854, Section 2 (United States, *Statutes at Large,* X, 332–33).

[49] California, *Sen. Jour.,* 1854, 24–25.

hostilities, the legislature passed an act on February 15, 1851, authorizing the state treasurer to negotiate a loan of not more than $500,000, at twelve per cent interest per annum. The claim of the state on the federal government was pledged for the payment of the principal and interest of the loan.[50] Under this act $200,000 worth of bonds were sold up to May 3, 1852, when it was repealed and a new act passed appropriating $600,000 to pay the expenses. Under the new act the bonds were to bear seven per cent interest per annum, and were to be paid out of the money to be appropriated by Congress to defray the expenses of the state in suppressing Indian hostilities. Only in case the amount to be paid by Congress should appear insufficient were the bonds to be valid claims against the state.[51]

By 1854 the total amount of the war debt, principal and interest, had reached the sum of $924,259.65.[52] The state authorities were confident that the federal government would assume the debt, for abundant precedents in the form of appropriations made for similar purposes[53] were to be found in the proceedings of Congress. Governor Bigler urged the legislature to demand that the government should assume the war debt. He also appointed Pierce as agent to collect and arrange the original documents connected with the several punitive expeditions in the years 1850, 1851, and 1852, and to proceed to Washington to endeavor to secure the payment of this money.[54]

In his interviews with some of the members of Congress Pierce found many of them prejudiced against the California claims. In both houses of Congress the California members intro-

---

[50] California, *Statutes*, 1851, 520–21.

[51] California, *Sen. Jour.*, 1852, 21, 75–76; 1852, 12–13.

[52] California, *Sen. Jour.*, 1854, 12.

[53] California, *Sen. Jour.*, 1852, 21, 75–76.

[54] California, *Sen. Jour.*, 1854, 18–19. In Browne's *Report* the amount of gold shipped in 1853 is given as only $57,330,034 (*H. Ex. Doc.* 29, 39 Cong., 2 Sess., 50 [1289]). See correspondence in reference to the war debt, California, *Sen. Jour.*, 1855, 63–64.

duced bills providing for the assumption of the California war debt by the federal government. They pointed out that this debt of about a million dollars was incurred by California because the federal government was not able to provide the necessary military aid, hence it was the duty of the federal government to assume this debt. After some discussion an amendment to the army appropriation bill of 1854 was adopted directing the Secretary of War to "ascertain the amount of expenses incurred by the State of California in the suppression of Indian hostilities" prior to January 1, 1854, and pay the amount not above $924,259.65 into the state treasury.[55]

In accordance with the provisions of the act of August, 1854, Secretary Jefferson Davis asked the state authorities to forward to him all the amounts, vouchers, and papers requisite to establish the claim. Instead of the vouchers the state authorities transmitted to the Secretary of War a certified statement of the amount paid by the state in suppressing Indian hostilities. Secretary Davis informed the governor of California that the requirement of the act could not be fulfilled upon the "evidence showing nothing more than that the State has made certain bonds and warrants" to satisfy certain claims; that unless he should be placed in possession of the vouchers on which the original warrants and bonds had been issued, he could not order the payment of the money appropriated by Congress. Other states, he said, in presenting similar claims against the government, had produced the original bills paid by them.[56]

The state authorities objected to transmitting the original bills to Washington, for in the settlement of the accounts before the board of examiners and legislature committees much of the testimony in behalf of the claimants was oral and had not been preserved. They feared lest, if Secretary Davis should assert the

[55] United States, *Statutes at Large*, X, 582–83.

[56] California, *Sen. Jour.*, 1856, 227 (letter from Jefferson Davis to the governor of California).

right "to go behind the act of the Board of Examiners, and inquire whether the demands were such as ought to have been allowed . . . . the exacting requirements of the Secretary and his auditing officers would find abundant pretexts to reduce the sum materially." They held that the act of Congress of August 5, 1854, did not require the Secretary of War to inquire into the necessity or expediency of some of the payments, which, owing to the peculiar conditions in California, were in some cases enormous.[57]

Realizing, however, that stubborn resistance to the demands of the Secretary of War would only delay the payment of the money and thereby increase the war debt, the state authorities decided to transmit to the Secretary all the documentary evidence and original vouchers. To save the cost of transporting the money to and from the state, and the further accumulation of interest on the bonds, an act of the legislature instructed the commissioners to advertise in the daily papers of Washington, Boston, New York, and Philadelphia inviting the bondholders to present the bonds for redemption. After the entire issue of the twelve per cent bonds had been redeemed, the commissioners were to apply the residue of the fund appropriated by Congress to the redemption of the seven per cent bonds. The reasons for giving preference to the twelve per cent bonds were (1) that the entire appropriation was pledged to their redemption, and (2) it was more advantageous to the state to redeem first the bonds bearing the higher rate of interest. The seven per cent bonds would not be due for several years, and since there was no permanent fund for their redemption, they would, it was assumed, be offered by their holders on terms that would enable the state to

[57] *Ibid.*, 28, 228. See also the report of the board of examiners in appendix to *Sen. Jour.*, 1855, Doc. 15, pp. 1–25. The board stated that the vouchers were in a state of confusion, and many irregularities had been committed in connection with this subject. A later committee of the legislature asserted that notorious frauds were committed in the issuance of these bonds (California, *Assembly Jour.*, 1864, App. to Vol. II, Doc. 38).

cancel the whole debt with the fund appropriated by Congress, thereby saving to the state some $200,000.[58]

But the state authorities reckoned without the host. The holders of the seven per cent bonds contended that the state of California had no right to apply preferentially to redemption of the twelve per cent bonds money appropriated by Congress for all the California creditors merely because such a transaction would benefit the state. Also the Senate Committee on Military Affairs, which had charge of a bill to provide for the settlement of the California war debt, held that the policy advocated by the state of California would involve the government in liabilities above the sum appropriated. The Committee further held that the United States government was not liable for any interest accrued since the appropriation was made, for it had accrued because the state authorities had not made the proper application for this fund.[59]

Since, under the act of Congress of 1856,[60] none of the money appropriated by Congress under the act of August 5, 1854, could be applied to the redemption of bonds issued after January 1, 1854; and since, by the ruling of the third auditor, interest could be allowed only up to January 1, 1854, there was no need to make any discrimination between the two kinds of bonds, for the appropriation of Congress was sufficient to pay the principal and interest on all the bonds due on January 1, 1854. But in consequence of the delay of two years from the time the appropriation was made until it was collected by the state, a large amount of interest had accumulated on the bonds. The coupons

---

[58] California, *Sen. Jour.*, 1856, 230–32; California, *Statutes*, 1856, 206–10. This action, he thought, was necessary, on account of the delay in collecting the appropriation, which resulted in the accumulation of a large amount of interest on the bonds, so that the funds appropriated by Congress would then not be sufficient to discharge the whole debt, interest and principal.

[59] *Cong. Globe*, 34 Cong., 1 Sess., 1777.

[60] *Ibid.*, 1846, 2238–39; United States, *Statutes at Large*, XI, 91.

falling due between January 1, 1854, and September 1, 1856, amounting to an aggregate sum of $172,828.54, were cut off and returned to the holders of bonds still outstanding against the state.[61] The state authorities were, however, confident that Congress would make provision for the remainder of the war debt.

New Indian disturbances.—Meanwhile fresh Indian hostilities broke out in the northern counties. In response to appeals for military aid, the legislature authorized the governor to call out a volunteer company of fifty men.[62] Knowing, however, how difficult it was to induce Congress to assume the war debt, Governor Johnson decided to appeal first to General Wool. Wool promised to do all he could to protect the frontier settlers.[63] Governor Johnson then decided to resort to volunteers, whom he thought would prove more effective than regular troops of the United States army.

On April 25, 1857, the legislature passed an act authorizing the state treasurer to issue bonds for a sum not exceeding $410,000 to pay the expenses incurred in suppressing Indian hostilities dating from 1850 to 1857 inclusive. The bonds were to be "payable out of any money hereafter to be appropriated

---

[61] See the several *Reports* of the Commissions of California War Debt, *in* California, *Assembly Jour.*, 1858, 65–69; California, *Sen. Jour.*, 1860, App., Doc. 12; *Sen. and Assembly Jours.*, App., 1872, Doc. 8. According to the *Report* of Adjutant General Kibbs in 1862 (California, *Sen. and Assembly Jours.*, 1862, Doc. 31), the Secretary of War paid out $781,650 on the bonds and $119,497 interest thereon up to January 1, 1854, thus making the total of $901,147.38 paid on bonds and interest. The course of Commissioners Denver and Smith was criticized severely in a minority report of a legislative committee on war claims. They were accused of collusion (see *Report* in California, *Sen. and Assembly Jours.*, 1864, App., Doc. 38).

[62] California, *Assembly Jour.*, 1856, 133, 149; California, *Statutes*, 1856, 42–43.

[63] California, *Assembly Jour.*, 1856, 327–28 (Wool to Johnson, Jan. 21, 1856). *Ibid.*, 328–29.

by Congress for the payment of such expenses.''[64] In 1858 the legislature adopted a resolution requesting Congress to appropriate a sum of money sufficient to discharge the war debt.[65]

The act of Congress of March 2, 1861, providing for a sum of $400,000 to defray the expenses incurred by the state of California in the suppression of Indian hostilities within the state during the years of 1854, 1855, 1856, 1858, and 1859 passed without much opposition, for it was the general belief that the federal government was liable for all such indebtedness. There was, however, a prevailing opinion in Congress that many of the frontier wars were instigated from ''motives of speculation in order that large claims may be made against the Government.''[66] California sent to Washington a board of commissioners with the necessary vouchers. But the third auditor found the prices for supplies and transportation exorbitant in many cases. In spite of the remonstrances of the California commissioners that the high cost of supplies and transportation was due to the peculiar conditions in the state, the third auditor allowed only $229,987 upon vouchers representing claims of over $400,000.[67]

Failure of the military reservations.—The promises which the system of military reservations held out at its inauguration had not been realized. Only a small percentage of Indians were on the reservations. Nor were these reservations self-supporting, as they were expected to be. The Indian Department attributed the failure of the reservation system to the mismanagement of the government employees on the reservation, to the interference of the white settlers, and to the indolence of the Indians. To secure the Indians from improper interference, it recommended application to the state of California for the relinquishment to

---

64 California, *Statutes*, 1857, 262–64.

65 California, *Statutes*, 1858, 358.

66 *Cong. Globe*, 36 Cong., 2 Sess., 478.

67 *Ibid.*, 479, 1130; United States, *Statutes at Large*, XII, 199–200; California, *Assembly Jour.*, 1863, 39.

the federal government of all jurisdiction over the reservations in the state.[68]

In California there were always many who deprecated the reservation policy. In 1855 the *Alta* pronounced it a failure. In 1857 Governor Johnson urged the legislature to demand the removal of Indians from the state. The Sacramento *Union* and San Francisco *Herald* advocated the abolishment of the reservation system, for it neither protected the whites nor the Indians; it only withheld from white settlers over two hundred thousand acres of the best farming land.[69]

In a concurrent resolution the legislature instructed the state delegation in Congress to "urge upon the federal authorities to cede to the State of California the entire jurisdiction over Indians and Indian affairs within our borders, together with such appropriations of land and money as will be adequate for the proper management and support of the Indians."[70] Latham introduced a bill in the Senate proposing to transfer the management of Indian affairs within California to the state government for an annual compensation of $50,000, to be paid for a period of twenty years.[71] He told the Senate that when the people who were "engaged in getting up these wars," understood that the legislature could send investigating committees to find out whether the wars were justifiable and whether the Indians were well cared for, then there would not be Indian wars.[72]

---

[68] Estimates of the number of Indians on reservations differed considerably. Superintendent of Indian Affairs, Henley, in his report for 1856, estimated the number of Indians within his jurisdiction at 61,000. Of these, only 10,000 were on reservations (Hayes, *Collection*, XLII, no. 100). Five reservations had been established in California, on which 11,239 Indians had been located up to March, 1858, at a cost of $1,173,000 (*Report* of Commissioner of Indian Affairs, *H. Ex. Doc.* 1, 35 Cong., 2 Sess., 357 [997]).

[69] *Alta*, Oct. 13, 1855; Sacramento *Union*, Jan. 26, 1855; California, *Assembly Jour.*, 1857, 25–26.

[70] California, *Statutes*, 1860, 423–24.

[71] *Cong. Globe*, 36 Cong., 1 Sess., 1549.

[72] *Loc. cit.*

Congress admitted that the federal Indian policy in California was unsuccessful but it doubted the wisdom of the policy of transferring the control of the Indians to the state. Under the act of June 19, 1860, California was divided into two Indian districts, a northern and a southern, with a superintendent agent for each district.[73] The condition of Indian affairs in California continued to be unsatisfactory. Commissioner of Indian Affairs Dole reported that some of the reservations within the northern districts were becoming worthless, that the buildings had fallen into decay, and many settlers were intruding upon the reservations. Congress passed an act consolidating the two districts under one superintendency,[74] and in August, 1866, the Indian Department dispatched a special agent to California to investigate the Indian situation.[75]

During the sixties the federal Indian policy was undergoing fundamental changes occasioned by the rapid progress of the construction of the continental railroads. In 1869 all superintendents of Indian affairs and all Indian agents, except those in Kansas and Nebraska, were officers of the United States army. The act of Congress of July 15, 1870, relieved the officers of the army from these duties. The President then decided that all the agencies should be filled by appointment upon the recommendation of some Christian denomination. The California Indians were entrusted to the care of the Methodists.[76] Meanwhile the frontier was becoming more thickly settled, and the Indians were becoming weaker and weaker.[77]

---

[73] United States, *Statutes at Large,* XII, 57.

[74] United States, *Statutes at Large,* XIII, 39–41. April 8, 1864.

[75] *H. Ex. Doc.* 1, 40 Cong., 2 Sess., 9 (1326).

[76] *H. Ex. Doc.* 1, 42 Cong., 3 Sess., 460 (1560).

[77] The Indian Commissioner estimated the number of Indians in California in 1869 at 20,000 (*H. Ex. Doc.* 1, 41 Cong., 2 Sess., 459 [1414]). The Indian question, however, left a legacy in the form of a controversy between the state and the federal government concerning the Indian war claims. We have already seen how after every settlement of the Indian war debt there remained, as a result of the disagreements between the state and federal officials, a large unpaid balance. By 1893 the entire

Summary and conclusions.—It is thus seen how troublesome the Indian question in California was for about two decades, giving rise to considerable controversy between the state and federal governments. California demanded military protection against the Indians but the federal authorities could not or would not respond to every call of the frontier settlements for military aid. Moreover, the two authorities differed considerably with regard to the causes of the Indian disturbances and the methods of dealing with this question. The state authorities claimed that the Indian hostilities were due to the inherent predatory character of the red man and that these racial collisions would continue until the Indians were removed or exterminated. But the federal authorities held that the Indian hostilities were due to the aggressive behavior of the reckless white adventurers, and that they were merely a "transitory inconvenience" experienced by many frontier communities. The state authorities believed that volunteer rangers were better fitted to cope with the Indians in their mountain fastnesses than were the regular United States military forces, while the federal authorities opposed the use of volunteer frontiersmen for punitive expeditions against the Indians on the grounds of economy, efficiency, and expediency.

Because of the failure of the federal government to supply the desired military aid, the state authorities resorted to the expensive volunteer service, accumulated large war debts, and then asked "Uncle Sam" to foot the bill. The controversy did not, generally, end with the assumption of the debt by the gov-

amount which California claimed to be due to her from the United States on this account aggregated the sum of $660,376.57. The controversy concerning these claims was a source of dispute between the state and federal authorities for over a half a century, and constituted the subject matter of various reports and resolutions in the state legislature and in Congress. Almost every session of Congress until 1917, saw some bills on this matter. But all the efforts of the California delegation in Congress were unsuccessful (*Report Third Auditor,* April 17, 1894, *Sen. Ex. Doc.* 84, 53 Cong., 2 Sess., 6–7 [3163]); *Cong. Record,* 56 Cong., 1 Sess., 1245; 59 Cong., 1 Sess., 6492, 8363; 60 Cong., 1 Sess., 16, 105; 61 Cong., 3 Sess., 1911; 65 Cong., 1 Sess., 611.

ernment. The exorbitant prices paid for supplies and services, and the irregularities connected with the vouchers, afforded sufficient cause for a conflict of opinion between the federal and state authorities, which prevented the state from getting the full benefit of the several appropriations made by Congress.

A good many of the Indian difficulties in California undoubtedly could have been avoided. But in spite of the good intentions of the federal government, and to a certain extent of the state government, the Indian question in California was not handled in a way to be proud of. This was due partly to the fact that the federal agents were not always appointed for their competency and honesty, but often for partisan reasons. Partisanship was also responsible for much of the discord between the Democratic state government and the Whig administration concerning the reservation system. Its inefficient handling was also partly due to the lack of sufficient information to work out a well-devised policy with regard to the Indians, and of the courage to carry it out in spite of opposition.

Most of the Indian difficulties, however, were perhaps unavoidable. Here we have the old story of a struggle between a native backward race and a civilized intruding race for the possession of the soil. Each side clamored that the other "must go." Those moralists and humanitarians who personally had never experienced any Indian trouble were apt to criticize too harshly the bellicose frontiersmen.

CHAPTER VI

THE CIVIL FUND AND THE MINT

THE CIVIL FUND

Origin of the civil fund.—During the war with Mexico the United States officers collected duties in California by executive authority. The collection of such duties was commonly admitted as a right belonging to the conqueror of the conquered territory. But after the termination of the war and the cession of the territory to the United States, Colonel Mason believed that he had no authority to collect duties. However, since no instructions with regard to this matter had come from Washington, and there was need of funds to support the existing government, he decided to substitute the United States revenue laws of 1846. Such a course, he thought, was also necessary to prevent an influx of foreign goods duty free, which would hurt the interests of the American merchants.[1]

It seems that Mason's course was neither approved nor disapproved in Washington. In his circular of October 7, 1848, Secretary of the Treasury Walker declared that:

> Although the Constitution of the United States extends to California, and Congress have recognized it by law as a part of the Union, and legislated for it as such, yet it is not brought by law within the limits of any collection district, nor has Congress authorized the appointment of any officers to collect the revenue accruing on the import of foreign dutiable goods into that territory. Under these circumstances, although this depart-

[1] Mason to Adjutant General Jones, Aug. 19, 1848 (*H. Ex. Doc.* 17 31 Cong., 1 Sess., 597–98); Halleck to the Committee of the Legislature, Jan. 23, 1850; California Legislature, *Jours.*, 1850, 820–21. Riley continued Mason's policy for the same reasons.

ment may be unable to collect the duties accruing on importations from foreign countries into California, yet, if foreign dutiable goods should be introduced there and shipped thence to any port or place of the United States, they will be subject to duty, as also to all the penalties prescribed by law when such importation is attempted without the payment of duties.[2]

The instructions given in this circular are anything but explicit and were naturally subject to misinterpretation. Importing merchants of San Francisco addressed a letter to Commodore Jones, the commander-in-chief of the United States Navy on the Pacific Coast, inquiring whether he would seize and confiscate goods landed at the port of San Francisco without payment of any duties thereon. According to Walker's circular, they said, no duties could be collected legally in California.[3] Jones replied that he fully approved of Mason's course, and that he would employ all his force "to enforce the revenue laws of the United States, at every point on the coast of California."[4] In a circular issued on April 1, 1849, General Smith announced that, in the absence of the necessary machinery to collect customs, dutiable goods could not be admitted at all. But, inasmuch as such a course would work great hardship on consumers and importers, he would allow the entry of goods subject to a deposit of the duties "to await the action of Congress on the subject."[5]

The people of California, of course, protested against the enforcement of the tariff laws without any action by Congress. Semple, the editor of the *Californian,* asserted that the moment the war ceased, the military officers had no right to collect custom-house duties.[6] Complaints of taxation without representation were not wanting.

---

[2] *H. Ex. Doc.* 1, 30 Cong., 2 Sess., 45 (537).

[3] Letter of Gillespie to Jones, Feb. 23, 1849, quoted in *Cong. Globe,* 31 Cong., 2 Sess., App., 277.

[4] Jones to Gillespie, Feb. 26, 1849, *ibid.*

[5] Circular to United States Consuls, April 1, 1849 (*H. Ex. Doc.* 17, 31 Cong., 1 Sess., 719–20 [573]).

[6] *Californian,* Oct. 21, 1848.

The duties were, however, paid regularly until November 12, 1849, the date when the revenue laws of the United States went into operation. This fund was more than sufficient to maintain the existing government, for since practically all articles of consumption had to be imported, the revenue from this source was very large. The military governors used this money for the purposes of the "civil government" and held whatever remained in a separate fund subject to the order of the President or to final disposition by Congress. Both General Riley and General Smith were in favor of turning over to California a part or the whole of the unexpended money in the civil fund to enable her to put the new government into successful operation.[7] But Secretary of War Crawford instructed Riley to place this fund in the Treasury Department to be held subject to the final action of Congress.[8]

Claims of California to the civil fund.—The question of the disposition of the civil fund was discussed at great length at the constitutional convention. McDougal offered a resolution declaring that the money collected as duties on foreign goods in the ports of California between August 7, 1848, and November 12, 1849, by right belonged to California. Gwin held that, since the general government had failed to organize a territorial government for California, it had no right to extend the revenue laws to California. The revenue act of March 3, 1849, was therefore an "act of usurpation," and the money unjustly collected should be returned to the people of California. Larkin argued that the money belonged to the merchants from whom it was

---

[7] Riley to Jones, June 30, 1849 (*H. Ex. Doc.* 17, 31 Cong., 1 Sess., 751, 819). He contended that the money properly belonged to the people and not to the merchants who had paid the duties. He pointed out that to refund the money to the importers would be a virtual gift to a few individuals who had sold their goods at a price high enough to cover the duties paid.

[8] Crawford to Riley, Nov. 28, 1849 (*H. Ex. Doc.* 17, 31 Cong. 1 Sess., 281–82 [573]).

illegally collected. For various reasons the resolution was laid on the table.[9]

But early in the session of the first legislature both houses adopted resolutions declaring that all the money collected upon imports in California up to September 9, 1850, belonged to the state of California.[10] A special committee in the assembly, appointed to examine into the "nature of any legal claim or moral right" of California to the civil fund, reported that from their inquiries they had come to the conclusion that this fund rightfully belonged to California. The argument was as follows: With the termination of the war the people of California became citizens of the United States entitled to the same privileges enjoyed by the people of any other state in the Union, and the power to collect duties must be either declared by Congress, or must be given by the consent of the people of California. The right of the President, as head of the army and navy, to levy military contributions on the conquered territory had ceased. Now, since Congress had not legislated for California, the President had no power to continue the collection of duties. Nor had the federal government any right to collect duties from November 12, 1849, to September 9, 1850, for it had no power to tax a "sovereignty" with which it had formed no political connections.[11]

In his annual message of 1849 President Taylor recommended that the balance of the civil fund be expended within California.[12] Soon after the California Senators took their seats, Fremont introduced a bill for the refund to California of the revenue collected in her ports prior to November 12, 1849. His colleague Gwin went farther in his bill, demanding the payment to California of the revenue collected in her ports since the

---

[9] Browne, *Debates*, 317–20, 322.

[10] California Legislature, *Jours.*, 1850, 28.

[11] *Ibid.*, 817–28.

[12] Richardson, *Messages*, V, 19.

ratification of the treaty with Mexico and prior to the admission of the state.[13] No action was taken on this bill.

The embarrassed condition of the state finances induced the state authorities to persist in the demand for the civil fund. In his annual message of January 7, 1851, Governor Burnett urged the legislature to insist upon the refund of this money. He asserted that the extension of the revenue laws over California, without giving her representation in Congress, was a "plain and palpable violation of the most prominent principle, the disregard of which by the mother country led to the American revolution." A resolution to this effect was adopted in both houses of the legislature.[14]

Congress and the civil fund.—The question of the civil fund came up for discussion at the end of the second session of the thirty-first Congress in connection with a bill to settle accounts with the officers who had charge of the fund. The bill provided for the transference of the money to the treasury of the United States after deducting the sum of $175,000, which had been expended for the support of the civil government and for the constitutional convention, and $100,000 expended for the relief of immigrants. In view of the fact that Congress had neglected to take care of California, the Committee of Finance thought it was proper and just to allow the state this money, though it had been expended without authority. Moreover, since these sums had been already expended, it would be in vain to attempt to reclaim them.[15] Gwin then offered an amendment to pay to California the duties collected within her ports between August 6, 1848, and November 12, 1849, after the several allowances were deducted from the same. He contended that no duties could be collected legally in California prior to the extension

---

[13] *Cong. Globe,* 31 Cong., 1 Sess., 1828. Fremont's bill was criticized in California on the ground that it only asked for a part of the money which rightfully belonged to California (*Picayune,* Oct. 23, 1850, Jan. 22, 1851; *Pacific News,* Nov. 5, 1850; *Courier,* Oct. 26, 1850).

[14] California, Legislature, *Jours.,* 1851, 30–32.

[15] *Cong. Globe,* 31 Cong., 2 Sess., App., 275–78.

of the revenue laws, and that the government of the United States, being one of limited powers, could not receive these illegal collections without an express provision in the Constitution. But since these duties had been already paid, he thought it would be just and proper to refund them to the state of California. To be sure, the duties had been paid by the importers, but indirectly they had been paid by the consumers who were forced to pay prices high enough to cover the duty charges. He pointed out that the money justly belonged to California on the ground that she had none of the benefits of territorial government; no roads had been built, no public buildings had been constructed from the money of the federal government. Partly as a result of this neglect California was heavily indebted. He also believed that California had a just claim to the duties collected between November 12, 1849, and September 9, 1850, because Congress had failed to give her a system of government.[16]

The opposition, however, argued that the extension of the revenue laws over a newly acquired territory was not essential, because the moment the treaty was completed the Constitution was *proprio vigore* extended over the ceded territory and with it all the laws of the United States, among which were the revenue laws. According to the case of *Fleming* v. *Page,* which merely decided the question of coasting trade, California was to be considered *quasi* foreign in regard to the coasting trade; in all other respects she was a part of the United States, where foreign goods could not be unloaded without payment of duties. Moreover, if the duties had been collected illegally they should be refunded to the merchants who had paid them. California had not even a moral claim to the money, for the government had already expended large sums for her benefit. And after all the measures passed for California, complained Walker of Wisconsin, Congress was still charged with injustice.[17]

---

[16] *Cong. Globe,* 31 Cong., 2 Sess., App., 276–78. The revenue collected from November 12, 1849, to September 9, 1850, amounted to $1,603,561.08.

[17] *Cong. Globe,* 31 Cong., 2 Sess., App., 279–82.

When the amendment was rejected, Gwin offered another one proposing to pay to the state of California $300,000 out of the duties collected within the ports of California for the expenses of the state government. The Committee on Finance recommended this appropriation on the ground that California had not had the benefit of territorial government nor of the internal improvements usually made by the general government. The southern Senators, who still resented the admission of California, opposed this proposition, too, contending that such appropriations would constitute precedents for paying money to states without any good claim. They complained that Californians were asking too much from the general government and that, all the while, they were digging gold without paying any rent to the government. "Is it because she has erected a government without the authority of Congress, in violation of the laws of the United States, that we should pay her this money?" asked Davis of Mississippi. "This merely proves that the South was right in claiming that California was not ripe for statehood," said Borland. "Why confer upon California so much money that we would not confer upon any other state?" asked Dawson of Georgia. "And yet it is cried out 'Oppression, oppression, and cruelty on the part of the General Government'." Seward, Douglas, Cass, and Ewing advocated the adoption of the measure on the ground that since Congress had not extended the land system over California previous to her admission into the Union, there was little property subject to taxation for the support of her government.[18] The amendment passed the Senate, but it was not taken up in the House.

The bill came up again at the next session of the Senate. The Committee on Finance recommended the payment of the $300,000 merely as a gratuity in lieu of the public buildings which, except in the case of California, were furnished to all

[18] *Cong.* Globe, 31 Cong., 2 Sess., App. 282–86.

territories before their admission as states. Again the bill passed the Senate but failed in the House.[19]

At the second session of the thirty-second Congress Gwin introduced his amendment to the deficiency bill. Some offered to vote for it provided California relinquished her claim to the rest of the civil fund. But Gwin refused to consent to this, contending that such a course would involve a violation of the pledged faith of California, for by the law of the state the proceeds of the civil fund were set apart for the payment of the bonds issued to put the state government into operation. After considerable opposition the amendment was agreed to.[20]

But again it met with strong opposition in the House, where McCorkle of California moved to amend the Senate amendment by increasing the sum to $470,000, which he said was the actual amount expended for the state government prior to its admission. The southern members objected to such appropriations. "California should not get more than a dollar; nobody invited the people to go there before a territorial government had been organized," said Meade of Virginia. California, he contended, constantly pointed to the fact that she was sending millions of dollars to the east, but this gold belonged to the miners who dug it out of "our mines, which cost us $15,000,000." And the question was whether they or the Government of the United States had a claim the one upon the other. "We have been liberal to her," said Hibbard of New Hampshire, "profusely so. But the cry is still, 'Give! Give!' It seems to me, at times, that nothing would satisfy this call for appropriations but a course of measures which would divert the whole revenue of the nation to the use of this favored state—literally overturning the Treasury and pouring its contents into her overflowing lap." The House disagreed on the amendment and again the measure was killed.[21]

---

[19] *Cong. Globe,* 32 Cong., 1 Sess., 676–77.
[20] *Cong. Globe,* 32 Cong., 2 Sess., 542, 543, 558, 568, 621.
[21] *Cong. Globe,* 32 Cong., 2 Sess., 923, 924, 1053.

Persistent efforts of California.—The people of California, however, persisted in pressing the demand for the return of the civil fund. In the press, party conventions, executive messages, and legislative resolutions Congress was urged to return to California the money "extorted from her citizens before her admission . . . . levied without color of law, the enormity of which has no parallel in the history of our government."[22] In its report of May 17, 1853, the joint committee of the two houses of the state legislature, declared that with the raising of the Bear Flag and the signing of the Declaration of Independence on June 5, 1846, California virtually became an independent republic. This independent republic, with her army of six hundred men and abundance of munitions of war, could fully and successfully retain her independent existence without relying on the United States or any other nation. Moreover, with the vast mineral wealth at her command, "she could have resisted successfully the combined armies of the civilized world."[23]

Final disposition of the subject.—The California delegation in Congress also persisted in demanding the return of the civil fund. Bills to this effect were introduced by them in both houses during the first session of the thirty-third Congress. In a speech printed and laid on the desks of the members of the House, Latham contended that the collections between August 6, 1848, and November 12, 1849, belonged to California because they had been exacted at the mouth of the cannon and at the point of the bayonet without any color of law, a worse grievance than the one experienced by the colonies at the hands of the mother country. He admitted that in many respects the Constitution and laws of the United States were *proprio vigore* extended to the newly acquired territories. But the revenue laws, he held, require auxiliary legislation prescribing and establishing the

[22] Davis, *Political Conventions in California,* 20–21; California, *Sen. Jour.,* 1853, 185–86.

[23] *Ibid.,* 1853, App., Doc. 73.

whole machinery of collecting duties. Until this machinery is established the ports of the newly acquired territory must be considered for revenue purposes as foreign territory. The claim of California to the duties collected between November 12, 1849, and September 9, 1850, he based on the ground that during this period California was not represented in Congress nor was she provided with the outfit given to almost all other territories.[24]

The House Committee of Ways and Means reported the bill with the recommendation that it should not pass. The Committee stated that it could find no legal or equitable ground on which the claim of California to the civil fund could be recognized. For if the money had been rightfully collected between May 30, 1848, and November 12, 1849, then it legally belonged to the United States government. And if the money had been collected illegally, then it must be refunded to the merchants who had paid it. Hence it was a question between the federal government and the importer who had paid the duties and not between the general government and the state of California. As to the rights of California to the money collected upon imports from November 12, 1849, to September 9, 1850, the Committee held that California had no better claim to it than any other state in the Union.[25]

The California claim received its strongest blow by the decision of the United States Supreme Court in *Cross et al.* v. *Harrison*. In this important case, which involved the question of the legality of the collection of duties by the military authorities in California between February 3, 1848, and November 13, 1849, the court denied the validity of all the arguments against

---

[24] *Cong. Globe,* 33 Cong., 1 Sess., App., 571–74. According to Latham, the general government had appropriated for the support of the territories the following sums: Mississippi, $142,213.75; Indiana, $101,836.66; Louisiana, $56,068.64; Orleans, $129,018.35; Michigan, $514,536.01; Illinois, $66,349.43; Missouri, $64,880.07; Alabama, $16,069.73; Florida, $1,321,790.20; Wisconsin, $638,557.99; Iowa, $561,601.65 (*loc. cit.*).

[25] *H. Rep.* 168, 33 Cong., 1 Sess., (743).

the legality of the collection of such duties. The court held that the

.... civil government of California, organized as it was from a right of Conquest, did not cease or become defunct, in consequence of the signature of the treaty or from its ratification. We think it was continued over a ceded conquest, without any violation of the Constitution or laws of the United States, and that until Congress legislated for it, the duties upon foreign goods imported into San Francisco were legally demanded and lawfully received by Mr. Harrison.

The court denied the argument that the United States revenue laws covered only so much of the territory of the Union as had been divided into collection districts and that until the revenue laws are extended over a newly acquired territory no duties could be legally collected and no authority was given to prevent the landing of foreign merchandise.

By the ratification of the Treaty, [it said] California became a part of the United States .... it became instantly bound and privileged by the laws which Congress had passed to raise a revenue from duties on imports and tonnage. It was bound by the eighteenth section of the act of 2d of March, 1799. ....

The right claimed to land foreign goods within the United States at any place out of a collection district, if allowed, would be a violation of that provision in the Constitution which enjoins that all duties, imposts and excises, shall be uniform throughout the United States.[26]

California, however, still kept on pressing the demand for the civil fund. The newspapers still talked of "taxation without representation," the violation of a principle for which the forefathers shed their blood at Bunker Hill, Lexington, and Yorktown. In their messages the executives urged the legislature to memorialize Congress upon this question. Governor Johnson recommended that the legislature should pass an act authorizing the payment of the state bonds from this fund when

[26] *Cross* v. *Harrison*, 16 *Howard*, 194–201. Cross, Hobson and Company attempted to recover from Harrison, who had been appointed by Mason, the then military governor, as collector of the customs at the port of San Francisco, the tonnage and duties upon goods imported between February 3, 1848, and November 13, 1849.

allowed by Congress. Such a measure, he held, would make every bond-holder interested in the success of the application to Congress for the return of the fund to the state.[27] In Congress Senator Broderick made an effort in this direction but without success.[28] There the question rested.

THE MINT

There were many things in the way of internal improvements which California greatly desired. She asked for lighthouses, fortifications, coast survey, a marine hospital, a navy yard, and a dry-dock. As a member of the Committee on Finance and chairman of the Committee on Naval Affairs, Gwin managed to obtain appropriations aggregating several million dollars for these purposes.[29]

Demand for a mint.—It was far more difficult, however, to influence the government to establish a branch mint in California. Yet a mint had been the great desideratum ever since the discovery of gold. As early as 1848 a memorial was drawn up and signed by many citizens of California, asking Congress to establish a mint, which would protect the interests of the miners and

---

27 California, *Sen. Jour.*, 1855, 29–30; California, *Assembly Jour.*, 1857, 32–34; 1858, 40–41; 1859, 41–42; California, *Statutes*, 1859, 384, asking for the refund of $2,706,512 revenue collected prior to the admission of the state.

28 *Alta*, Jan. 10, 1859.

29 In 1850 Congress appropriated $90,000 for the erection of lighthouses on the coasts of California and Oregon. Additional appropriations were made during the following years. But the government was slow in erecting these lighthouses. In 1859 there were fourteen lighthouses in operation on the Pacific Coast. The amount appropriated by Congress for fortification of the San Francisco harbor, up to June 30, 1858, was $2,695,800 (California, *State Register*, 1859, 139, 147, 160, 135–36.) The marine hospital was erected in San Francisco at a total cost of $224,000 (*ibid.*, 160). The navy yard at Mare Island was one of the largest in the world. Together with the dry-dock it cost the government several million dollars. Gwin urged its construction, claiming that in time of peace it would add to the security of the United States merchant marine and vessels engaged in the whale fisheries on the Pacific; and in time of war with a maritime nation it would serve as a base for American naval construction (*Sen. Rep.* 14, 32 Cong., 1 Sess. [630]; California, *Register*, 1859, 135–36).

supply the territory with a circulating medium.[30] With the increase of population and in the volume of commercial transactions, the scarcity of currency became increasingly troublesome. Merchants found it difficult to procure sufficient coin to pay the duties on imported goods. In ordinary daily transactions gold dust became a circulating medium, taken, of course, at a rate much lower than its actual worth.[31] It was estimated that by the establishment of a mint the miners would save about $6,250,000 annually, on an output of $50,000,000 worth of gold dust per annum. In their messages Presidents Polk and Taylor recommended the establishment of a mint in California.[32]

When the bill for the establishment of a branch mint in New York was under consideration in the Senate during the first session of the thirty-first Congress, Benton offered an amendment providing for an assay office and branch mint in San Francisco. The amendment passed the Senate.[33] In the House, however, the bill met the determined opposition of the Pennsylvania delegation, who were afraid that the establishment of a branch mint in New York would affect the interests of the Philadelphia mint. The California delegation then agreed on a temporary measure empowering the Secretary of the Treasury to make a contract with an assayer in California, to assay gold dust, for a reasonable charge, under the supervision of the United States assayer who was to stamp on the ingots a statement of their real value.[34]

Opposition in California to the assay office.—The people of California were opposed to the assay office, contending that it would not benefit the miners and would merely jeopardize the establishment of a mint. The California delegation in Congress was convinced that the chief obstacle to the passage of

30 *Californian*, Sept. 16, 1848.

31 *Report* of Secretary of the Interior Ewing, Dec. 3, 1849 (*Sen. Ex. Doc.* 1, 31 Cong., 1 Sess., 12 [550]); *Alta*, Jan. 28, 1851.

32 Richardson, *Messages*, IV, 636–37; V, 19.

33 *Cong. Globe*, 31 Cong., 1 Sess., 1109.

34 United States, *Statutes at Large*, IX, 531.

the mint bill was the California assay office whose agents were lobbying in the capital. They were therefore determined to break up the assay office. In the absence of a mint the miners were compelled to sell their gold at $15.50 an ounce, while its real worth was about $17.50 an ounce. "This is what we denominate the proscription of the people of California," reads an address of the Democratic party in California. As usual the press complained that California was being neglected and mistreated. "It is a burning shame, a great national wrong . . . . a wanton and foolhardy oppression," said the *Alta*.[35] The Democratic and Whig parties at the state conventions adopted resolutions advocating a mint.[36] In their messages to the legislature both Governor Burnett and Governor McDougal criticized Congress for neglecting to pass a mint bill. "For the want of a Mint," said Governor Burnett, "the industry of the state has been severely taxed, and we have been forced to become tributary to the other portions of the world to the amount of millions."[37]

The mint bill passes.—The mint was considered almost as a panacea for all ills.[38] In the first place, from it the miners would receive full value for their gold dust. According to the president of the San Francisco Chamber of Commerce, the average value of gold dust in California prior to October, 1850, never ranged higher than sixteen dollars an ounce, and from October, 1850, to March, 1852, its average value was $16.55 an ounce, while the value of California gold dust at the United States mint was $18.32 an ounce.[39] The miners of California were really suffering heavy losses by the difference in the true value of their gold and the amount they actually received for it. Second, it would

[35] *Courier*, Nov. 13, 1850; *Alta*, Dec. 18, 1850; *Pacific News*, Dec. 28, 1850; Sacramento *Transcript*, Nov. 14, 1850; Jan. 17, 1851.

[36] Davis, *Political Conventions in California*, 14, 20.

[37] California Legislature, *Jours.*, 1851, 30; California, *Sen. Jour.*, 1852, 19, 80.

[38] California, *Sen. Jour.*, 1852, 19, 80; *Herald*, Jan. 21, 1851; *Pacific News*, Feb. 1, 1851.

[39] Statement of Beverly Sanders, president of the San Francisco Chamber of Commerce (California, *Sen. Jour.*, 1852, App., 653).

make unnecessary (*a*) the transportation of gold thousands of miles, and mostly to foreign countries, in order to have it coined; and at the same time (*b*) the importation of specie for exchange purposes, saving thereby the heavy cost involved, which sometimes amounted to seven per cent.[40] Three advantages would thus be gained: California gold would be kept in the state; the rate of interest would be reduced; the investment of capital would be made more attractive; third, the mint would safeguard the state against the circulation of depreciated gold and silver coins of foreign and private coinage. On account of the scarcity of United States specie for the ordinary uses of trade quantities of depreciated foreign coins entered California. There were Spanish, Mexican, Peruvian, and Bolivian dollars; French *francs,* Spanish *piestas,* Austrian *zwanzigers.* These circulated for amounts above their intrinsic value. The *pistareen,* worth nineteen cents, circulated as a twenty-five cent piece. The Spanish *real,* worth twelve and a half cents, circulated at fifteen cents.[41] The scarcity of coin also induced the issue of private coins.[42] As early as 1849, five and ten-dollar pieces were coined by various coining companies. Their deficiency in value, or lack of confidence in the ability of their issuers to redeem them, resulted in their depreciation, and inflicted heavy losses upon the community. They were not accepted at the custom house nor at the post office. Many mercantile firms refused to take them at their par value.[43] Some considered them to be counter-

[40] Wright, *Banking in California,* 8; Fankhauser, *A Financial History of California,* 125.

[41] *Alta,* Oct. 9, 1852; Wright, *Banking in California,* 8.

[42] In spite of the fact that the privilege of coinage was specifically withheld from the states and confined entirely to the national government, the government of the United States apparently did not interfere with the right of private coinage which was in operation for many years in Georgia and North Carolina.

[43] Adams, *Private Gold Coinage of California,* p. IX. Among these were: ''Great Salt Lake City Pure Gold'' pieces. The net value of the twenty-dollar piece was a little over seventeen dollars; ''Ormsby Tens,'' $9.37; ''Moffat Tens,'' $9.777 (*Alta,* Jan. 26, 1850).

feit coins. The state legislature, attempting to cope with this problem, passed the act of April 20, 1850, which prohibited private coinage,[44] but it soon became a dead letter and was repealed in 1851.[45] Of course the advocates of the mint overestimated the benefits to be derived from it. They overlooked the fact that California was an importing state, importing practically all her goods, for which she could pay only with her gold. They also overlooked the fact that rates of interest are high in all frontier communities, due to the great demand for capital to develop the natural resources. Where profits are large, rates of interest are high. It is easily seen, however, that the monetary situation in California at this time was very unsatisfactory.

President Fillmore recommended the establishment of a branch mint in California. He believed that the lack of it was an unjust tax upon the miners who were "compelled to dispose of their gold dust at a large discount." As a temporary measure of relief he recommended that Congress should authorize the receipt of assayed and stamped gold bullion in payment of government dues. Such a provision, he said, would not hurt the interests of the government treasury and would be of great benefit to the people of California by raising bullion to its par value.[46]

After strenuous efforts on the part of the New York and California members, the House took up the Senate mint bill. But again it met with the opposition of the Pennsylvania members. It was argued that there was sufficient coin in California to supply the local market and that it was much cheaper to transmit bars of ingots than coin. The opposition was mainly to the New York mint. The attempt to divide the question so as to bring in a direct vote on the two proposed branches was opposed

[44] California, *Statutes*, 1850, 274.

[45] California, *Statutes*, 1851, 404; Adams, *Private Gold Coinage in California*, p. XIV.

[46] Richardson, *Messages*, V, 85.

by the New York members.[47] It was not until July 3, 1852, that the California mint bill passed Congress and became a law.[48] The mint went into operation in April, 1854, and the monetary question was settled.

[47] *Cong. Globe,* 31 Cong., 2 Sess., 367–68, 380–83, 391–400, 412–19, 420–21.

[48] United States, *Statutes at Large,* X, 11–13.

CHAPTER VII

THE VIGILANCE COMMITTEE AND FEDERAL INTERFERENCE

The Vigilance Committee of 1856.—For several years San Francisco had suffered from political corruption, but about 1856 matters came to a crisis. In order to purge the city of corruption a number of citizens established an organization known as the Vigilance Committee. Anticipating a riot, Commander Gibson of the San Francisco presidio issued, at the request of the mayor of San Francisco, a supply of cannon ammunition and musket cartridges for the use of the California Guards.[1] Only a few of the militia responded to the call of the mayor; some of them joined the Vigilance Committee taking with them the arms and accoutrements of the state.[2] The Vigilance Committee seized and hanged two prisoners and proceeded to arrest several other offenders, disregarding a writ of habeas corpus issued by the state supreme court for one of the prisoners. Unable to quiet matters Governor Johnson decided to appeal to the federal officials for military aid.[3]

The Governor's appeal to the army and navy officers.—Governor Johnson and General Sherman visited General Wool, commander of the Pacific division at Benicia, and Commodore Farragut, commandant of Mare Island navy yard, asking for military supplies. Commodore Farragut immediately declined to lend any assistance declaring that he had no authority, with-

[1] *Sen. Ex. Doc.* 43, 34 Cong., 3 Sess., 19 (881).

[2] California, *Sen. Jour.*, 1857, 59.

[3] California, *Sen. Jour.*, 1857, 59. Sherman, *Memoirs*, 1, 125.

out orders from Washington, to interfere in domestic troubles.[4] General Wool seemed to be at a loss to know what to do. According to the testimony of Governor Johnson and General Sherman, Wool had distinctly promised them to supply the necessary arms and ammunition, believing that, although under ordinary circumstances no one but the President could issue arms to a state in case of emergency, he was justified in assuming the responsibility in this case because California was so far from Washington.[5]

A few days later Governor Johnson issued a proclamation declaring the city and county of San Francisco to be in a state of insurrection. He also ordered all the volunteer military companies in San Francisco to report for duty to General Sherman. A copy of this proclamation together with a requisition for arms was forwarded to General Wool. The governor promised that all the arms and ammunition to be furnished would be returned or deducted from the quota of arms which the state of California expected to receive from the general government.[6]

The San Francisco press, generally, was against the intervention of the federal forces. Woe to the man who dares to oppose the Vigilance Committee, be he governor of the state, or general of the United States, said the *Chronicle.* "The Union chord between the hearts of our people and the home Government," it said, "has been very much weakened by the neglect and abuse we have suffered, and a foray upon us by U. S. troops and men-of-war would snap it like a burned tow string."[7]

General Wool's refusal to intervene.—After thinking the matter over and examining more carefully the laws applicable to

---

[4] Commander Boutwell to Secretary of the Navy Dobbin, July 3, 1856 (*Sen. Ex. Doc.* 101, 34 Cong., 1 Sess., 20 [824]). Sherman, *Memoirs,* 1, 126. But he promised to keep the sloop John Adams abreast of the city of San Francisco for "*moral effect.*"

[5] Sherman's testimony on June 11 (*Sen. Ex. Doc.* 43, 34 Cong., 3 Sess., 26–28 [881]); Statement of Governor Johnson, Oct. 17 (California, *Sen. Jour.,* 1857, 52).

[6] California, *Sen. Jour.,* 1857, 50–51.

[7] *Alta,* June 1, 1856; *Chronicle,* May 31, 1856.

such an emergency, General Wool decided to keep out of the domestic brawls and not to issue any arms to the state authorities.[8] He decided, however, to prepare for any emergency by concentrating more troops at Benicia and at the presidio of San Francisco. He also ordered special protection for the government buildings in San Francisco.[9]

Governor Johnson felt enraged when he was informed that General Wool had refused to supply the expected arms and ammunition. A heated controversy between the governor and the general took place. General Wool denied that he had promised any arms; he had merely stated that under certain conditions he might "deem it proper to assume the responsibility of issuing arms." But upon examination of the law and regulations on the subject, he found that the President had the power to furnish arms only in the case of an insurrection within a state.[10]

The Governor appeals to the President.—Governor Johnson then addressed a letter to the President of the United States, informing him of the state of affairs in San Francisco and asking him to instruct the United States commander of the Pacific division to "issue to the State authorities, on the requisition of the Executive, such arms and ammunition as may be needed for the purpose of suppressing the existing insurrection." Without the required aid, he said, the state would be helpless to protect its citizens. He also stated that the "most violent harangues and inflammatory appeals are indulged, both against the General and State Governments."[11]

---

[8] *Sen. Ex. Doc.* 43, 34 Cong., 3 Sess., 17–18 (881). Johnson believed "outside influence" induced the general to change his mind (California, *Sen. Jour.*, 1857, 52–54). Rowe stated that General Wool had told him on June 4 that he could not furnish the state with arms, because "men in San Francisco could not be trusted or relied upon," and that "it was not safe to place arms in their hands, as they might be turned against the authorities themselves" (*ibid.*, 56–57).

[9] *Sen. Ex. Doc.* 43, 34 Cong., 3 Sess., 9, 15 (881).

[10] General Wool to Governor Johnson, June 9, 1856 (*Sen. Ex. Doc.* 43, 34 Cong., 3 Sess., 6–7 [881]).

[11] The letter is printed in California, *Sen. Jour.*, 1857, 58–60.

Boutwell's attitude.—Meanwhile the Vigilance Committee had arrested Dr. Ashe, the United States navy agent, and Judge Terry, of the supreme court of California. Dr. Ashe was set at liberty upon the request of Boutwell, commander of the United States sloop-of-war "John Adams." But Terry was under charge of stabbing one of the police of the Vigilance Committee, while defending himself when attacked by several members of the committee. Judge Terry addressed a strong appeal to Captain Boutwell to protect him from the Vigilance Committee. He claimed the right of a native-born citizen of the United States to invoke the protection of the flag of his country. He reminded Captain Boutwell of the noble and gallant Captain Ingraham, who had interfered to save the life of Kostza,[12] who was not yet a full citizen of the United States. To make the appeal more effective, he warned the officer that the Vigilance Committee was even threatening "to seize the *forts* and *arsenals* of the United States as well as the ships of war in port and secede from the Federal Union."[13] Governor Johnson also appealed to Captain Boutwell in behalf of Terry, pointing out that the judge was held in confinement "in utter violation of his rights under the Constitution of the United States and this State, and the laws enacted in pursuance thereof."[14]

Appeals of Governor Johnson, Judge Terry, and his "distressed wife" had such an effect on Captain Boutwell that he was almost ready "to batter the city down" with the guns of the "John Adams," if he could have done so "without destroying the lives and property of the innocent with the guilty."[15] He addressed a letter to the Vigilance Committee asking the com-

[12] Kostza, a Hungarian refugee, was arrested in Turkey and placed on board an Austrian warship. The American consul demanded and obtained his release on the ground that Kostza had taken out his first naturalization papers in the United States.

[13] *Sen. Ex. Doc.* 101, 34 Cong., 1 Sess., 26–27 (824).

[14] *Ibid.*, 23–24.

[15] Boutwell to Secretary of the Navy Dobbin, July 3, 1856 (*Sen. Ex. Doc.* 101, 34 Cong., 1 Sess., 21 [824]).

mittee, in a somewhat officious tone, to restrain from shedding the blood of an American citizen on American soil, and either place the prisoner on board of the "John Adams," or surrender him to the "lawful authority of the State." He reminded the committee that

. . . . if the action of Captain Ingraham in interfering to save the life of Kostza (who was not an American citizen) met the approbation of his country, how much more necessary is it for me to use all the power at my command to save the life of a native born American citizen, whose only offense is believed to be in his effort to carry out the law, obey the governor's proclamation, and in defense of his own life.[16]

The Vigilance Committee did not relish the menacing tone of Commander Boutwell and referred his letter to Captain Farragut. The latter was more tactful. He pointed out to the committee that its procedure did not comply with articles five and six of the amended Constitution, which says: "No person shall be held to answer for a capital or otherwise infamous crime, unless on a presentment or indictment of a grand jury . . . . nor be deprived of life, liberty, or property, without due process of law." And "in all criminal prosecutions, the accused shall enjoy the right to a speedy and public trial, by an impartial jury of the State . . . ." while article four, section four, of the Constitution provides that the United States shall guarantee to each state a republican form of government, and on the application of the proper authorities should protect the state against "domestic violence." In view of the remoteness of the seat of the national government, the officers of the government must decide for themselves in such an emergency. He assured the committee, however, that he would "always be ready to pour oil on the troubled waters, rather than do aught to fan the flame of human passions, or add to the chances of the horrors of civil war."[17]

[16] *Sen. Ex. Doc.* 101, 34 Cong., 1 Sess., 25–26 (824).
[17] *Ibid*, 18–19.

On the same day he addressed a letter to Commander Boutwell, pointing out that it had always been the policy of the federal government to avoid any interference with the strictly domestic troubles of states when there was no collision with the laws of the United States. Until further instructions from the government, he felt it was his duty to avoid any interference in the San Francisco disturbances; and it was his duty likewise to restrain the commander of the "John Adams" as long as the ship lay within the waters of his command.[18]

Boutwell could not see anything wrong in the attempt of a federal officer to interfere in behalf of an American citizen. As a "states' right" man himself, he did not believe that it was any part of the creed "to overturn the laws of the State, hang men without trial by jury, and imprison a judge of the supreme court." Moreover, he claimed that the committee had interfered with the federal government in arresting Dr. Ashe, a navy agent of the port of San Francisco. However, to avoid any further complications because of his presence, he decided to go to sea as soon as possible. But before he had time to leave the harbor he received orders from Farragut not to sail until further orders, for his "presence may be necessary in the harbor."[19]

The press on government interference.—The news that Governor Johnson had appealed to the President for military assistance created considerable excitement in San Francisco. The *Alta, Bulletin,* and Sacramento *Union* warned the federal authorities that any attempt to call out federal troops to suppress a movement to reform domestic abuses would result in fearful consequences; it would rend asunder the bonds which bound California to the Union. The *Alta* asserted that the thousands of men under the control of the committee, who were well armed with muskets and cannons, would fight till the last drop of blood

[18] *Sen. Ex. Doc.* 101, 34 Cong., 1 Sess., 28–29.

[19] *Sen. Ex. Doc.* 101, 34 Cong., 1 Sess., 20. The correspondence cited in the last few pages is given also in *Life of David S. Terry . . .*, compiled and edited by Wagstaff, pp. 110–18.

and would annihilate the federal forces.[20] The opponents of the Vigilance Committee, on the other hand, favored government interference. ''The course of President Pierce in the Kansas difficulty,'' said the San Francisco *Sun*, ''gives a sufficient earnest of what his action will be in the premises. He will put his foot on this shop keeper's rebellion.'' The *Sun* and the *Democratic State Journal,* among others, held that it was the duty of the President to protect states in case of domestic violence.[21] At various times reports were circulated of anticipated attacks by the federal forces upon the Vigilance Committee. One day a rumor spread that a federal army was on the way to San Francisco. On another day it was rumored that every gun upon the ''Warren'' and ''Decatur'' was shotted and ready for further orders.[22]

A Pacific republic.—In order to discredit the Vigilance Committee its enemies accused it of secession tendencies, and of having the intention of establishing a Pacific republic.[23] Nor were these accusations entirely unfounded. Mr. Coleman, head of the Vigilance Committee, stated in his memoirs that there was a strong undercurrent of secession in the Vigilance Committee. Some of the advocates of a ''Western Republic'' approached him with this project arguing that California, being geographically separated from the east, should also be separated politically. Flattering pictures of an independent existence were held up but the committee discountenanced the project.[24]

The rumors that California was contemplating the establishment of an independent republic reached even the east. The

[20] Sacramento *Union,* June 9, 20, 1856; *Alta,* July 10, 25, Aug. 5, 1856; *Bulletin,* June 24, 1856.

[21] Quoted in Sacramento *Union,* June 20, 1856; Sacramento *Democratic State Journal,* Aug. 4, 1856.

[22] *Alta,* July 24, 25, 26, 1856.

[23] *Herald,* June 11, 13, 30, 1856.

[24] Coleman, *Vigilance Committee,* 79–81. MS in Bancroft Library. This is confirmed by Dempster in his manuscript on the Vigilance Committee, 3. Also in Bancroft Library.

New York *Herald* urged the government to dispatch a strong army to arrest the movement for secession.[25] On July 28 the Senate adopted a resolution requesting the President to inform the Senate whether he had received any application from the governor of California for military aid against the Vigilance Committee of San Francisco.[26] On August 29 a memorial was presented from the Texas legislature asking Congress and the President to interfere for the liberation of Judge Terry.[27] Senator Weller and Representative Herbert, both of California, urged federal interference in San Francisco. They asserted that the Vigilance Committee had secession tendencies. On the other hand, Bell of Tennessee believed that there was no danger of disloyalty in California and that no contingency requiring executive interference had arisen. Any attempt of the President to suppress the Vigilance Committee would result in considerable bloodshed and possibly the separation of the Pacific Coast from the Union.[28]

President's refusal to intervene.—President Pierce was reluctant to intervene in the domestic troubles of California. He probably remembered the protests occasioned by President Tyler's intervention in Rhode Island during the Dorr rebellion.[29] Since it was close to the presidential election of 1856, he decided to move cautiously and referred the matter to the Attorney General.

In his written report Attorney General Cushing held that while the acts of the Vigilance Committee constituted a "lawless

25 San Francisco *Herald,* Aug. 29, 1856.

26 *Cong. Globe,* 34 Cong. 1 Sess., 1799. On August 6, the President transmitted to the Senate reports from the Secretaries of Navy and State (Richardson, V, 383). These reports form Document 101, cited in this chapter.

27 *Cong. Globe,* 34 Cong., 2 Sess., 69.

28 *Cong. Globe,* 34 Cong., 2 Sess., 69–70.

29 President Tyler claimed he did not interfere with the naval or military forces in Rhode Island (*Cong. Globe,* 28 Cong., 1 Sess., 504). According to Burke's report the President did interfere. See *Report* in *H. Rep.* 546, 28 Cong., 1 Sess. (447).

usurpation of the powers of the State,'' there was no evidence in all the information received from California that the committee had threatened to resist the laws of the United States and the official authority of the federal government. There were therefore two difficulties. In the first place, the application of the governor was not in due form, for there was no statement that the legislature could not be convened, and according to the California constitution he had the power to call the legislature. But the President could act only upon the application of the legislature of the state in insurrection, or upon the call of the executive of the state when the legislature could not be convened.[30] In the second place, the application of the governor was not for military forces but for arms and ammunition. It was therefore questionable whether the President was empowered to furnish to the state authorities, in time of an insurrection, arms and ammunition distinct from and not in the hands of officers and troops of the United States. He admitted that an emergency might arise when the President might furnish arms alone, but the circumstances in California ''did not afford sufficient legal justification for acceding to the actual requests of the governor of the State of California.''[31]

[30] The act of February 28, 1795, provides that ''in case of an insurrection in any state, against the government thereof, it shall be lawful for the President of the United States, on application of the legislature of such State, or of the executive (when the legislature cannot be convened), to call forth such number of the militia of any other state or states, as may be applied for, as he may judge sufficient to suppress such insurrection'' (United States, *Statutes at Large*, I, 424). The second act of March 3, 1807, is entitled ''*An act* authorizing the employment of the land and naval forces of the United States in case of insurrection or obstruction to the laws of the United States or of any state or territory'' (United States, *Statutes at Large*, II, 443). In his annual message of 1857, Governor Johnson claimed that the reasons for not calling the legislature in extra session were that it would involve a great expenditure of money and a loss of time. Moreover, he did not think that an application for arms and ammunition must necessarily be made by the legislature. A requisition of the executive of the state to the President he thought was sufficient (California, *Sen. Jour.*, 1857, 25).

[31] *Sen. Ex. Doc.* 101, 34 Cong., 1 Sess., 8–13 (824).

Upon the receipt of the opinion of the Attorney General, Secretary of State Marcy wrote to Governor Johnson that he was deeply impressed by the disturbed conditions in San Francisco, and "was prepared, whenever exigency arises demanding and justifying his interposition, to render assistance to suppress insurrection against the government of a State," but in the present case the President believed that there were "insuperable obstacles" to the action desired of the federal authorities.[32]

Secretary of the Navy Dobbin instructed Commander Mervine, commanding the Pacific squadron, to exercise the most "extraordinary circumspection and wise discretion," in order to prevent a collision between the federal officers and the people of California. He emphasized the fact that no officer of the naval forces could interpose on the mere request of the state executive and without any instructions from the Navy Department. The officers were further instructed to see that the United States property was fully protected and the federal laws sustained. In order to be prepared for any emergency, there were to be stationed at Mare Island or San Francisco several vessels, to be kept there until the disturbances in San Francisco were over.[33] Similar instructions were issued by Secretary of War Jefferson Davis to General Wool. The general was ordered to concentrate at Benicia and Fort Point sufficient federal troops and arms to meet any emergency. But he was not to interfere with the domestic affairs unless it should be necessary to protect government property against revolutionary attacks.[34]

The refusal of the President to interfere in the affairs of San Francisco avoided unnecessary complications which undoubtedly would have resulted from such a policy. This episode is of some interest in a study of the relations of a state with the

[32] *Sen. Ex. Doc.*, 101, 34 Cong., 1 Sess., 7–8; California, *Sen. Jour.*, 1857, 57–61.

[33] *Sen. Ex. Doc.* 101, 34 Cong., 1 Sess., 13–15.

[34] *Sen. Ex. Doc.* 43, 34 Cong., 3 Sess., 8–9 (881); *Alta*, Aug. 15, Oct. 12, 1856.

federal government, for here we have a case wherein the executive of the general government was called upon to construe article four, section four, of the Constitution; namely, when and how far should the federal government interfere within a state "against domestic violence." The act of February 28, 1795, vests in the President power to carry out the provision in the Constitution; it is left to his discretion to decide when interference is necessary. We also see how reluctant are the federal authorities to interfere in domestic troubles within states. This seems to have been especially true before the Civil War when the doctrine of states' rights was of paramount importance.

CHAPTER VIII

MEANS OF COMMUNICATION AND TRANSPORTATION

Early demand for mail facilities.—One of the hardest fights California had to make was the struggle to secure, for social and commercial purposes, adequate means of communication between the Atlantic and Pacific coasts. Yet her extreme remoteness from the centers of population and industry made this problem more urgent in California than in other frontier communities.

As early as 1847, when California was still held by military occupation, Congress passed an act providing for a semimonthly mail between New York and Chagres, and a monthly mail between Panama and Astoria with stopovers at Monterey and San Francisco.[1] Shortly after California was ceded to the United States, Congress provided for post offices in California. The charge on each single letter not exceeding half an ounce in weight, conveyed between the Atlantic and Pacific coasts, was to be forty cents; and twelve and a half cents for every letter conveyed from one place to another on the Pacific Coast.[2] In accordance with this act of August 14, 1848, the Postmaster General appointed a special agent to make the necessary arrangements in California for the establishment of post offices, and for the receipt and conveyance of mails in that territory. He was

---

[1] United States, *Statutes at Large,* IX, 200, Act of March 3, 1847. In accordance with this act contracts were made with Sloo, of Cincinnati, Ohio, for the transportation of mail from New York to New Orleans and then to Chagres; and with Harris, of Arkansas, for similar service from Panama to Astoria. The mail service between Panama and Astoria commenced in October, 1848. The company launched three ships: the "California," the "Panama," and the "Oregon." The "California" arrived in San Francisco Feb. 28, 1849 (*Sen. Ex. Doc.* 50, 32 Cong., 1 Sess., 1–11 [619]).

[2] United States, *Statutes at Large,* IX, 320.

ordered to practice economy and limit the expenditure to the revenue from the postage. But owing to the high cost of labor and material in California, the agent found the means at his disposal entirely inadequate for the service, and was unable to establish a mail service satisfactory to California.[3]

California complained against the exorbitant charges and poor transportation facilities. A joint resolution of the legislature asked for a reduction in the rate of letter postage, better facilities in the interior, and the establishment of a semimonthly mail from Panama to California.[4]

Postmaster General Collamer recommended that provision be made for a more satisfactory service in California even should the expenses exceed the income from the postage; he also recommended provision for a semimonthly mail service between Panama and San Francisco.[5] In accordance with these recommendations a bill was introduced in the Senate providing for a semimonthly mail between Panama and California, and for the establishment of a branch Post Office Department to be devoted exclusively to the mail service in California and Oregon.

The Committee on Post Offices and Post Roads recommended the passage of the bill and pointed out that the rapidity with which California was being settled justified an increase in the

[3] Voorhees to Postmaster General Johnson, March 13, 1849 (*H. Ex. Doc.* 17, 31 Cong., 1 Sess., 959 [573]). Voorhees pointed out that in view of the high cost of living in California, the government could not get men to devote all their time to their office for the same salaries paid in other parts of the Union. As an illustration of the high cost of living in California, he pointed out that boarding per week was $17.50; washing from $6 to $8 a dozen pieces; rent for a small room $100 a month. The prices as given by Allen are even higher than those quoted by Voorhees. Allen gives the ordinary salary of clerks as from $300 to $500 a month (*ibid.*, 961–64).

[4] *H. Ex. Doc.* 17, 31 Cong., 1 Sess., 969; *Alta,* Dec. 21, 1850, Jan. 18, July 8, 1851; *Pacific News,* Oct. 29, 1850, Jan. 31, 1851; California, *Statutes,* 1850, 464; *Cong. Globe,* 31 Cong., 2 Sess., App., 17.

[5] *Ibid.*, 19. The Post Office Department estimated the average monthly mail from New York to California at over 10,000 letters and 12,000 newspapers in 1849 (*Sen. Ex. Doc.* 1, 31 Cong., 1 Sess., 796 [569]); *Sen. Rept.* 97, 31 Cong., 1 Sess., [565]).

mail service and that many unnecessary delays in the service could be avoided by having on the coast some "controlling power" to which all local difficulties might be referred. But the opposition contended that there was no need for an increase in the mail service in California, and that the establishment of a branch office of the Post Office Department on the Pacific Coast would be considered an acknowledgment that the government was unable to manage its peripheral territories from one common center, and might lead to disunion on the Pacific Coast. The bill was defeated.[6]

Postmaster General Hall attributed the unsatisfactory conditions of the mail service in California and Oregon "to the difficulties incident to the new and very peculiar state of affairs in that distant region." In his report of November 30, 1850, he recommended reducing the rate of postage to and from the Pacific Coast to twenty cents the single letter. In both houses were offered resolutions providing for some reforms in the Pacific Coast mail service. As a result California succeeded in obtaining two important measures. In the first place, the service from Panama to California and Oregon was made semimonthly.[7] Secondly, the act reducing the rate of postage throughout the United States provided that there should be a charge of three cents when prepaid, and five cents when sent collect, on all single letters of half an ounce in weight when conveyed in the mail any distance between places of the United States not exceeding 3000 miles; and double that rate when the distance exceeded the 3000 mile limit.[8]

---

[6] *Sen. Rept.* 97, 31 Cong., 1 Sess., (565); *Sen. Ex. Doc.* 1, 31, Cong., 2 Sess., 407–10 (587).

[7] United States, *Statutes at Large,* IX, 623. In pursuance of this act the proper authorities entered into a contract with Aspinwall, head of the Pacific Mail Steamship Company, by which the mail service from Panama to California and Oregon was increased to a semimonthly service at the increased cost of $149,250 (*H. Ex. Doc.* 1, 31 Cong., 2 Sess., 629 [778]).

[8] Act of March 3, 1851 (United States, *Statutes at Large,* IX, 587–91).

The reduction of postage from forty cents to six and ten cents was a result of the strong opinion in Congress that pioneer communities should have the advantage of a cheap postage, irrespective of the great expenditure in transmitting the mails. Postmaster General Hall, however, thought that the high cost of mail transportation to the Pacific Coast did not permit such a reduction. He pointed out that during the month of September, 1850, the number of letters received and sent by the New Orleans, New York, and Chagres lines was 112,085, and postage thereon was $44,385.60; while during the month of September, 1851, after the reduction took place, the postage on 118,934 letters was only $12,854.81. He further pointed out that while the government received only five cents for a pound of printed matter transported to and from the Pacific Coast, it paid twenty cents for the same transported only across the Isthmus.[9]

But the Californians denied the justice of the principle that the mail service of the Pacific Coast must pay its way, contending that distant communities should enjoy a cheap postage. Moreover, California contributed to the welfare of the nation in other ways than postal revenue. It was also pointed out that the distance overland from the Atlantic states to the Pacific Coast did not exceed 3000 miles, therefore California should not be asked to pay double rate merely because the Postmaster General transported the mail by a circuitous route of over 3000 miles.[10]

---

[9] *Sen. Ex. Doc.* 1, 32 Cong., 1 Sess., 427–28 (612). According to the Postmaster General, comparative costs of mail transportation in California and other parts of the Union were as follows: in steamboats, thirteen cents and eight mills a mile; in coaches, about twenty cents a mile; and in modes not specified above, thirty-four cents and six mills a mile. The cost of similar service in other parts of the United States, except Oregon, Utah, and New Mexico, was: in steamboats, nine cents a mile; in coaches, five cents and five mills; and in modes not specified above, four cents and seven mills a mile (*ibid.*, 418, also serial nos. 692, 705).

[10] *California*, Sen. Jour., 1852, 18; *Courier*, Jan. 24, 1851; *Herald*, April 14, 1855; *News*, Feb. 12, 1855. The legislature passed several resolutions asking Congress for a uniform postage rate of two cents on the letter (California, *Statutes*, 1856, 238–39; 1857, 367).

There was also a great deal of complaint of the inadequacy of the mail service. It was acknowledged even by the Postmaster General that the government was too slow to keep pace with the rapid spread of the mining settlements. The number of distributing offices was too few and they were often injudiciously located. There were many large communities with no post offices.[11] People were therefore compelled to use private expresses for the transmission of their mail. These private expresses were always at hand but for this accommodation the miners had to pay an exorbitant rate ranging, according to distance, from one to five dollars a letter.[12] Even after the government offices and mail routes had penetrated the new settlements, the miners still resorted to the private expresses. This was due, largely, to the corrupt practices of the postmasters at the central offices, who were very tardy in forwarding the mail from the states; while the letters sent by the expressmen were delivered promptly. In return for this service, the postmasters received from the expressmen a commission for each letter. In his annual report for 1853, the Postmaster General complained against the encroachments of the private expresses. He issued orders to the postmasters in California to discontinue the vicious practice of withholding the mail in order to encourage the employment of expresses.[13]

The people of California were of course complaining against the poor service and demanding more extensive interior mail facilities as well as a weekly mail between the east and the Pacific Coast.[14] ''California has many grievances to complain

[11] *Sen. Ex. Doc.* 1, 33 Cong., 1 Sess., 705–6 (692); *Herald,* June 3, 1853; *Alta,* Nov. 14, 1853, Oct. 15, 1855; Sacramento *Transcript,* Feb. 14, March 14, 1851. According to the report of the Postmaster General for 1851, there were thirty-four post offices in California up to June 30, 1851 (*H. Ex. Doc.* 2, 32 Cong., 1 Sess., 419 [635]).

[12] *Sen. Ex. Doc.* 1, 32 Cong., 1 Sess., 705 (692).

[13] *Ibid.* This illegitimate business of the postmasters was partly explained by the meager salaries they received from the government.

[14] California, *Statutes*, 1854, 268, 275.

of at the hands of the General Government," said the *Alta*, "but the most prominent, as well as the most annoying, is our defective postal arrangements. Will it be believed that there are whole counties in the State that are totally deprived of mail facilities? . . . . Were it not for our admirably arranged express companies, we do not know what the State would have done."[15]

In response to the demands McDougal of California introduced in the House during the first session of the thirty-third Congress, a bill for increased mail facilities that, together with the existing arrangement, would provide a weekly mail service for the Pacific Coast. The California representatives contended that a weekly mail service would contribute greatly to the prosperity of the Pacific Coast. But the opposition argued that it would be unfair to tax the Post Office Department over a million dollars in order to increase the mail service in California at a time when many districts were ill supplied with mail facilities, and when that department was already suffering a yearly deficit of $200,000. The bill was laid on the table.[16]

Early Pacific railroad projects.—Long before the acquisition of California enterprising men had advocated the construction of a transcontinental railroad to facilitate commercial and social intercourse between east and west. In 1835 Hartwell Carver, a grandson of the explorer, Jonathan Carver, laid before Congress a plan for a Pacific railroad and telegraph line from Lake Michigan to South Pass, with branches to San Francisco Bay and the mouth of the Columbia River. Carver was not the only one who caught the vision of this great enterprise. A similar project was advocated by Plumb of Iowa. But of all these early dreamers the outstanding one was Asa Whitney, a New York merchant, who had resided for a number of years in China. His plan, presented to Congress in 1845, provided for a grant of land sixty miles wide along the entire road from Lake Michigan to the

[15] *Alta*, March 6, 1854; April 20, June 9, 13, July 13, Oct. 25, 1855.

[16] *Cong. Globe*, 33 Cong., 1 Sess., 854–55, 1433–34, 1560.

Pacific. The road was to be built from the proceeds of the sale of this land.[17]

Whitney's project was discussed fully in Congress and at railroad conventions. Among its opponents were those who, fearing that such a vast undertaking by private individuals would result in a dangerous monopoly, advocated a national road. On February 7, 1849, Benton introduced a bill in the Senate for the construction of a "central national road from the Pacific Ocean to the Mississippi river." Wherever practical it was to consist of an iron railway, otherwise it was to be a macadamized road. The funds for the construction of this road were to be derived from the sale of public lands. The bill died in the Committee on Military Affairs.

Agitation in California for a continental railroad.—By this time the movement for a transcontinental railroad had gained considerable impetus from the Pacific Coast. As early as 1850 the press and the legislature began to voice the demand for an interoceanic railroad as a bond between the Atlantic and Pacific coasts. The failure of Congress to provide for the construction of such a railroad, said Colton, would make the interests of the Atlantic and Pacific slopes "forever independent of and opposed to each other," and result in the formation of "an independent nation on the Pacific."[18]

As time went on the agitation for a transcontinental railroad became one of the vital issues in California. Such a road, it was contended, would remove the necessity of a toilsome journey through the desert or the expensive circuitous voyage by way of the Isthmus. There was a prevailing belief that California could not have justice done to her by the central government so long as communication between her and the national capital was slow and inadequate. Such a state of things, said

---

[17] Bancroft, *California*, VII, 498–500. For a brief and spirited account of these early schemes see Sabin, *Building the Pacific Railway*, chap. 1.

[18] *Alta*, May 24, 1850; *Courier*, Aug. 5, 1850, Sept. 14, 1851; *Pacific News*, Oct. 25, 1849; Colton, *Three Years in California*, 456; California, *Statutes*, 1850, 465.

the *Alta,* was "calculated to engender an unkind state of feeling between our State and the General Government—which might finally be fostered to a frightful extent."[19] In a memorial to Congress adopted at a special Pacific railroad meeting held at San Francisco November 28, 1851, it was contended that a transcontinental railroad would bind together the large unoccupied and sparsely settled territories; that in case of a foreign war California would be easily invaded and without a railroad the federal government would not be able to afford aid. The memorialists stated that without such a bond the Pacific Coast could not be governed, and it would be "better, far better for us, and for the world, ... to cut these adjacent provinces loose, and permit us, in our own strength to organize a Pacific Union of States."[20]

There were, however, considerable differences of opinion as to the most appropriate route and means of accomplishing the object. Some were in favor of a northern route, others favored a middle route, and still others preferred a southern route. In a resolution the legislature advocated that the cost of constructing the railroad should be a tax on the revenue or credit of the federal government, leaving the public domain to be granted to actual settlers.

Congress and the railroad.—The federal government was not insensible to the needs and demands of the Pacific Coast. President Fillmore and Secretary of the Interior Stuart pointed out the need of a transcontinental railroad.[21] On December 16, 1850, Benton introduced in the Senate his bill for a national

[19] The prices of passage between Panama and San Francisco fluctuated. According to the statement of Aspinwall, the president of the Pacific Mail Steamship Company, the prices in 1851 were as follows: first-class, $250; second-class, $200; steerage, $100 (*Sen. Rep.* 267, 32 Cong., 1 Sess. [631]). Then there was the unpleasant journey across the Isthmus on mules and in small boats. The Pacific Mail Steamship Company later connected Navy Bay with Panama by a railroad. This saved the immigrant time and inconvenience, but it was very expensive.

[20] California, *Assembly Jour.*, 1853, App., Doc. 58.

[21] *Annual Message* of Dec. 2, 1850, Richardson, *Messages,* V, 86; *Report* of the Secretary of the Interior, *Cong. Globe,* 31 Cong., 2 Sess., App., 7–8.

road to the Pacific Ocean between the parallels thirty and thirty-nine degrees of north latitude. This route, he said, was laid off not by engineers but by the buffalo, elk, deer, and antelope, which by mere instinct always discovered the lowest passes in the mountains and the shortest lines between two points. Gwin protested against any attempt "to commit the Government prematurely to any route which subsequent developments may prove impracticable." The bill and the joint resolution of the California legislature urging the organization of a corps of engineers to explore and survey the several proposed routes were referred to the Committee on Roads and Canals.[22]

Several bills for overland communication were introduced in the Senate during the thirty-second Congress. One of these was a bill offered by Douglas for the "protection of the immigrant route, and a telegraphic line, and for an overland mail between the Missouri river and the settlements in California and Oregon." The object of the bill, said Douglas, was to bind together the two divisions of the republic. The western Senators supported the bill; the southern Senators opposed it on the ground of constitutionality, and that it "would be a bounty upon immigration to encourage new swarms to leave the old hive."[23]

A second bill introduced by Gwin, provided for the establishment of two railroads between the Mississippi Valley and the Pacific Coast. One route was to start at the Red River, near the southwest corner of the state of Arkansas; the other route was to commence at a point on the western boundary of Missouri or Iowa. "Upon the completion of one or more railroads," asserted Gwin, "depends the existence of this Union." The bill was laid on the table.[24]

Early in the next session Gwin introduced a new bill providing for a main trunk line from San Francisco to Memphis

[22] *Cong. Globe,* 31 Cong., 2 Sess., 58.
[23] *Cong. Globe,* 32 Cong., 1 Sess., 1161, 1756, *et seq.*
[24] *Cong. Globe,* 32 Cong., 1 Sess., 2467, 2469.

and several branches to St. Louis, Dubuque, Texas, New Orleans, and Oregon. The purpose of the several branches was to connect the main trunk with the various parts of the country as required by local needs and preferences.[25] It was hoped that by conciliating all sections the bill would gain strength. The California Senators resisted all attempts to refer it to a committee. There had been enough committee reports on this subject, said Gwin, "the time has come for action."

A number of prominent senators pledged their support to the railroad bill, believing that the government owed to the citizens of California the construction of this great route and that the exigencies of the whole country called for the undertaking of this project. But the bill met with a stubborn opposition from various quarters for it involved many mooted difficulties. In the first place, there was the question of cost. The opponents contended that no project for the construction of a railroad with branches aggregating a route of over five thousand miles could be financially accomplished. "One simple road is all that the country needs at present," said Senator Cass. Then, there was the troublesome question destined to wreck many railroad bills—the question of the precise location of the route and the eastern terminus. Many friends of a transcontinental road believed that before a project of such magnitude could be undertaken there should be some preliminary reconnaissance by a corps of topographical engineers to determine upon the best and the most practicable route. Finally, there were the constitutional scruples of the Democrats, particularly those from the south. They questioned the constitutional right to take money out of the government treasury for the purpose of constructing railroads within the states. "The whole character of the Government will be changed. . . . . The Constitution will be gone. There will be no appeal to that, and the

[25] *Cong. Globe,* 32 Cong., 2 Sess., 127, 280–84, 314–21, 330, 340–43, 350–55, 420–24, 671–82, 695–715, 740–56, 765–75, 814–23.

Government will be one of unlimited powers,'' declared Mason of Virginia. ''I would perish sooner than I would suffer any foreign influence to have a corporation within my State,'' exclaimed Butler of South Carolina. In vain did the friends of the project argue that under the power to make a military road, the federal government possessed the full constitutional power to build such a road.[26]

To remove some of the constitutional objections Shields of Illinois offered, at the eleventh hour, an amendment that the $20,000,000 appropriated by the bill should not be expended in the construction of the road within the states, and that the road within any state should be made under the authority of the state legislature.[27] This amendment created a split in the camp of the railroad friends. Gwin and Rusk contended that the adoption of such an amendment would actually kill the whole bill. ''Why come in with an amendment that knocked the whole thing into a cocked hat—that disjointed and destroyed the bill?'' argued Rusk. On the other hand Senator Weller declared that he would not sacrifice long cherished principles in order to obtain the railroad.[28]

The Shields amendment was rejected and other amendments were introduced. But the sum total of positive result of all the ''noise and confusion'' during the whole session was the adoption of an amendment to the army appropriation bill authorizing the Secretary of War to employ topographical engineers to survey the various proposed routes to the Pacific, and ascertain which was the most practicable and economical route.

---

26 *Cong. Globe,* 32 Cong., 2 Sess., 285–86, 678, 680.

27 *Cong. Globe,* 32 Cong., 2 Sess., 714, Feb. 19, 1853.

28 Gwin, *Memoirs,* 86. MS in Bancroft Library. Gwin holds that, but for this amendment, the bill would have passed both houses and have become a law in 1853, but the new provision killed the whole measure (*Cong. Globe,* 32 Cong., 2 Sess., 741–43). It was feared that the road would be built in the states only and that the money would all be spent there, before the work would be begun in the territories.

Their reports were to be submitted to Congress in February, 1854.[29]

Vain hopes of California.—The people of California considered this measure as the first positive step of the government toward the realization of the great project. Railroad conventions were held at San Diego and San Francisco in 1853 to concert measures for advancing the project. A senate committee asserted that from 1849 to 1853 no less than 40,000 lives had been "sacrificed to the pestilential and sickening influences of the routes of travel" to and from California and this loss of life could be prevented only by supplying the needed railroad. The railroad question became one of the cardinal principles in state politics. At their state conventions both parties passed resolutions favoring the great project. The Democratic party took the position that such a measure would be justified on the ground that it was a means of defense. In their messages the governors urged the legislature to press the subject upon Congress. The legislature usually responded with joint resolutions.[30]

There was, however, a difference of opinion as to the most practicable route. Generally the southern counties advocated a southern route; while the people of the central and northern portions of the state favored the central route. Others contended that the road was practicable by more than one route. It was suggested that the legislature should provide for a preliminary survey of the various passes through the Sierra Nevada.[31]

Results of the exploring expeditions.—Under the instructions of the act of March 3, 1853, Secretary Jefferson Davis sent out, in 1853, five expeditions under the guidance of able officers to

[29] The bill was adopted in the Senate by a majority of 31 to 16, and in the House by 82 to 42 (*Cong. Globe*, 32 Cong., 2 Sess., 841, 998). For the law *see* United States, *Statutes at Large*, X, 219, 579.

[30] *Herald*, June 15, 1853; *Alta*, Oct. 4, 5, 1853; California, *Statutes*, 1853, 315; 1854, 276; California, *Sen. Jour.*, 1853, 25, App., Doc. 5, 72; *ibid.*, 1854, 31; *ibid.*, 1855, 45.

[31] *Herald*, June 15, 1853; *Alta*, Jan. 30, Nov. 4, Dec. 13, 15, 1854, Jan. 29, 1855; Sacramento *Union*, Dec. 14, 16, 1854.

"ascertain the most practicable and economical route for a railroad from the Mississippi River to the Pacific Ocean." The five routes selected to be reconnoitered were: (1) the northern trail, between parallels forty-seven and forty-nine; (2) the route between the forty-first and forty-second parallels; (3) the Benton "Buffalo trail," between the thirty-ninth and thirty-eighth parallels; (4) the thirty-fifth parallel trail; (5) the southern trail, near the thirty-second parallel.[32]

The surveys began in 1853 and were carried on for several years. On February 27, 1855, Secretary Davis submitted to Congress the printed reports of the several exploring expeditions together with a brief summary of the results of the several surveys, and his own conclusions. A comparison of the results of the explorations, asserted the Secretary of War, "conclusively shows that the route of the thirty-second parallel is, of those surveyed, 'the most practicable and economical route for a railroad from the Mississippi river to the Pacific Ocean'." He claimed that it was the shortest and least costly of all the routes and that it passed through territory of the most favorable climate for the construction and preservation of the road.[33] The net results of these extensive explorations and estimates were to satisfy the country that from an engineering point of view transcontinental railroads could be constructed over several routes. Henceforth the question was not whether it was possible to build the road but how and where it should be constructed.

---

[32] *Report* of the Secretary of War (Jefferson Davis), Feb. 27, 1855 (*Sen. Ex. Doc.* 78, 33 Cong., 2 Sess., 1–30 [758]).

[33] *Sen. Ex. Doc.* 78, 33 Cong., 2 Sess., 29–30 (758). The following figures are given in the table of the length and comparative costs of the several routes: Route near 47° and 49° parallels, 2025 miles, cost $140,-871,000; from St. Paul to Vancouver, distance 1864 miles, cost $130,781,000; route near 41° and 42° parallels, from Council Bluffs to Benicia, distance 2,032 miles, cost $116,095,000; route near parallels 38° and 39°, from Westport to San Francisco, a distance of 2,290 miles, cost, very great; route near 35° parallel, from Fort Smith to San Francisco, distance, 2,174 miles, cost around one hundred and seventy millions; route near the 32° parallel from Fulton to San Francisco, distance 2,039 miles, cost $93,120,000 (*ibid.*, 107).

Secretary Davis, perhaps influenced by his sectional predilections, favored the southern route. The attitude of President Pierce was less encouraging. While admitting the importance of a transcontinental railroad from a commercial and military point of view, he declared that no considerations "can have any appreciable value, when weighed against the obligation strictly to adhere to the Constitution and faithfully to execute the powers it confers." He doubted whether the federal government had the power to undertake a work of this nature even within the limits of the territories.[34]

In the Senate select committees each member had his own plan. To reconcile the different sections Douglas reported a bill providing for three routes. One road to be called the "Southern Pacific," was to commence on the western border of Texas and terminate in California. The second to be called the "Central Pacific," was to commence on the western border of the state of Missouri, or of Iowa, and terminate at the Bay of San Francisco. The third road, to be known as the "Northern Pacific," was to commence on the western border of the state of Wisconsin and terminate in Oregon and Washington. Each road was to be accompanied by a telegraph line. To aid the construction of these several lines the bill provided for a grant of land of twelve miles on each side of the road in alternate sections. The completion of the construction of these railroads was not to exceed ten years.[35]

While this plan had the strength of conciliating the several sections it also had the weakness of being too gigantic a project. It was contended, even by many friends of a Pacific railroad, that under the existing conditions such a project was not physically nor fiscally possible; that there would be a shortage of capital and labor to construct the three roads; that the travel and transportation on these lines, running through an unin-

[34] Richardson, *Messages*, V, 221–23.

[35] *Cong. Globe*, 33 Cong., 2 Sess., 749. The bill is given in full.

habited country, would not be sufficient to pay the upkeep of the roads. The bill passed the Senate, however, but failed in the House.[36]

At the thirty-fourth Congress the Pacific railroad question attracted less attention. Weller of California reported a bill for the construction of one road to be selected by the contractors. But in spite of his warnings that unless direct communication between the Atlantic and Pacific was established, "there will be an independent government on that coast in less than fifteen years," his project failed.[37]

Nor was Denver of California, chairman of the select committee in the House, more successful with his railroad bill. The committee did not think proper to "step aside from the long established system of the government in granting lands only, to aid in the construction of the road" while Wood of Maine in his minority report contended that the work could be accomplished only with the financial aid of the government. He also maintained that the central route was the most favorable for the Pacific railroad, for the selection of the route should be governed not so much by the facility and cheapness with which the project could be carried out, but rather by the amount of population to be accommodated and the amount of service to be performed to support the enterprise when completed.

On the other hand, Kidwell of Virginia in his minority report took the ground of an extreme strict constructionist. He maintained that the Constitution conferred no authority upon Congress to provide for the construction of the railroad, that such a project was not feasible at a "reasonable" cost for its construction and subsequent support.[38]

California protests.—The long debates and the fruitless efforts to secure a bill for the construction of the railroad

[36] *Cong. Globe,* 33 Cong., 2 Sess., 750, 815; *Cong. Globe,* 33 Cong., 2 Sess., 281–82, 355, 356.

[37] *Cong. Globe,* 34 Cong., 1 Sess., App., 477–81.

[38] *H. Rep.* 274, 34 Cong., 1 Sess., 1–23 (870).

irritated the people in California. During the years 1854 and 1855, California lived through a period of financial depression. The product of the mines began to diminish;[39] immigration decreased so that during the year 1855 the number of arrivals and departures was almost equal.[40] There were a number of bankruptcies;[41] the market was glutted with goods; real estate fell in value; interest and rent declined. There were many reasons to account for this depression. It was partly due to over-speculation on the part of California and eastern merchants which resulted in ill adjustment of the market.[42] It was also due to the want of more adequate means of communication. Without adequate means of communication, contended the California merchants, the market could not be well adjusted. Moreover, as long as the back country was not filled up by a regularly settled population the cities were bound to retrograde, the resources of the country would not be developed, and the growth of the state would be retarded.[43]

The Californians believed that the government at Washington was not sufficiently attentive to the needs of their state. The *Herald* complained of the "madness and ingratitude of the Eastern States in opposing every measure for the benefit of California." Comparing California with Australia, the *Chronicle* claimed that the greater progress of the latter was due to the

---

39 During 1854 the yield of the mines amounted to $64,000,000, while in 1855 it fell to $49,000,000. Shipment via Panama in 1854 was $51,328,653; in 1855, $43,080,211 (*State Register,* 1859, 264).

40 During 1855 the number of arrivals was 29,198; the number of departures was 22,898 (*State Register,* 1859, 122).

41 Some of the principal banks had suspended payment. There was a stagnation of business. See *Herald,* Feb. 23, 1855.

42 The California merchants frequently complained that the eastern exporters glutted the markets by "inundating us with goods we do not want, and then denounce us as swindlers if they do not realize a hundred per cent profit on their shipments. They cunningly duplicate the orders sent by our merchants and stupidly manifest them as unspecified merchandise" (*Herald,* Feb. 28, 1855).

43 Sacramento *Union,* Jan. 11, 12, Oct. 1, 1855; *Herald,* Jan. 28, March 15, 1855; *Chronicle,* Jan. 22, 1855; *Alta,* Aug. 4, 1854.

differences in the attitudes of the American and British governments. "In Australia," it argued, "the British government promotes the construction of railroads; but in California the American government stands aloof in spite of the fact that its treasury is overflowing."[44]

A movement was set on foot in California to organize a new party, which should "go for California first, last, and all the time." The main issue of the new party was to be the Pacific railroad question. Without this road, declared the *Chronicle,* California would not be settled for a hundred years and instead of lands dotted with cottages and green fields the back country would be occupied by the bear and coyote.[45] The same paper warned the "great selfish East that it is pursuing the course of England which alienated thirteen of her colonies."[46]

At times these grumblings and complaints took on a tone of open secession. In a letter published in the *Bulletin* "Caxton" drew a gloomy picture of the prospects of California, and he warned the people that the only alternative for them was ruin or a continental railroad to connect California with the emporiums of America. "Caxton" called upon the people of California to take bolder steps than mere begging, praying, and supplicating high officials. These means, he said, had been tried in vain for five years.

> Begging for it [he asserted] will not lay a single rail, or it would have had a double track, long ago, from shore to shore. . . .
>
> *Let us demand as a Right what has been refused as a boon* . . . .
>
> The government must do something for our defence, or it cuts loose from us, casts adrift, and in effect bids us shift for ourselves.
>
> If such be the alternative, we are ready for it. The sooner it comes, the better. . . .[47]

---

[44] *Chronicle,* Dec. 1, 1854.

[45] *Chronicle,* Nov. 29, 1854.

[46] *Chronicle,* April 18, 1855.

[47] *Bulletin,* April 9, 1856. "Caxton" was a well-known political writer in California.

Demand for wagon roads.—Realizing that many years would elapse before all the difficulties in connection with the railroad project would be adjusted and the construction completed, many began to direct their energies temporarily to the accomplishment of a speedy construction of a good military road across the plains to California. The project was discussed throughout the state. Meetings for the purpose of carrying into Congress the demand for a wagon road were held in 1854 in San Francisco, Sacramento, and in other places. A resolution adopted at a meeting held in San Francisco declared that the project of a Pacific railroad would be a work of years, therefore as a temporary means of safe travel from the eastern states to California, an immigrant road protected by military posts should be constructed. "The people do not ask the wagon road as a boon," said the *Bulletin*, "they demand it as a right, for California enriches the nation."[48]

In his annual message Governor Bigler emphasized the need of military roads. The legislature debated this question. The memorial accompanying the Senate resolution argued that, as a result of the inadequate means of communication, the intercourse between the Atlantic and Pacific coasts must necessarily be reduced to a minimum, retarding the advancement of the Pacific slope. But "when the road is once completed," proceeds the memorial, "flourishing settlements would spring up on the fertile lands contiguous to it, and in a very few years these lands will produce food for the consumption of the laborers who will grade the track for the great railroad."[49]

The resolution adopted by the legislature urged the construction of three or more military roads across the deserts leading into California through the northern, middle, and southern por-

[48] *News*, Jan. 3, 4, 1855; Sacramento *Union*, Jan. 11, 1855; *Bulletin*, April 5, 1855; *see* Sacramento *Union*, Oct. 1, 1855. The *Alta* hinted at the probability of the establishment of a Pacific republic in case Congress should refuse to supply adequate means of communication between the Atlantic and Pacific coasts (*Alta*, Feb. 21, April 12, 17, 1855).

[49] California, *Sen. Jour.*, 1855, 231; Sacramento *Union*, Feb. 8, 1855, quotes portions of the memorial.

tions of the state. The government was granted the right of way for the construction of these roads through any portion of the state.[50]

It was felt that an expression on the subject coming directly from the people of California would appeal to Congress more than the usual resolutions of the legislature. Such a petition was drawn up at a wagon-road meeting held in San Francisco during the month of March, 1856. The memorial told of the conditions under which California, as an outpost upon the frontier of the United States, was laboring and the danger to which she was exposed in case of war with a foreign maritime power. It urged the establishment of a military wagon road between Missouri and California.[51]

The memorial was carried throughout the state for signatures. The press devoted considerable space in its columns arguing the great need of a wagon road and urging the people to sign the petition. On April 21 the monster petition, signed by tens of thousands[52] of people, was, amidst speech-making and festivity, dispatched to Washington.

> Upon the receipt of this memorial [said the *Herald*], depends the loyalty of the Pacific Coast to the federal government. If our earnest petition is once more scouted, it will remain for the exiles in this far distant land to adopt measures for their own salvation regardless, if needs must be, of the fraternal ties that once bound us to the Union.[53]

In presenting the memorial to the Senate Weller declared that the seventy-five thousand "freemen" who had signed the

---

[50] California, *Assembly Jour.*, 1856, 35–38.

[51] The memorial is printed in *Cong. Globe,* 34 Cong., 1 Sess., 1297; Sacramento *Union,* March 31, 1856.

[52] *Alta,* April 21, 1856; *Herald,* April 21, 1856. The *Alta* estimated the number of signatures from 60,000 to 80,000. The signatures were pasted into two large blank books of fourteen by twenty inches. Each volume contained one thousand leaves. The books were bound in fine morocco, with gilt edges. The first volume, designated part I, contained the signatures from San Francisco, Sacramento, and El Dorado counties (*Alta,* April 22, 1856).

[53] *Herald,* April 21, 1856; Sacramento *Union,* May 1, 1856.

petition, were "earnestly demanding the construction of a wagon road immediately." He criticized the federal authorities for their lack of interest in the welfare of the people on the Pacific Coast. As an instance of the tardy action of the government he referred to an appropriation of $50,000 made during the thirty-third Congress to construct a road from Fort Riley to Bridger's Pass, but fifteen months had elapsed without the work being even begun.[54]

Immediately after the memorial was laid on the table, Weller reported from the Committee on Military Affairs a bill for the construction of a military road from some point in the state of Missouri, via Salt Lake, to Carson Valley, and for the establishment of military posts thereon. A sum of $300,000 was to be appropriated for this purpose. He also introduced a bill for the construction of a military road from El Paso, on the Rio Grande, to Fort Yuma, at the mouth of the Gila River. The first bill passed the Senate without much discussion. In the House the Committee on Military Affairs recommended its passage on the ground that such a road would not only serve as a means of transit for social and commercial intercourse, but also for military purposes, and by helping to allay the feeling of estrangement among the people of California, would discourage any dreams of an independent Pacific republic. But the attempts to take up the bill were unsuccessful.[55]

During the third session of the thirty-fourth Congress the California delegation succeeded in passing a bill appropriating the sum of $300,000 for the construction of a wagon road from Fort Kearney in Nebraska, via the South Pass of the Rocky Mountains, to the eastern boundary of California at Honey Lake. A sum of $200,000 was appropriated for the construction of a wagon road from El Paso to Fort Yuma; and $50,000 were

---

[54] On May 26, 1856 (*Cong. Globe,* 34 Cong., 1 Sess., 1297, 1299).

[55] *Cong. Globe,* 34 Cong., 1 Sess., 1485; *H. Rept.* 358, 34 Cong., 1 Sess. (870). It was reported by Denver, of California.

appropriated for the construction of a road from Fort Defiance, in New Mexico, to the Colorado River, near the mouth of the Mohave River.[56] In accordance with this act the Secretary of the Interior appointed a superintendent, organized a corps of operatives on each road, and proceeded with the construction. The act of Congress appropriating $550,000 for the construction of wagon roads to California attracted considerable attention in California. It was considered as a good start toward more adequate communication facilities. Several conventions were called in the interior counties, and almost every county claimed the privilege of having a wagon road constructed through its territory.

Overland mail.—The next move of the California delegation in Congress was for a semi-weekly overland mail. "The wagon road bill," said Gwin, on the floor of the Senate, "will be considered in California as a bright era in the history of the Pacific Coast, but without the constant use of the roads by mail wagons, the Indians will destroy them." He pointed out that the contract with the New York–Chagres Company would expire in October, 1858, and that unless the overland system was inaugurated, California would continue to suffer from the gigantic monopoly of the steamship companies. His colleague, Senator Weller, maintained that as a member of the Union California had a right to demand the privilege of more adequate communication facilities.[57]

But the southern Senators contended that it would be unwise to embark upon an expensive, immature scheme when the Post Office Department was laboring under an annual deficit of over $2,000,000; that California was already sufficiently supplied with mail facilities which cost the government about a million dollars annually (twice as much as the income from postage in

[56] United States, *Statutes at Large,* XI, 162–63, Feb. 17, 1857.

[57] *Cong. Globe,* 34 Cong., 3 Sess., App. 307–8, 313–14. The railroad charge across the Isthmus of Panama was $25 a passenger.

that state), and that it would be folly to run a semi-weekly mail coach through a territory of 2000 miles of desert and hostile Indians.[58] The friends of the measure admitted that California cost a great deal, but they argued that all new territories cost a great deal. Moreover, at a time when the federal treasury was overflowing and all kinds of visionary schemes were being indulged in, the government should not hesitate to inaugurate a system of communication that would settle the lines of travel between the Atlantic and Pacific coasts and bind them together.[59]

The friends of the overland mail succeeded in having a bill passed which authorized the Postmaster General to contract for the transportation of mails from a point on the Mississippi River, to be selected by the contractors, to San Francisco. The contract was to be made for six years at an annual cost not exceeding $300,000 for a semimonthly mail; $450,000 for a weekly mail; and $600,000 for a semi-weekly service. The Postmaster General was to decide upon the amount of service. The time limit for each trip was to be twenty-five days. The mail was to be carried in "good four horse coaches, or spring wagons suitable for the conveyance of passengers."[60]

The purpose of leaving to the contractors the selection of the starting point on the Mississippi was to avoid a sectional conflict, for each section desired to have the eastern terminus in its own territory. But it was of course well known that the final choice would be made by the Postmaster General. The friends of a northern or central route hoped that President Buchanan would appoint a northern man for Postmaster General. They were therefore disappointed when Aaron V. Brown was appointed for that office. Their apprehension was increased when they noticed in the advertisement of the Postmaster General inviting express companies to offer bids, a proposition that

---

58 *Ibid.*, 307, 313, 315, 316.

59 *Cong. Globe.*, 34 Cong., 3 Sess., App. 307–20.

60 *Ibid.*, 321. It passed the Senate by a vote of twenty-four to ten. The opposition came mainly from the south.

the bidder should state in the bid the starting point on the Mississippi River and designate the course of the route.[61]

In response to the advertisement of the Postmaster General, bids were offered by a number of the largest express firms engaged in freighting on the plains. In most of the bids, St. Louis and Memphis were designated as the starting points on the Mississippi River.[62] The Postmaster General, with the concurrence of the President, selected the extreme southern route, from St. Louis, Missouri, and Memphis, Tennessee, converging at Little Rock, Arkansas; thence via Preston, Texas, to the Rio Grande above El Paso; thence to Fort Yuma; thence through the best passes to San Francisco.[63] The President and the Postmaster General claimed that the route was selected because it offered "more advantages and fewer disadvantages than any other, on account of its temperate climate, freedom from snow and other obstructions." Still another reason pointed out by the Postmaster General was that

. . . . The southern location of the route, especially if it shall be followed by the construction of a railroad, may serve a valuable purpose in reference to the neighboring Republic of Mexico. In time of peace it will shed its blessings on both nations, whilst in time of war it will furnish a highway for troops and munitions of war, which might enable us to vindicate our rights, and preserve untarnished our national honor.[64]

On September 16, 1857, the Postmaster General awarded the contract to the Butterfield express firm at $600,000 per annum for a semi-weekly letter mail.[65] The company was given a year's time to stock the route.

While the Butterfield company was making preparations for the great overland mail, the Postmaster General had the Utah

---

[61] *H. Ex. Doc.* 2, 35 Cong., 1 Sess., 986–87 (944).

[62] Memphis was selected probably to flatter Postmaster General Brown, who was a native of that city. But St. Louis was a logical place for the terminus.

[63] *H. Ex. Doc.* 2, 35 Cong., 1 Sess., 989–90 (944).

[64] *H. Ex. Doc.* 2, 35 Cong., 1 Sess., 993–1003 (944).

[65] *Ibid.*, 989–92.

route—the route between St. Joseph, Missouri, and Salt Lake City, and between Salt Lake and Placerville—so improved that the trip could be made once a week in thirty-eight days each way, at the cost of $310,000 per annum.[66] The first mail stage on this route arrived in Placerville, California, on July 19, 1858, making the trip in twenty-nine days. The event was celebrated by the people of Placerville in the most enthusiastic fashion. The press of the north and of the interior proclaimed this route as far superior to the pet of the administration, the Butterfield route.[67]

Meanwhile the Butterfield route had been completed and on September 15, 1858, the coaches left the opposite ends of the route. On October 10 the long hoped-for overland mail arrived in San Francisco, making the trip of over 2795 miles in twenty-three days and twenty-three hours.[68] It was still early in the morning when the residents of the southern part of San Francisco were disturbed in their Sabbath slumber by the tearing gallop of the four-horse, heavy mail coach, and by the resounding peal of the coachman's horn "Behold I bring you glad tidings of great joy!" Immediately the news flashed over the whole city, which was soon thrown into ecstasies of joy. Men congratulated each other. The *Alta* issued an extra describing in detail the great event. The Home Guard celebrated the occasion by firing two hundred guns.[69]

---

[66] *H. Ex. Doc.* 2, 35 Cong., 2 Sess., 722–23 (1000). The mail left St. Joseph and Placerville every Saturday. Its schedule was from St. Joseph to Salt Lake, 22 days; from Salt Lake to Placerville, 16 days.

[67] The mail arrived in Placerville at eleven o'clock at night. On its arrival the houses were illuminated, and the citizens formed in two lines, and welcomed it with loud cheers (Sacramento *Union*, July 22, 1858; *Alta*, July 23, 1858).

[68] *Herald*, Oct. 11, 1858; *Bulletin*, Oct. 11, 1858; *Alta*, Oct. 12, 1858; Sacramento *Union*, Oct. 18, 1858. The contract called for twenty-five days. No mail was carried and the only passenger was W. L. Ormsby, a special correspondent of the New York *Herald*. The coach left St. Louis, September 16; El Paso, September 3; Fort Yuma, October 5; Los Angeles, October 7; San Jose, October 10, in the morning. *See* Sacramento *Union*, Oct. 13, 1858.

[69] *Alta*, Oct. 11, 1858; *Bulletin*, Oct. 11, 1858; *Herald*, Oct. 11, 1858. The *Alta's* extra "went off like hot cakes."

On the following day an enthusiastic mass meeting was held in San Francisco to express the sentiments of the people in regard to the great benefits California would derive from this means of communication. The resolutions unanimously adopted expressed gratitude to the enlightened Postmaster General Aaron Brown. They recommended that the government should not renew the contract with the steamship companies for the transmission of the mails from New York to San Francisco, but instead improve the overland mail. They declared that the overland mail routes were destined to emancipate California from the thralldom of the steamship companies and make unnecessary the circuitous route through foreign territory of semi-civilized nations, while they would bind together, with firmer ties, the east and the west. But, they continued, while expressing their gratitude for these advantages, California considered them as mere preliminaries to the great desiderata—the transcontinental railroad and telegraph lines, the only ties strong enough to defy sectionalism.[70]

The first overland mail coach from San Francisco was received in St. Louis with considerable enthusiasm. It was escorted to the post office by a long procession led by a band of music.[71] In answer to a telegram from John Butterfield, informing the President of the great event, Mr. Buchanan telegraphed: "I cordially congratulate you upon the result. It is a glorious triumph for civilization and the Union. Settlements will soon follow the course of the road, and the East and West will be bound together by a chain of living Americans which can never be broken."[72]

In general the Butterfield overland mail worked with great regularity; but frequently it was detained for many hours on account of hostile Indians along the road. The people in Cali-

[70] *Herald,* Oct. 12, 1858.

[71] Root and Connelley, *Overland Stage to California,* II.

[72] *Ibid.,* 13

fornia urged the federal government to dispatch adequate military forces to protect the mail. The necessity for military protection was foreseen by Postmaster General Brown and in a letter to the Secretary of War he pointed out the need for establishing military posts along the mail route to insure its safety.[73] On October 12, Senator Gwin addressed a letter to President Buchanan soliciting him in forcible terms to dispatch immediately sufficient military forces to guard the mail route from Fort Smith to Fort Yuma, and save not only the great enterprise but also hundreds of lives. "From this time forth *forever* regular overland communication will exist between California and the Mississippi States," he said. "Neither hostile Indians nor subsequent government neglect can undo what has been wisely accomplished."[74]

Opposition to the overland mail service.—The Butterfield mail service soon had to defend itself in Congress. The friends of the St. Joseph-Placerville route resented the particular attention paid by the Postmaster General to the southern route. They contended that there was no good reason why the Placerville-St. Joseph route, which was much shorter and better than the Butterfield line, should not work on a twenty-five day schedule. Efforts were made to induce the Postmaster General to increase the speed for the central route but they were unsuccessful.[75]

A resolution was introduced in the House by Craig of Missouri directing the Postmaster General to order an increase of speed on the mail route between St. Joseph and Placerville from thirty-eight to thirty days, at a pro rata increase of compensation to the contractors. The resolution passed the House[76] but met with opposition in the Senate. The southern Senators resented the statement that the Butterfield route had been

[73] *Herald,* Oct. 19, 1858; *Bulletin,* Nov. 13, 1858; Los Angeles *Star,* Oct. 1, 1859.

[74] Portions of the letter are quoted in the *Bulletin,* Nov. 13, 1858.

[75] *Cong. Globe.,* 35 Cong., 1 Sess., 2805.

[76] *Cong. Globe.,* 35 Cong., 1 Sess., 3002.

selected for sectional reasons. They asserted that the route was selected because it was known to be the cheapest and most practicable, and that the transportation of mail should have nothing to do with the question of a route for emigration. The resolution finally passed the Senate[77] but it was pocket vetoed by the President.

At the next session a proposition was offered in the House to permit the Butterfield company to carry mail from the Mississippi River to San Francisco by any route it might select. Broderick of California declared that, in establishing the several overland routes in the southern territory, the Postmaster General had considered more the interests of the jobbers than the interests of California, and had made the best and shortest central route too slow for any postal use.[78] The southern Senators threatened to break up the whole contract should the attempt to move the Butterfield route prove successful.

In view of the increasingly larger deficits of the Post Office Department, which amounted to $4,500,000 for the fiscal year ending June 30, 1858, some members in Congress proposed to discontinue entirely the expensive overland routes. Postmaster General Brown pointed out that the deficit was due to the departure from the original policy of making the Post Office Department self-sustaining by adjusting its expenditure to its income from postage. Thus, while the rate of postage had been reduced in 1851, the cost of transportation was constantly mounting higher and higher. He contended, however, that the Post Office Department should not be looked upon as a mere business proposition and its usefulness measured by mere postal receipts, for it was becoming an important instrument in the development of the great west and a consolidating influence for the several sections of the country. Such an important agency should not be expected to subsist wholly on its own resources.

---

[77] *Ibid.*, 3002–5.

[78] *Cong. Globe.*, 35 Cong., 2 Sess., 1500. It was even intimated that the Postmaster General was personally interested in the southern route.

To reduce the annual deficit, he recommended that the franking privileges be discontinued or modified and that a uniform rate of five cents a letter for all distances be made, thereby avoiding the inconveniences of several rates and removing a source of dissatisfaction on the part of correspondents between the Atlantic and Pacific coasts. As a further means of saving a million dollars annually he suggested contracting for conveyance of mail without regard to transportation of passengers. The effect of such a policy would be to substitute two-horse coaches or even horseback conveyance for the more expensive four-horse coaches.[79]

But the northern men protested against raising the postal rates, and advocated retrenchment, beginning with the overland mail to the Pacific. "We pay just as much," said Hale of New Hampshire, "for driving an empty wagon from Memphis to San Francisco, across the plains, to carry nothing, and bring nothing back and get nothing for it, as we do for the whole ocean steam service of the United States, with all the rest of the world together."[80]

California resented the attack on the overland mail, contending that the line was of importance to the emigrant trains and to the War Department. She not only demanded a uniform rate of postage but also more mail facilities. The legislature of 1859 adopted a joint resolution urging Congress to increase the number of trips and reduce the scheduled time of the St. Joseph–Placerville route, and the route from Kansas City to Stockton, placing them on an equal footing with the Butterfield line.[81]

---

[79] *Cong Globe.*, 35 Cong. 2 Sess., App., 23–24.

[80] *Cong. Globe.*, 35 Cong. 2 Sess., 1304, 1310. So small was the income from postage on this line that it was calculated that every letter conveyed by the Butterfield route cost the government from sixty to seventy cents (*ibid.*, 1501). The press advised the people to forward their letters overland instead of by sea and thereby assure the existence of these routes (*Alta*, April 29, 1859; *Herald*, April 3, 1859).

[81] California, *Statutes*, 1859, 387–88, 384; *Alta*, Oct. 25, 1858; Sacramento *Union*, Jan. 29, 1859.

The failure of Congress to pass the post office appropriation bill, and the appointment of Holt of Kentucky, as Postmaster General, who was less in sympathy with the overland mail enterprise than his deceased predecessor had been, were not very promising to the interests of the California mail service. Upon his examination of the California mail service, Holt found it was too excessive for the needs of that community and too costly in comparison with its receipts. He found that the gross annual disbursements for the six routes conveying the mails to and from the Pacific Coast amounted to $2,184,697. And when to this sum was added $508,697.13, the annual expenditure for local mail service in California, Oregon, Washington, and Utah, the gross annual disbursements for the Pacific Coast mail service aggregated $2,693,394.13, while the revenue from postage on these routes amounted to only $339,747.66. The department was suffering an annual loss of $1,844,949.66! Estimating the total population of the Pacific Coast around six hundred and fifty thousand souls, the postal expenditure would then amount to $4.14 for each person, while the remaining $12,271,099.20 of the gross annual expenditure supplied mail facilities for thirty millions of people, amounting to forty-one cents for each person.[82]

In view of these facts, the Postmaster General decided to curtail the Pacific mail service. Instead of extending the

[82] *Sen. Ex. Doc.* 2, 36 Cong., 1 Sess., 1408 (1025). The table of the annual costs and receipts for the six Pacific mail routes is interesting:

1. From New York and New Orleans, via Panama to San Francisco, semimonthly, annual cost, $738,250; annual receipts, $299,972.69.
2. From New Orleans to San Francisco, via Tehuantepec, semimonthly, annual cost, $250,000; annual receipts, $5,276.58 .
3. From San Antonio, via El Paso to San Diego, semimonthly, annual cost, $196,448; annual receipts, $601.
4. From St. Louis and Memphis, via El Paso to San Francisco, annual cost, $600,000; annual receipts, $27,229.94.
5. From Kansas, Missouri, to Stockton, California, monthly, annual cost, $79,999; annual receipts, $1,255.
6. From St. Joseph, Missouri, to Placerville, weekly, annual cost, $320,000; annual receipts, only $5,412.03.

expensive contract for the New York-New Orleans-San Francisco monthly mail service, he made an agreement with Vanderbilt for the conveyance of the Pacific mail, thereby saving annually some $387,250. The Postmaster General also refused to continue the mail service by the Tehuantepec route at an annual cost of $250,000, believing that this service was too costly and unnecessary. The San Antonio-San Diego route was reduced to a semimonthly mail at an annual rate of $120,000. Likewise the central route was reduced to a semimonthly service at an annual compensation of $205,000. The Kansas-Stockton route was discontinued. Postmaster General Holt also recommended that Congress should consider the matter of reducing the Butterfield overland mail to a weekly service by compromising with the Butterfield company.

By this curtailing of the Pacific mail service, the Post Office Department reduced the annual expenditure to $1,276,000, making a yearly saving of $908,697. And even this the Postmaster General thought was "far beyond what an enlightened and just administration of the finances of the department would warrant." He believed that "until a railroad shall have been constructed across the continent, the conveyance of the Pacific mail overland must be regarded as wholly impracticable."[83]

Protests of California.—California protested against Holt's policy. "It is adding injury to insult," said the *Alta*, "we grow sick and tired of such kind of treatment. What say our readers? Will they longer submit with patience and resignation to the inflictions that are being heaped upon them?" It was argued that the overland mail service being a new experiment could not be expected to be self-supporting and that a government subsidy of half a million dollars for such an important purpose was worth while, especially when the government was ready to pay $30,000,000 for Cuba, and indulge in other similar visionary

[83] *Annual Report* of Postmaster General for 1859 (*Cong. Globe*, 36 Cong., 1 Sess., App., 23).

schemes. England, France, and Russia, they said, would never manifest such a niggardly spirit toward such a precious child as California, that produces $50,000,000 of gold bullion per annum.[84]

In a petition to the Postmaster General the memorialists remonstrated against the reduction of the Butterfield route to a weekly service and demanded the establishment of a daily overland mail as an "inalienable right." Only such improved mail service, it was contended, could satisfy the needs of trade and commerce, induce a greater immigration into California, and thus help to develop the resources of the state.[85]

Although the President and the Postmaster General believed that it would be impossible to attempt to carry all the mail matter overland, the members in Congress from California and from the western states in general began to advocate discontinuing the ocean mail service and conveying the entire mail by overland route. In the Senate Gwin offered a bill providing for a semi-weekly mail on the central route. His colleague, Latham, offered a bill providing a tri-weekly mail on the central route, and a trimonthly steamer mail for printed matter, while Hale of New Hampshire offered a bill providing for the conveyance of the entire mail matter between St. Louis and San Francisco via the central route, tri-weekly, in twenty days' time, at a cost of $600,000 the first year, and $800,000 per annum thereafter. A second tri-weekly mail was to be carried over the southern route at a cost of $400,000; thus giving California a daily overland mail. It also provided for the conveyance of the entire mail matter from St. Paul to Oregon once a week at a yearly cost of $200,000[86]

Hale's plan was satisfactory to northern and central California though some questioned the wisdom of having three dis-

---

[84] *Alta,* June 8, July 7, Dec. 5, 1859, Jan. 25, 1860; *Bulletin,* Oct. 8, 1859.

[85] *Herald,* June 29, 1859.

[86] *Cong. Globe,* 36 Cong. 1 Sess., 3148.

tinct routes. A group of Californians in New York memorialized Gwin to work for the passage of Hale's bill. But it met the opposition of the steamship companies and of the Post Office Department. Holt was opposed to the overland mail project, especially to the lines above the Butterfield route. He held that, owing to the rigorous climate, the character of the road, and the heavy bulk of matter the project would prove a failure and result in embarrassment to the Post Office Department. Gwin was blamed for the failure of Hale's bill, for as a member of the Senate Committee on Post Offices and Post Roads it was believed that he could have succeeded in having the bill passed.[87]

By the terms of an act of Congress of June 15, 1860, the compensation of the ocean mail service to and from the Pacific Coast was limited to the postage received on the mails conveyed. The steamship companies declined to accept the offer of the Post Office Department claiming that, in consequence of the conveyance of a considerable part of the overland mail by the overland routes, the postage rates would not afford sufficient compensation.[88] Meantime the mail to the Pacific, most of it printed matter, was being piled up by the ton and the situation was quite awkward for the Post Office Department. Gwin addressed a letter to the President reminding him of his former promises and urging him to provide for carrying the entire mail overland.[89] Finally an agreement was concluded with Vanderbilt for the transportation of the mail between New York and San

---

[87] *Alta*, July 11, July 24, 29, Aug. 19, Sept. 1, 1860; Sacramento *Union*, July 28, 1860.

[88] The postal receipts from the ocean service were constantly diminishing, from the overland service, constantly increasing. For instance, during the March quarter of 1860, the postal receipts from ocean and Isthmus service were $39,773.97, while the receipts from the overland service were $30,772.49. During the June quarter, the former dropped to $33,607.12, and the latter rose to $34,509.73. During the September quarter the former again dropped to $25,644.20, while the latter reached the sum of $37,010.28. This is accounted for by the order of the Post Office Department of December 17, 1859, to forward by overland mail letters which had previously been transported by steamer (*Sen. Ex. Doc.* 1, 36 Cong., 2 Sess., 434 [1080]).

[89] The letter was printed in the *Alta*, July 29, 1860.

Francisco by way of the Isthmus of Panama upon the terms of the act of June, 1860, with the assurance that the President would recommend that Congress make such additional allowances as might be deemed a fair remuneration for the service.[90]

Pony express and daily overland mail.—While Congress was debating the question of a daily overland mail, the great overland freighting company, Russel, Majors, and Waddell, established a pony express carrying letters weekly from St. Joseph, Missouri, to Sacramento, and making the trip in ten days. On April 3 the first pony expresses left simultaneously the eastern and western terminals. The arrival of the first pony express at Placerville and Sacramento was an occasion for considerable enthusiasm. At Sacramento the legislature adjourned on that day in honor of the great enterprise. At 5:30 in the afternoon, amidst the noise of firing cannon, pealing of bells, and shouting of the multitude on the streets, balconies, and roofs, the pony express was escorted by a group of mounted citizens into the heart of town, which was decorated with flags and bunting.[91]

For over a year the pony express performed its service faithfully, save when, now and then, it was interrupted by Indian attacks. It brought news and letters two weeks sooner than the mail coach. But unprotected by military forces, it was always at the mercy of the Indians. Moreover, the high charge of five dollars for a letter half an ounce in weight, in addition to the government postage, was too expensive for ordinary correspondence. California demanded a cheaper and more rapid means of communication.

After the secession of several southern states, Congress succeeded in passing a law providing for a daily overland mail to the Pacific Coast. Section nine of the act of March 2, 1861, making appropriations for the service of the Post Office Department, directed the Postmaster General to order the Butterfield com-

---

[90] *Cong. Globe,* 36 Cong., 2 Sess., App., 13. Vanderbilt was criticized by the New York press for his refusal to take the mails.

[91] Sacramento *Union,* April 13, 14, 1860.

pany to discontinue its mail service on the southern route and to transport the entire letter mail on the central route in twenty days' time, six times a week, for eight months of the year, and in twenty-three days during the remaining four months of the year. The remainder of the mail matter, also to be carried by the same company, could, under the act, be conveyed semi-monthly within a period not exceeding thirty-five days. Until the completion of the telegraph line to the Pacific, the company was required to run a pony express semi-weekly, making the trip in ten days during eight months of the year, and within twelve days during the remaining four months. On every trip it was to carry free of charge five pounds of mail matter for the government. Private letters were to be charged for at a rate not higher than one dollar a half-ounce. The annual compensation for the whole service was one million dollars. The service was to be paid for from the United States Treasury.[92] In accordance with this act, the first daily overland mail began its service on July 1, 1861. The act of June 16, 1860, authorized and directed the Secretary of the Treasury to advertise for proposals to construct a telegraph line from San Francisco to some point in western Missouri, connecting it with the big cities in the east. For the use of the line the government was to pay $40,000 per annum for a period of ten years. The line was to be open to the use of all citizens of the United States on the payment of three dollars for a dispatch of ten words, with the usual proportionate charge when the dispatch exceeded that length.[93]

The lines were built by two companies acting in concert. Although the real work did not commence in earnest until the beginning of the summer of 1861, it was carried on so rapidly that by October, 1861, the lines from California east and from Omaha west met at Salt Lake City. During the latter part of the month the through line was opened for operation. "Today,

[92] United States, *Statutes at Large,* XII, 169, 206.
[93] United States, *Statutes at Large,* XII, 41–42.

California is but a second's distance from the National Capital. Her patriotism with electric currents throbs responsive to that of her sister States, and holds civil liberty and the Union above all price." Thus spoke Leland Stanford, in behalf of the people of California, in a message to President Abraham Lincoln on October 23, 1861.[94] On the next day San Francisco read a dispatch from Great Salt Lake, flashed across the wires at 7 P.M., that General E. D. Baker, an adopted son of Oregon and California, "was killed in the battle on the 21st, while in the act of cheering on his command."[95]

The establishment of a daily overland mail and the completion of the long cherished telegraph line to the Pacific Coast were important steps toward a closer unification of the two extremes of the Union. There now remained to take the next step—the construction of the Pacific railroad. "Give us the transcontinental railroad and we shall be satisfied," clamored the people of California. We shall now turn to the final episodes in the struggle for adequate communication and transportation facilities.

Renewed agitation for a Pacific railroad.—The clamor for the continental railroad was really never abated in California. The wagon roads and overland mail were considered merely forerunners of the railroad. Governors Weller and Latham emphasized the need for the great project. The legislature adopted resolutions urging its construction and the platforms of the two political parties included railroad planks.[96]

---

[94] "May the golden links of the Constitution ever unite us as one happy and free people," read Governor Downey's telegram to the President on October 25. The several telegrams were printed in the *Alta*, Oct. 25; *Bulletin*, Oct. 24, 25, 1861.

[95] *Bulletin*, Oct. 24, 25, 1861.

[96] California, *Sen. Jour.*, 1859, 40–41; 1860, 60–64, 111; California, *Assembly Jour.*, 1857, App., Doc. 12; California *Statutes*, 1857, 370–71; 1859, 395–96; Davis, *Political Conventions in California*, for the Republican party, 60–61, 63, 66, 93–94, 98, 175; for the resolutions of the Democratic party, see pp. 57, 72, 120, 106, 112, 170; for the other parties, see pp. 82, 92, 100, 121.

In Congress the California delegation took the leading part in pushing the railroad question to the front. The project was advocated in all western states and territories. President Buchanan believed that without it California could not be protected against foreign invasion.[97] To get around the constitutional scruples of the strict constructionists and to escape the question of the location of the route, Gwin, in 1858, reported a bill in the Senate authorizing the President to invite propositions for carrying the mail and military and naval stores of the government between the Atlantic and Pacific by railroad. The route was to be selected by the contractors.[98] The southern Senators objected to the policy of leaving the matter of the route to the decision of the President, and also to the cost of such an undertaking. The Senate finally passed a bill authorizing the Secretary of the Interior to secure proposals for northern, central, and southern routes to the Pacific Coast and to submit the proposals to Congress.[99] The House refused to consider the bill.

California felt indignant at the failure of Congress to pass its "idol of worship" the railroad bill.

> We have petitioned, begged, prayed, [said the *Alta*] and petitioned again, and been driven from the national Capitol in disgrace. Where is the heart so dead as not to rebel? . . . .
>
> . . . . Let us do as our forefathers did in Boston harbor, and in the war of Independence. Let us use as little as possible of their goods—send them only as much of our gold as cannot be helped, and by touching their pockets learn [teach] them to place a proper estimate on California.[100]

The *Bulletin* and other papers argued in a similar vein, threatening the United States government that if California should be

[97] Richardson, *Messages,* V, 456–57.

[98] To make it thus not a measure for internal improvement, but an agency to carry the mail and for defensive purposes—clearly within the power of Congress (*Cong. Globe.,* 35 Cong., 1 Sess., 329 [1535]).

[99] *Ibid.,* 627. The amendment was introduced by Doolittle, of Wisconsin, "whose name seems to describe his capacity," said the *Bulletin.*

[100] *Alta,* Feb. 27, 1859.

doomed to remain in isolation the bonds which held her to the east would gradually grow weaker.[101]

A railroad convention representing California, Oregon, and Washington Territory was held in San Francisco in September, 1859. The convention issued a memorial to the President of the United States, and to Congress, declaring that the failure of the government to supply the necessary means of communication was responsible for retarding the growth of the whole Pacific Coast. And then the memorial proceeded with the usual warning of the possible separation of California, for "a free people will not long endure a Government which refuses to afford them that protection for which Governments were instituted." The memorial also suggested that the government should assist the construction of the railroad through the territories by land grants and by money guaranties. To enable California to assist the construction of the railroad within her borders the government should donate to her all the public lands within her boundaries and should refund the civil fund, amounting to $2,706,512.[102]

The final act.—By the opening of the year 1862 the Pacific railroad question became a vital issue. The project had been before the American people for several decades. It had been discussed in legislative halls and at public meetings. The Republican and Democratic parties inserted railroad planks in their national platforms of 1856 and 1860. While in some respects the secession of the southern members from Congress and the increased military necessity of binding together the Atlantic and Pacific coasts furnished impelling motives for the construction of the road, nevertheless the actual outbreak of the war—when all the financial and human resources were strained

---

[101] *Bulletin,* Feb. 24, 1859; Stockton *Weekly Democrat,* March 6, 1859; Nevada *Democrat,* March 2, 1859. *See also* Nevada *Journal,* March 11, 1859.

[102] The memorial may be found in *Pamphlets on California Railroads,* III, Doc. 3.

to the utmost—acted rather as an unfavorable influence upon the great undertaking.

The final and successful effort in behalf of the great project was made by the California members in the second session of the thirty-seventh Congress. McDougal, chairman of the Senate Pacific Railroad Committee, and Sargent, a member of the House Pacific Railroad Committee, were ably assisted by Theodore Judah, the chief engineer of the California Central Pacific Railroad Company, who supplied them with the necessary technical information. Both members had prepared railroad bills. On January 31, 1862, Sargent delivered an eloquent speech contending that the construction of the road was a war measure to retain and protect California. He pictured the undefended portion of California and the dire results which would follow in case of an invasion.[103]

These eloquent arguments, coming at a moment when the Union was threatened with dissolution, aroused considerable interest in the railroad question. A bill prepared by Sargent, with the aid of Judah, was reported in the House on March 4.[104] In answer to the argument of some members that it would not be advisable to embark during war-time upon such a vast undertaking, Sargent contended that unless the road was built immediately the Pacific Coast might secede from the Union. On May 6 the bill passed the House by a vote of 79 ayes to 49 nays. On June 20 it passed the Senate by a vote of 35 ayes to 5 nays.[105] The bill was signed by President Lincoln and became a law on July 1, 1862.

By this act the construction of the main line from the Missouri River westward was given to the Union Pacific Railroad Company, while the road eastward from Sacramento River was to be constructed by a California corporation, the Central Pacific

[103] *Cong. Globe.*, 37 Cong., 2 Sess., 599–603.

[104] *Ibid.*, 1062.

[105] *Cong. Globe.*, 37 Cong., 2 Sess., 1971, 1983, 2840.

Railroad Company. In aid of the undertaking the government granted to the companies a right of way four hundred feet wide through the public lands and ten alternate sections of public lands for each mile of track constructed. As a further subsidy the government was to lend to the companies United States bonds to run thirty years at six per cent interest at the rate of $16,000 for each mile east of the Rocky Mountains, and, west of the Sierras, $32,000 for each mile in the foothills between the two mountain sections; and $48,000 for each mile in the mountains.[106]

Thus under the inspiration of California was passed the act for the transcontinental railroad. The passage of this act terminated a twelve-year struggle and agitation which had caused considerable complaint against the federal government. "I congratulate you, upon the fact that the great wish for which California has so long earnestly labored, is commenced, and will be urged, I trust, as far as our State is concerned, to a rapid completion," said Governor Stanford in his annual message to the legislature in 1863.[107]

On July 10 San Francisco celebrated the passage of the railroad act by an eleborate and enthusiastic torchlight procession with brass bands and firing of cannons.[108] On January 8 the great work began in Sacramento when Governor Stanford, "amid the lusty cheering of the crowd, deposited the first earth for the embankment."[109]

The work, however, did not progress rapidly. In fact the Union Pacific Company did not begin work until 1865. As further inducement to action Congress passed the act of July 2,

---

106 United States, *Statutes at Large*, XIII, 489–98. The act was amended July 2, 1864, increasing the land grants from ten to twenty sections per mile of railway constructed (*ibid.*, 356).

107 California, *Sen. Jour.*, 1863, 43.

108 *Alta*, July 11, 1862; *Bulletin*, July 11, 1862. Some of the mottoes carried by the procession were. "The Railroad completed! California is impregnable against foreign foes." "The American Union! From sea to sea, clasped by bonds of iron and hooks of steel."

109 Sacramento *Union*, Jan. 8, 1863, gives *in extenso* the speeches delivered on that occasion.

1864,[110] which amended the act of July 1, 1862, by increasing the aid to the companies. Stimulated by this generous aid, the companies began the real work of tunneling and scaling the mountains, building trestles, air bridges, and snow sheds. It was a race between the two companies, each one trying to outdo the other in track-laying.

Completion of the first transcontinental railroad and the union of the two coasts.—A little over six years after the ground-breaking the country celebrated the completion of the great transcontinental railroad. On May 10, 1869, in the Utah desert at Promontory Point, took place the dramatic event of laying the last rail. At 2:27 P.M., eastern time in Washington, a message was flashed from Promontory Point throughout the country: "Almost ready. Hats off; prayer is being offered." After a short interval another message was sent: "We have done praying. The spike is about to be presented." Chicago responded: "We understand. All are ready in the East."[111] At 2:47 P.M., witnessed by a motley crowd of railroad directors, army officers, frontiersmen, Indians, Mexicans, and Chinese, Dr. Durant, of the Union Pacific, and Leland Stanford, of the Central Pacific, drove with a silver sledge the last spikes, made of gold, silver, and iron from California, Nevada, Montana, Idaho, and Arizona.[112] By means of a connection between the

[110] United States, *Statutes at Large,* XIII, 356. The act doubled the donation of the lands and authorized the companies to issue bonds equal to the amount issued by the government, the former being a first lien on the road.

[111] The messages are quoted in Sabin, *Building the Pacific Railway,* 221; "The Last Spike," in *Pamphlets on California Railroads,* II, No. 15, p. 29.

[112] Sabin, *Building the Pacific Railway,* 221–22. The gold spike of California was about six inches long, and half an inch square, worth about $400 in gold. On the first face were inscribed the names of the officers of the road. On the second face were inscribed the names of the directors of the road. On the third face were the words: "May God continue the unity of our country as this railroad unites the two great oceans of the world" and on the fourth face were: "The Central Pacific Railroad: ground broken January 8th, 1863; completed May 10th, 1869." The nugget at the end of the spike was afterward detached and made into four rings, which were presented to President Grant, William H. Seward, Leland Stanford, and Oakes Ames. The last rail was of California laurel, well polished ("The Last Spike," in *Pamphlets, etc.,* p. 26).

hammer and the telegraph wires, every blow was heard at the telegraph offices of the big cities of the Union. The response was immediate. In Washington the crowd cheered when signaled by a magnetic ball on the dome of the Capitol. In Omaha, cannon boomed; in Chicago whistles sounded and brass bands led a procession; in Philadelphia the Liberty Bell pealed; in New York guns roared, and Trinity Church chanted the "Te Deum."[113] San Francisco and Sacramento were jubilant, though the great celebration in these cities had taken place on May 8.[114]

"The last rail is laid, the last spike driven. The Pacific Railroad is completed. The point of junction is 1086 miles west of the Missouri River, and 690 miles east of Sacramento City." This was the official message of the two companies to President Grant in Washington, telegraphed on May 10.[115]

Thus at last the great desideratum of California, for which she had begged and prayed for over a decade, was realized. "From today we may date a new era in the affairs of California," said the San Francisco *Bulletin*. "The great work is finished . . . . Railroads are now about to change the aspect of things in California . . . . we may rest assured we are no longer an isolated community." And in another place it said: "The States of the Pacific will no longer be divorced from the sympathies and the affections of 'the old States.' The iron road will be a bond of amity as well as of commerce, and it reaches its

---

[113] Accounts of the celebration are given by Sidney Dillon, "Historic Moment; Driving the Last Spike of the Union Pacific," *Scribner's Magazine*, 1892, 253–59; Sabin, *Building of the Pacific Railway*, 221–25; "The Last Spike," in *Pamphlets, etc.*, 29–30; Carter, *When Railroads Were New*, 255–58. Also the dispatches from the east in the Sacramento *Union* of May 12, 1869.

[114] The celebration at Promontory Point was to take place on May 8, but on account of the delay of the officers of the Union Pacific in arriving it was decided to postpone the ceremony to Monday, May 10. San Francisco and Sacramento, however, decided to hold the celebration on May 8 (*Bulletin*, May 8, 1861).

[115] The telegram is quoted in "The Last Spike," in *Pamphlets, etc.*, p. 30; Sabin, *Building the Pacific Railway*, 225.

highest utility in thus bringing together sundered kindred and communities.''[116]

> California [said the San Francisco *Alta*] was formally admitted by an act of Congress to the sisterhood of the States nineteen years ago, but that relation did not become a real, visible, tangible fact till the last rail was laid, and the last spike driven in the great continental road. We shall no longer hear the common expression when a person announces his intention of traveling to the East, ''I am going to the States—I am going to America'' . . . . We shall no longer hear of those longings and desires . . . . The provincialisms which have grown up in our long isolation are doomed to a speedy death.

The completion of this great project ended not only the decade and a half of federal legislation for California, but also the frontier era of California.

---

[116] *Ibid.*, May 11, 1869.
[117] *Alta,* May 12, 1869.

PART II

CIVIL WAR ISSUES

CHAPTER IX

SENTIMENT FOR A PACIFIC REPUBLIC

Forces behind the movement.—The peculiar situation in California during the Civil War period was due to her frontier position and to the character of her population. While politically California was a part of the Union, geographically she was an isolated community separated from the central government by thousands of miles of prairie, desert, and mountains unspanned by any railroad lines. This isolation naturally fostered a spirit of independence and self-reliance; a feeling that California had interests distinct from those of any other part of the Union, and a destiny of her own.

In addition to these peculiar geographical conditions, we must remember that California possessed a large population of native Californians who had little attachment for the Union, and a strong adventurous element always ready to countenance revolutionary projects. There had always been advocates of a Pacific republic, and these became especially vociferous whenever California felt she had a grievance against the United States government. And because of the conditions in California, which have already been pointed out, there was always a prevailing belief that the Pacific Coast was not getting fair treatment from the central government.

The idea of a Pacific republic was therefore not novel. But on the eve of the Civil War the question was discussed more seriously than at any previous time. Its advocates now were men high in the counsels of the state. California had a strong southern element,[1] men with pronounced southern views. This element dominated the politics of the state between 1850 and 1860. It was naturally to be expected that these southerners would favor an independent government for California in case of a war between the north and the south, in order to avoid the unpleasant situation of being called upon to support a war against their native states, friends, and relatives.

In spite of the fact that she was a free state and removed thousands of miles from the scenes of the conflict, the same sectional prejudices that agitated the east also existed to some degree in California. Political parties on the old lines were organized in California shortly after the establishment of a state government. The Democratic party, which was the ruling party in California from 1850 to 1861, always championed the interests of the south. The legislature of 1852 passed a fugitive slave act providing that state officers must assist in the return of persons "held to labor in any State or Territory of the United States under the laws thereof, [who] shall escape into this State." It also provided for the return of slaves brought to California prior to her admission into the Union.[2] The law was reenacted in the following years.[3] The legislature of 1858 passed a concurrent

---

[1] The southern population in California was estimated to be about thirty per cent of the entire population of the state, but this was probably an exaggeration.

[2] California, *Statutes*, 1852, 67–69. The claimants were, however, not allowed to hold the slaves in the state after their reclamation. In the very interesting case of the *matter of Carter Perkins and Robert Perkins*, the supreme court of California upheld the constitutionality of the act and assumed in this matter the position taken by the ultra southerners. *See* 2 California, 424–59, in the *matter of Archy, on Habeas Corpus*, 9 California, 147–71; Duniway, "Slavery in California after 1848." American Hist. Assoc. *Annual Report*, 1905, I, 243–48.

[3] California, *Statutes*, 1853, 94; 1854, 30; 1855, 201.

resolution indorsing President Buchanan's Kansas policy and instructing the California delegation in Congress to vote for the immediate admission of Kansas into the Union. At the Democratic convention of 1860, the whole California delegation stood on the side of the ultra pro-slavery wing of the party.[4] Abolition was not popular in California. During the middle of the sixth decade it was considered a disgrace for a citizen of San Francisco to announce himself a Republican.[5]

California's course should the Union be dissolved.—The Democrats, especially the radical wing of the party, advocated the establishment of an independent Pacific republic in case of a dissolution of the Union. In his last annual message Governor Weller predicted that in case the south seceded from the Union, California "will not go with the South or the North, but here upon the shores of the Pacific found a mighty republic which may in the end prove the greatest of all."[6] Senators Gwin and Latham asserted on the floor of the United States Senate that in case the Union was broken up the eastern boundary of the Pacific republic would be the Sierra Madre and the Rocky Mountains. "For," said Latham, "we have resources not possessed by any other State of the Union, while our population comprises the most enterprizing and energetic men of the country."[7] Undoubtedly Governor Weller and Senators Gwin and Latham expressed the sentiments of a goodly portion of their constituents. The more moderate ones, however, were against such immature predictions, maintaining that California could not afford to incur the enmity of either the north or the south.

The presidential election of 1860 was an exciting one in California. Two-thirds of the California votes were cast against

[4] Davis, *Political Conventions in California*, 121; Fite, *The Presidential Campaign of 1860*, 106.

[5] See *Alta*, July 16, Oct. 23, 1860.

[6] California, *Sen. Jour.*, 1860, 60.

[7] *Cong. Globe*, 36 Cong., 1 Sess., 1728; *Alta*, Feb. 3, May 6, 1860.

Lincoln, but the division in the Democratic ranks enabled him to gain the four electors of the state.[8]

When news of Lincoln's election reached California many of the most influential men in the state began to discuss seriously the establishment of an independent Pacific republic. Judge Butts, the state printer and editor of the Sacramento *Standard*, proposed that a convention should be called with a view to the establishment of a separate and independent republic on the Pacific Coast.[9] In a lengthy letter dated November 22, 1860, Congressman Burch advocated that California, Oregon, New Mexico, Washington, and Utah should "raise aloft, the flag of the 'bear' surrounded with the 'hydra' pointed cactus of the Western wilds, and call upon the enlightened nations of the Earth to acknowledge our independence . . . . the youthful but vigorous Caesarian Republic of the Pacific."[10]

When the California election returns reached Washington, Senator Latham acknowledged that his former prediction that California would secede was premature. He warned the north, however, that the failure to build a Pacific railroad might alienate the affections of the people of California for the Union.[11] Latham was severely censured by some of the California Democrats for pledging the state to the north. They maintained that it was for the people of California to decide for or against a Pacific republic. The Los Angeles *Star* asserted that in the southern counties one could not find a corporal's guard who would go with the north, for their sympathies were with the south.[12] Congressman C. L. Scott also disagreed with Latham.

[8] The highest vote for Lincoln's electors was 38,734; for Douglas' electors, 38,023; for Breckinridge's electors, 33,975; for Bell's electors, 9, 136 (Davis, *Political Conventions in California*, 127).

[9] *Alta*, Nov. 15, 1860; *Herald*, Nov. 15, 1860.

[10] The letter is printed in the San Francisco *Herald* Jan 3, 1861. The writer stated that Senator Latham had read the letter and had approved of it (*ibid.*, editorial).

[11] *Cong. Globe*, 36 Cong., 2 Sess., 27.

[12] *Herald*, Jan. 10, 11, 21, 1861; San Joaquin *Republican*, Jan. 5, 1861; Los Angeles *Star*, Jan.. 5, 1861. *In* Hayes, *Collection, Southern California, Civil War*, XLVIII, 6.

In a letter dated December 21, 1860, he wrote:

> If this Union is divided, and two separate confederacies are formed, I will strenuously advocate the secession of California and the establishment of a separate republic on the Pacific slope. Some may contend that we have neither resources nor population to set up for ourselves. In answer to this I say, that if California links her destiny with the Northern government, crippled and ruined as she must necessarily be by the separation and withdrawal of her Southern allies, California, instead of being benefitted and receiving aid from the Northern Confederacy, will be heavily taxed to carry on the machinery of their government. . . . I really believe that the programme proposed by Thomas Ewing, General Taylor's Secretary of the Interior, to exact a tax, in the shape of seignorage, from the miners of California, would be carried out to raise revenue for this bogus government. Again, if she stands alone and severs her ties from a Union dissolved and bankrupted, there will spring up a rivalry between the two sections, North and South, to connect with her by railroad, in order to secure the trade of the Pacific; and thus we would have intercourse and trade not only with the sixteen Northern States, but also with the fifteen Southern States. The distance between the western frontier of Texas and the eastern border of California is a little over 500 miles; a railroad could and would be constructed in a few years, and you would have the means of transporting your heavy products of grain, and would find a ready market in the Southern States, for New York and the middle States will always be supplied from the Northwest. . . . .
>
> Besides all this, we have one hundred millions of acres of public domain within our limits, our immense mineral and agricultural resources, and our geographical position with China, Japan and the East Indies, and the trade generally with the East. . . . .
>
> . . . . What course, then, would California pursue, her population consisting of nearly half a million, one-half of which are from the West, the Southwest and the South? Do you believe, does any sane man believe, that the gallant men from the above sections would tamely and quietly acquiesce in being taxed by the North and Northwest to raise troops and to carry on a civil war? to place arms in the hands of a Government to subjugate their fathers, to pay money to the incendiaries to burn the houses of their mothers, to aid and assist the ruthless ruffian to ravish their sisters, and to give power to the "Great North" to lay waste and desolate the fair land that gave them birth? Sir, let such taxation be once attempted and the beautiful valleys, hills and gulches of California will flow with blood, and all the horrors of civil war will be upon us in our Golden State.[13]

[13] The letter was printed in the San Francisco *Herald,* Jan. 17, 1861; *Bulletin,* Jan. 16, 1861.

Secession of South Carolina.—When word of South Carolina's secession reached California the Alameda *Gazette* came out with an editorial entitled "What Shall We Do?"

> The slave holding States [it said] have been literally driven out of the Union. . . . . The Union is dissolved. . . . . It would be idle, therefore, in case of hostile collisions, between the Atlantic States, to think of *uniting* California for or against one section or the other. There are 40,000 Southern born and 40,000 Northern born men in this State, more or less. Under no circumstances, and especially those which now surround us, could the one or the other be induced to take up arms against the *land of his nativity.* To join an army of invasion against the South, a Southerner must be a parricide. To join an army of invasion against the North, a Northerner must be the equal of his brother of the South in parricidal enormity. . . . .
>
> What then, the question occurs, is to be the course of California when hope of Union bids the world farewell as we believe it has already done? . . . .
>
> Our solution of the question—advanced with doubt and hesitation—is a Pacific Republic.[14]

The Sonora *Democrat,* the Carson City *Silver Age,* and the Los Angeles *Star* also argued in favor of a Pacific republic.

> We are for a Pacific Republic [said the *Democrat*] if, unfortunately, the Confederacy should be disrupted. We believe it to be the true policy of California, in such an event, to cut loose from both sections, and not involve herself in the general ruin. She has all the elements of greatness within her borders. Situated thousands of miles from the distracted States, she would be an asylum of peace and safety in the eyes of the people of the older States, and many thousands would flock to her shores,—the effect of which must be to build up on the Pacific a mighty, prosperous, and independent nation. These are our views. We shall never consent to pay taxes for the coercion of a sovereign State; neither do we desire to see California linked on to any fragment of this Union.[15]

The opponents of a Pacific republic maintained that the majority of the people of California were in favor of adhering to the north, for the interests of California were connected with

[14] San Leandro *Gazette,* Jan. 12, 1861.

[15] Quoted in the *Alta,* Jan. 8, 1861. *See also* Los Angeles *Star,* in Hayes, *Collection,* XLVIII, and the opinion of the *Silver Age,* quoted in the Nevada *Democrat,* Feb. 5, 1861.

that section; the bulk of the population came from the northern states, her imports came from them, her exports went to them, and their ships filled her harbors. Moreover, California and the rest of the Pacific Coast were too weak to stand alone. To be sure, so far as actual territory was concerned the Pacific slope was almost as large as Europe, but in respect to population the Pacific republic would not play an imposing part. With an aggregate population of 602,000 it would be impossible to defend a sea coast 1500 miles long. Nor would the taxable property be sufficient to cover the cost of an expensive government, and it would require many millions to equip a navy, organize an army, and complete the fortifications. Moreover the whole burden would fall upon California since it would cost more to collect taxes among the truculent Mormons and in the unexplored regions of Washington and northern Oregon than the taxes would amount to. California would become the prey of Louis Napoleon.[16]

The proponents of a Pacific republic attempted to refute many of the charges against the inexpediency of its establishment. In an open letter on the state of the Union, published in the San Francisco *Herald,* General Volney E. Howard contended that in case of a contest of arms between north and south it would be unwise for California to connect herself with either section, for then California would be exposed to the hostilities of one or the other section; her treasure passing through southern waters, for example, to a northern port would be continually liable to capture. Moreover, neither section would be able to construct a railroad to the Pacific, and without a railroad neither government could afford the necessary protection for California against any maritime power should war ensue.

He went on to show that the commerce of California was forced to the Atlantic states by the tariff system and navigation

[16] *Alta,* Nov. 15, 25, 1860; Nevada *Democrat,* Nov. 17, 1860; Nevada *Journal,* Jan. 25, Nov. 30 1860; Stockton, *Daily Argus,* Jan. 12, 15, 1861.

acts of the United States government. If these impediments were removed California could ship her gold direct to Europe and purchase European manufactures in return. Moreover, California was subjected to a great financial loss by the operation of the paper system in the Atlantic states: she was paying in gold for goods at the paper price of the Atlantic states. Were California to make her exchange with England, where a sounder currency prevailed, she would greatly benefit by such a transaction. He also refuted the assertion that California would not have adequate resources to keep up an independent existence. He claimed that California could collect annually from eight to nine million dollars in the form of tariff duties, a sum sufficient to support an independent government.[17]

Prompted by the loyal press in California, the legislature busied itself with resolutions on the state of the Union. The general tone of the resolutions introduced by the Republican and Douglas Democrat members was unconditional loyalty to the Union and repudiation of the Pacific republic project. But some of the Breckinridge Democrats were not willing to go that far. The resolution of the minority of the Assembly Committee on Federal Relations declared that the people of California were "not prepared to pledge" their allegiance to "either a northern or a southern fragment of a dismembered confederacy," nor would they "ever consent to become the ally of one section in waging a fratricidal war against another section of our common country." During the debate on these resolutions the Breckinridge members warned the assembly that if California did not stand aloof and occupy an independent position, her soil would be crimsoned with blood. "I will die," said Montgomery, "before I will ever contribute a dime to prosecute a wicked, unholy, unjust, blackhearted, abolition war upon my southern brethren." The loyal members repudiated the idea of a Pacific

[17] *Herald*, Jan. 17, 25, 1861.

republic, pointing out that such a government would not have strength enough to continue an independent existence.[18]

An animated discussion on the Union resolutions took place also on the floor of the senate. In an eloquent speech Thornton, a Breckinridge Democrat, denounced any attempt to coerce the seceding states, and advocated the establishment of a Pacific republic should the Union be dissolved. The loyal members pointed out that it would be inexpedient to establish a Pacific republic at this time and that the material advantages arising from the connection between California and the Union were in favor of the former. The federal government was suffering an annual loss on the mail system of California of $931,000 and the annual expenditure on the means of defense for California amounted to $2,000,000.[19]

Effect of the assault on Fort Sumter.—Meanwhile the news arrived that actual hostilities between north and south had broken out. The facts that the south had initiated the terrible war by capturing Fort Sumter and had forced the hauling down of the stars and stripes, considerably strengthened the Union sentiment among the lukewarm Unionists. On the day of the arrival of the news the excitement in San Francisco was intense. Extras were issued; knots of people were discussing the eventful news in the streets.[20]

Almost all the Republican and Douglas Democrat newspapers came out expressing unconditional loyalty. Meetings expressing loyalty to the Union, and discouraging all efforts having in view the establishment of a Pacific republic were held in San Francisco, Oakland, San José, Marysville, Placerville, and a number

[18] Speech of Z. Montgomery, delivered in the California Assembly, Feb. 11, 1861. *In* California Legislature, *Speeches on the Resolution upon the State of the Union,* no. 4, pp. 14–15. *See also* speech of T. Laspeyre delivered in the California Assembly, Feb. 16, 1861 (*ibid.*, no. 8, p. 7).

[19] See *Speeches on the Resolutions upon the State of the Union,* nos. 3, 5, 7, 10, 11, 12, 14, 16, 17.

[20] *Alta,* April 25, 26, 27, 1861; *Bulletin,* April 26, 27, 1861.

of other towns.[21] On May 11, 1861, San Francisco expressed her loyalty by a grand Union demonstration with elaborate military and civic processions, loyal speeches, and a liberal display of Union flags, bunting, and badges. Union concerts and balls were given at various places. Union clubs were organized in many towns to fight secession.[22] The legislature passed a resolution pledging the loyalty of California to the Union.[23]

But the Breckinridge organs still maintained that California should not take any part in the fratricidal war. Even the San Francisco *Herald* at first advocated that California should adopt the position of the fox, in the fable of the lion, the tiger, and the fox, who appropriated for himself the best portion of the dead stag when the two stronger animals were exhausted fighting between themselves.[24] The *Semi-Weekly Southern News* asserted that any attempt to force California to espouse the cause of either section, "would be attended with bloody consequences."[25] How it would be possible to remain in the Union and yet maintain an attitude of neutrality was difficult to see. The Sacramento *Standard*, the Sonora *Democrat*, and the Los Angeles *Star* were more logical in this respect when they advocated the establishment of an independent republic.[26] "Shall we, too, strike for independence, or like whipped spaniels, crawl at the feet of either a Southern or a Northern Confederacy?" asked the Los Angeles *Star*. In another issue, in an article signed "Peace" it was

21 Extracts from the editorials of the various papers were published in the *Alta*, April 28, May 3, 1861; Sacramento *Union*, April 29, May 6, 1861.

22 *Alta*, April 28, May 3, 4, 6, 10, 12, 17, June 9, 13, 21, 24, 1861; *Herald*, May 21, 24, 27, 28, 30, 31, June 1, 5, 10, 11, 13, 22, 1861; Sacramento *Union*, May 8, 9, 11, 13, 14, 15, 16, 22, 23, 25, 27, 28, 29, June 1, 4, 16, 1861.

23 California, *Statutes*, 1861, 686; passed by a vote of 24 to 5. California, *Sen. Jour.*, 841. In the assembly there were 12 votes against the passage of the resolutions.

24 *Herald*, April 25, 29, May 1, 1861.

25 Los Angeles *Semi-Weekly Southern News*, May 3, 1861; San Leandro *Alameda County Gazette*, May 11, 1861.

26 Quoted in the Sacramento *Union*, May 1, 1861.

asserted that "*no Southern man of spirit*" would submit to pay duties "which will go towards raising and equipping an army to lay waste the Southern States." Hence "the solution of the problem is the establishment of a Republic, independent of any and all powers in the universe."[27]

From time to time articles with "much food for serious reflection" appeared in the columns of the Los Angeles *Star*. But the stand taken by the legislature, which in resolutions pledged the loyalty of California to the Union; the monster mass meetings held throughout the state, where resolutions of loyalty were adopted; and the energetic activity of General Sumner showed the futility of further advocating the movement for an independent republic. It feebly persisted up to the gubernatorial election of September, 1861, but the victory of the Republican candidate, Leland Stanford, extinguished the last vestiges of the movement.

[27] Los Angeles *Star*, April 27, May 11, 1861. *In* Hayes, *Collection, Civil War*, XLVIII, nos. 11, 17; L, no. 195.

CHAPTER X

LOYALTY AND DISLOYALTY

The abandonment of the Pacific republic project did not mean, however, that its advocates had fully acquiesced in the war policy of the administration; they continued to manifest a hostile attitude toward the cause of the Union. At first the more moderate newspapers advised the people not to exhibit any unnecessary excitement and irritation, and thereby avoid strife on the Pacific Coast. But as the war progressed, and the war spirit waxed more vigorous in California, it became impossible to preserve an attitude of tolerance. During the war period there was continual strife in California between the loyalist group, which was fully in sympathy with the war policy of President Lincoln, and a smaller group of disloyalists actively displaying their sympathies with the south.

Attitude of the political parties.—Examination of the activities of the two groups and of the expressions of the various agencies of public opinion will give us light on California's attitude toward the Civil War. Let us first ascertain the *vox populi* as expressed in party platforms. The first election after the outbreak of the war was held on September 4, 1861, for congressmen, governor, and other state officials. The Republican and Union Democratic platforms repudiated the right of secession, justified the policy of coercion, and pledged the support of California to sustain the federal government in all necessary measures to defend the Union.[1] The platform adopted at the

[1] Davis, *Political Conventions in California*, 162–63, 174–75; *Alta*, June 19, 1861.

Breckinridge state convention favored the preservation of the Union upon "constitutional guarantees" which would be acceptable to both sections of the Union, but if that should be impossible, then it was in favor of the "recognition of the independence of the confederate states." It declared itself opposed to the policy of coercion, and maintained that it was the duty of California to "yield obedience to all constitutional acts of Congress, and to all constitutional and legal acts of the federal executive" and in the following resolutions condemned Lincoln's appropriation of money and raising of armies without the authority of Congress as "usurpation of power." Only two voted for the loyal resolution which was presented, condemning secession, repudiating the idea of a Pacific republic, and pledging the loyalty of California to the Union.[2]

The vote polled on September 4, 1861, was as follows: the Republican and Union Democratic gubernatorial candidates, running on platforms loyal to the Union, polled together 86,980 votes; while the Breckinridge candidate, running on a platform which was opposed to the war, polled 32,751 votes. In similar proportion were the votes of the three parties for Congressmen.[3] From these figures it seems that more than a third of the voters of California were opposed to the war.

At the election of September, 1863, the gubernatorial candidate of the Union party,[4] which was the former Republican party, running on a platform similar to the one of 1861, polled 64,283 votes; while the candidate of the fusion Democrats,[5] run-

---

[2] Davis, *Political Conventions in California*, 166–69; *Alta*, June 13, 1861.

[3] Davis, *Political Conventions in California*, 180.

[4] During 1862 a movement was going on in California favoring the abandonment of the two 'Union party' organizations and the formation of a new party upon the principle of pledging support to the Administration. Hence the name Republican was dropped, and the new Union party was formed, in the hope of uniting the Republican and Union Democratic elements. But a number of Union Democrats refused to unite with a party whose principles included abolition.

[5] Simultaneously with the movement to unite the Republican and the Union Democratic parties, there was also a strong movement for union

ning on a platform lukewarm in its loyalty to the Union, polled 44,622 votes. In the same proportion stood the vote for Congressmen.[6] The platforms of the two parties during the presidential election of 1864 were similar to the respective platforms of the previous years. The vote cast for Lincoln was 62,141; for McClellan 43,839.[7]

An examination of the several party platforms and the popular vote of the state cast in the gubernatorial and presidential elections seems to indicate that more than two-thirds of the voters were fully in accord with the war policy. Of the remaining third, which came mainly from the southern counties, probably half were lukewarm Unionists, loyalists with conditions.

Attitude of the press.—The platform of the Union party was fully endorsed by the loyal press. Indeed, the loyal newspapers frequently urged a more vigorous prosecution of the war, without regard to the sacrifice in men and money.[8] On the other hand, the radical platform of the Breckinridge party seemed too moderate to many of the outspoken disloyalists and ultra Breckinridge organs. The editorials of these papers justified secession, deprecated coercion, magnified Union defeats, belittled Union victories, and denounced President Lincoln as an idiot and despot.

---

among the Breckinridge and the Union Democratic parties. But the committees of the two parties were averse to union, and both wings of the Democratic party issued calls for state conventions. The rank and file, however, refused to abide by the decision of the leaders, and a movement was set on foot by some of the Democratic papers and clubs to hold a fusion convention. This fusion Democratic state convention met at Sacramento on July 8, 1863. The Breckinridge and Union Democratic parties went out of existence.

[6] Davis, *Political Conventions in California*, 201.

[7] *Ibid.*, 212. The Democratic vote was particularly strong in the southern counties of the state.

[8] *Alta*, July 15, 19, 1861; San Andreas *Register*, Oct. 8, 1861; Los Angeles *Semi-Weekly Southern News*, Oct. 2, 1861; Nevada City *Morning Transcript*, Oct. 17, 1862. According to the classification of the *Call*, and the *Herald*, there were eight Republican organs in the state, twenty-one Union Democratic papers, some six independent papers, and about half a dozen which leaned toward either the Republican party or the Democratic party. See *Herald*, July 26, 1861.

Thus far [said the Visalia *Equal Rights Expositor*] the South has sustained herself well. Their fathers won their independence under far greater disadvantages, and it is not even a supposable case that they will fail to do so. The sympathies of the civilized world are with them, and they must succeed. When they do so, they will be covered with immortal glory and honors, and the North will stand a monument of disgrace to the world, because she repudiates the grand principle for which their fathers fought—that of self government.[9]

The *Expositor* called upon the people to

stamp the seal of their indignation [upon the administration which] deluded them into the belief that the South could be conquered. [It is impossible to enslave a free people, it said; the result is that our government is ruined financially and outlawed in foreign money markets.] The bloody fields of Big Bethel and Bull Run rose like Banquo's ghost to the vision and affrighted consciences of the loyal bravomisimos of the Government, and the proud flag of the United States was made to trail disgracefully in the dust, and the loudly vaunted prowess of the Union soldiers was exhibited in shameful retreat.[10]

In its Thanksgiving issue the *Expositor* ridiculed the Union defeats.

O Lord [it said] we thank thee for letting the rebels wallop us at the battle of Pittsburg Landing—for letting them smite us hip and thigh, even unto the destruction of 9,600 of our good loyal soldiers, and 463 of our officers; and for giving speed to their legs through the awful swamps of Chickahominy; and, O Lord, most especially do we thank thee for the licking they gave us at Bull Run the second, and assisting our flight from that fatal field; and, O Lord, never while we live will we forget Antietam, where we had 200,000 and they only 70,000—if they, O Lord, had a happened to a had as many men as we, we'd a been a done gone in—and that friendly creek between us, the mountains that kept our men from running. . . . .[11]

Not less vehement in its denunciations was the Marysville *Express.* It characterized the Union army as a "whining running army, that has disgraced our flag, lowered our cause and dishonored Republican chivalry all over the earth!"[12] President

[9] Visalia *Equal Rights Expositor,* Aug. 30, Nov. 1, 1862. Quoted by Earle, *The Sentiment of the People of California with Regard to the Civil War,* 41, MS Thesis (M.A.), University of California.

[10] *Ibid.,* Nov. 22, 1862.

[11] Quoted by Earle.

[12] Marysville *Appeal,* Sept. 10, 1861. Quoted by Earle, 48–49.

Lincoln was denounced by these papers as a "narrow minded bigot," an "autocratic tyrant," an "unprincipled demagogue," an "imbecile creature" who "will die universally execrated."[13] The San José *Tribune* called Lincoln an "illiterate backwoodsman, who is not only destitute of the first requirements of a statesman, but who can scarcely write a sentence of the English language correctly."[14] The *Tribune* called upon the people to repudiate the "galling military despotism that now tries to subvert our liberties and reduce us to bondage."[15]

The loyal press complained against such incendiary and malicious expressions. Speaking of these disloyal papers, the *Alta* said:

> They have persistently maligned the men at the head of our Government . . . . they have denounced the war as wicked, and vain. They have declared that the Secessionists are morally and legally right. . . . . They refuse to give the title of "rebels" or "traitors" to the enemy. They speak of "Mr. Lincoln," and "President Davis." They publish few reports unfavorable to the enemy. While villifying the high officers of the Federal Government, they always mention the rebel officials with studious terms of respect. . . . .
>
> No appeal to the patriotism of the people is ever made. Whatever a secret traitor dares to do, that they do.[16]

On September 16, 1862, General Wright ordered that the Stockton *Argus*, the Stockton *Democrat*, the San José *Tribune*, the Tulare *Post*, and the Visalia *Equal Rights Expositor* should be excluded from the United States mails and expresses. He also cautioned the people of the Pacific Coast against committing treasonable acts which might involve the state in a civil war.[17] He claimed that their disloyal utterances tended to discourage

---

[13] Visalia *Equal Rights Expositor*, Oct. 4, 18, Sept. 6, Dec. 13, 1862; Jan. 16, 23, 1863; March 5. Quoted by Earle, pp. 45–49. See also *Sonoma County Democrat*, March 13, 1862; Mariposa *Gazette*, May 28, 1864; *Weekly San Joaquin Republican*, Sept. 7, 1861.

[14] Dec. 19, 1861.

[15] *Ibid.*, Oct. 24, 1861.

[16] *Alta*, Feb. 19, 1862.

[17] *Alta*, Sept. 17, 1862; *Records of the Rebellion*, ser. 1, Vol. L, part 2, pp. 456–57. A similar penalty had been imposed on the Los Angeles *Star*.

enlistment. The papers affected by this order protested vigorously against this arbitrary and despotic policy.

> This act of despotism [said the Visalia *Equal Rights Expositor*] has by no means astonished us. . . . . A free press has never yet been tolerated by any power that conspired against the liberties of the people. Will any one now dare say that they live under a free government, that thus outrages the liberties of the press and of free speech? . . . . Men who will continue their support of such a government, steeped in infamy as it is, are fit only for slaves.

The *Expositor* declared that regardless of threats of imprisonment it would continue to expose the "free negro party that outrages the Constitution," and the wickedness of the officials who trampled upon the Constitution and stole the people's money.[18] On January 5, 1863, the military authorities arrested Hall and Garrison, the editors of the *Expositor,* on the ground of disloyal practices, and they were placed in close confinement. Hall was released on taking the oath of loyalty. Garrison, who refused to take the oath, was retained a little longer.[19] But even after their brief confinement, the editors refused to keep silent. Shortly after his release Hall announced that he would continue to oppose the iniquitous war with all his zeal. The soldiers then decided to take the matter into their own hands. On the night of March 5, 1863, some thirty soldiers of Camp Babbitt, Visalia, completely destroyed the office of the *Expositor,* breaking the press and throwing the type, paper, and ink into the street.[20]

The Mariposa *Free Press* seemed to be a worthy companion of the Visalia *Expositor.* In an article on March 21, 1863, it said: "What cares Abraham Lincoln for the good of the country? A traitor to God and humanity, his hands dripping with the blood of his countrymen." And in its issue of April 23, 1863, it said: "Outrages, such as have been consummated by the

[18] Visalia *Equal Rights Expositor,* Sept. 20, 1862. Quoted by Earle, 51–53.

[19] *Records of the Rebellion,* ser. 1, Vol. L, part 2, p. 277.

[20] *Ibid.,* 341–42. It is said that the immediate cause of the attack was an article on the "*California Cosacs*" (*Bulletin,* March 16, 1862).

party in power, have shaken empires to their centers—cast kings from their thrones. The assumption of power whetted a dagger for Caesar and begat a Cromwell for Charles.''[21]

Disloyal speeches.—Then we have a number of disloyal speeches made by the ''secesh'' element. The most celebrated speech was that of Edmund Randolph, made at a Breckinridge convention shortly after the beginning of hostilities, which he concluded by saying:

> My thoughts and my heart are not here tonight in this house. Far to the east, in the homes from which we came, tyranny and usurpation, with arms in its hands, is this night, perhaps slaughtering our fathers, our brothers, and our sisters, and outraging our homes in every conceivable way shocking to the heart of humanity and freedom . . . . For God's sake, tell me of battles fought and won. Tell me of the usurpers overthrown; that Missouri is again a free state, no longer crushed under the armed heel of a reckless, and odious despot. . . . If this be rebellion, then I am a rebel. Do you want a traitor? then I am a traitor. For God's sake speed the ball; may the lead go quick to his heart, and may our country be free from this despot usurper that now claims the name of president of the United States [cheers].[22]

---

[21] Quoted in Mariposa *Gazette,* April 29, 1863.

[22] Randolph was one of the most prominent lawyers in the state. This extract is given in Davis, *Political Conventions in California,* 173. It is also found in the contemporary local papers. For other speeches at the convention *see* Sacramento *Union,* June 14, 1862. Similar suggestions were also made by many other sympathizers with the cause of the south. A poem under the title ''The Tread of Despotism,'' which appeared in the Los Angeles *Star,* in December, 1861, reads:

> ''Shall that same tyrant, with his yoke,
> Who spurned the public weal,
> And first the Constitution broke,
> That Negroes he might steal;
>
> Who basely forced the States apart,
> Espous'd the Negro cause,
> Stabbed our Republic in the heart,
> And overthrew our laws—
>
> * * * * * *
>
> Is he so maddened by defeat,
> That he'll insult the world,
> 'Till from his dictatorial seat
> To depths below he's hurled?''

In Hayes, *Collection,* L, no. 264. *See also* a poem, ''Coercion,'' by Caxton, printed in the Los Angeles *Star,* Aug. 17, 1861 (*ibid.,* no. 218).

Randolph was not molested but later disloyal speakers did not escape so easily. One of these was the Reverend Dr. Scott, pastor of the Calvary Presbyterian Church in San Francisco, one of the most distinguished pastors in that city. In his prayers, it is said, he invoked the blessing upon the Presidents and Vice-Presidents of the United States. And at a meeting of the California Presbytery he declared that Jefferson Davis was no usurper, but as much a President as Abraham Lincoln was; that there was no such thing as rebellion, but only rightful revolution.[23] Dr. Scott was severely criticized in the press, while around his church the mob held demonstrations and placed there an effigy bearing the inscription "Dr. Scott the Traitor." The strong popular demonstration compelled Dr. Scott to resign his post and leave the state.

Another case was that of James H. Hardy, judge of the sixteenth judicial district. The judge was impeached by the legislature on several charges. Some of these charges were: that he had shouted "huzzas" for Jefferson Davis, that he had publicly given a toast "Here's to Jefferson Davis and the Southern Confederacy," that he had called the American flag "an old woman's rag, and ought to be torn down," and that he had called himself a rebel. He was found guilty and was removed from office.[24]

Military arrests.—The military authorities arrested and confined in Fort Alcatraz a number of persons because of alleged

---

[23] *Alta,* Sept. 19, 23, 1861; *Bulletin,* Sept. 23, 1861; *Herald,* Sept. 23, 1861. In his statement to the moderator of the Presbytery, he declared that there was no authority from the "Church or from Christ to decide what is the difference between a needful revolution and a rebellion;" that he found no "authority from the Bible, nor from the standards of the Church, to say that Jefferson Davis is a traitor, any more than George Washington was . . . . If George Washington had been unsuccessful he would have been hung. If Jefferson Davis fails you will hang him, I suppose. What history will call him depends on success or failure" (*The Pacific Expositor,* 191–93. In *California Miscellany,* III).

[24] The official report of the proceedings, testimony, and arguments in the trial of Judge Hardy is published in California, *Sen. and Assembly Jours.,* 1862, App. (Doc. 37). Article 15 is on pages 674–75, 705.

treasonable expressions. On November 29, 1861, Major Rigg captured near San Bernardino Dan Showalter with a party of eighteen men, all well armed and of southern birth. It was commonly believed that they were traveling toward Texas with the intention of enlisting in the Confederate army. They were released after taking the oath of allegiance to the federal government.[25] Dan Showalter, however, finally succeeded in enlisting in the Confederate army.[26]

Some of the notable persons arrested for alleged treasonable utterances were Bishop Kavanaugh of the Methodist church south, Colonel Kewen, assemblyman from Los Angeles; Senator Baker, of Visalia; Major Gibbs, the editor of the Los Angeles *Star* and the Visalia *Expositor,* Dr. Gwin, and C. L. Weller, chairman of the Democratic state committee.[27] Dr. Gwin was arrested by General Sumner, who believed that Gwin was on his way to meet Slidell at Cuba. Gwin appealed to the Granada authorities but the latter were unsuccessful in their attempt to obtain his release.[28]

Weller was arrested and lodged at Alcatraz on July 25, 1864, on the charge that in an address delivered by him in San Francisco he had appealed to southern sentiment and had urged the people to arm themselves "to resist the high arm of the military tyranny in California."[29] The Democrats held an indignation meeting and adopted resolutions condemning the acts of the military authorities and the practice of imprisoning men with-

---

25 *Records of the Rebellion,* ser. 1, Vol. L, part 1, pp. 30–33, 38–39; *Bulletin,* Dec. 5, 1861.

26 *Records of the Rebellion,* ser. 1, Vol. L, part 2, pp. 1078, 1079–80. A number of other Californians had enlisted in the Confederate army, McDuffie, David S. Terry, H. I. Thornton, and others.

27 Merced *Morning Transcript,* Oct. 17, 1862; *Bulletin,* Nov. 30, 1861, Oct. 11, 15, 1862; Sacramento *Union,* July 27, 1864; *Alta,* Oct. 11, 1862; San Andreas *Register,* July 30, 1864; *Herald,* Nov. 28, 1861.

28 *Herald,* Nov. 28, 1861; *Bulletin,* Nov. 27, 30, 1861.

29 *Records of the Rebellion,* ser. 1, Vol. L, part 2, p. 948; *Alta,* July 26, 27, 1864. The Sacramento *Union,* July 27, 1864, gives extracts from his speech.

out trial. Weller was released after taking the oath of allegiance to the federal government and giving a bond for $25,000.[30] A number of persons were imprisoned at Fort Alcatraz for alleged rejoicing over the assassination of President Lincoln.[31] At their state convention the Democrats protested against the military arrests.[32]

War hysteria.—One of the most spectacular manifestations of disloyalty in California was the Chapman case. Several ultra southerners in San Francisco purchased the swift schooner "Chapman," equipped her with cannons, ammunition, and twenty fighting men, and were planning to sail for Manzanillo where they were to exhibit their letters of marque and commission from the Confederate navy and then lie in wait for the Pacific mail vessel, capture her and equip her for privateer purposes. But the military authorities in San Francisco were on the lookout for such schemes, and on March 15, early in the morning as the vessel was getting under way, she was seized and towed to Alcatraz Island. Upon search it was found that the several cases invoiced as merchandise contained cannons, revolvers, muskets, powder, and shrapnel.[33] The leaders of the

---

30 *Alta,* Aug. 3, 1864; *Records of the Rebellion,* ser. 1, Vol. L, part 2, p. 948.

31 The news of the assassination of the President produced considerable excitement in California. In San Francisco all the main business houses closed their doors immediately; the flags were at half-mast, and the bells of the city hall and various churches tolled mournfully. About three P.M. a mob wrecked the offices of some "secesh" papers: the Democratic *Press,* the *News Letter,* the *Monitor,* the *Occidental,* and the French paper *L'Union Américaine.* The French *Echo du Pacifique* was also threatened by the mob, but was saved by the editor of the *Alta,* whose office was located in the same building (*Records of the Rebellion,* ser. 1, Vol. L, part 2, p. 1198; *Alta,* April 16, 1865; *Bulletin,* April 16, 1865). It was reported that at Colusa a number of "seceshes" celebrated the assassination of Lincoln by cheers and the firing of guns (*Records of the Rebellion,* ser. 1, Vol. L, part 2, pp. 1012–20; Mariposa *Gazette,* May 20, 1865; San Andreas *Register,* April 29, 1865).

32 Davis, *Political Conventions in California,* 212.

33 *Records of the Rebellion,* ser. 1, Vol. L, part 2, pp. 363–64. A full account of the affair is found in *Alta,* March 16, 17, 1863. The *Alta* of March 17 published some of the papers found on the "Chapman." One of these was a solemn oath of secrecy; another paper was an oath of fellow-

plot were tried before the United States Circuit Court in San Francisco and were each sentenced to ten years' imprisonment and a fine of $10,000.[34]

The news of the Chapman affair produced considerable excitement in San Francisco. People began to think of the exposed state of the harbor. A proposition to raise $600,000 to put the harbor in a state of defense was considered at a meeting of the board of supervisors. The legislature, also, was considering means of defense for the state.[35] Rumors were spread that other privateering vessels were being fitted out to prey upon California commerce and mail steamers. An hysterical atmosphere prevailed throughout the state. Anyone who dared to express the least disapproval of the policy of the administration was denounced by the ultra loyalists as a "secesh." All kinds of rumors were circulated and believed. It was reported that in some localities bear flags had been raised; that at a ball some women had appeared in dresses representing the flag of the Confederacy; that in some places "secessionists had sung 'Dixie' to the obnoxious words," and had cheered for Jefferson Davis and South Carolina, and denounced the "absolute" government of the United States; that upon the arrival of news of the defeats of the Union army they congratulated each other; that the secessionists held nightly meetings with the expectation of uniting their forces with those of the Confederates; that conflicts between secessionists and loyalists had taken place at different places in the state.[36]

ship, swearing allegiance to the Confederacy. The third paper was a rough sketch of a conspiracy plot. The plan as outlined in the draft was to raise a thousand men, and take possession of Benicia and the two forts commanding the harbor of San Francisco. The capture of these strategic places, it was thought, would bring about the withdrawal of California from the Union.

[34] For the reports of the proceedings of the trial see *Alta*, Sept., 1863. Harpending's account of the trial is found in his book, *Great Diamond Hoax*, 83–88.

[35] *Bulletin*, March 16, 17, 19, 1863.

[36] *Alta*, May 24, July 4, Aug. 9, 10, 15, 21, 25, 29, 30, 31, Dec. 20, Oct. 5, 1861; *Journal*, Aug. 23, 1861.

Secret disloyal organizations.—Rumors were widely current of the existence of secret organizations for revolutionary purposes. The *Alta* called upon all loyal citizens to arm themselves for the conflict. "We have in this State," it asserted, "a larger number of persons who sympathize with the enemies of the Government than in any other free State in the whole Union. They are active, energetic, and wily. They are at work night and day."[37] Commenting on the El Monte incident,[38] the San Bernardino *Patriot* said: "Fellow citizens we must arouse ourselves; a secret organization, we learn, exists here in Southern California, whose object it is to raise the secession flag among us . . . . Let every man who owns a good horse keep him ready at hand at a moment's warning."[39]

There were many who considered it their duty as loyal citizens to warn the federal authorities against danger from secessionists in California. From Los Angeles they wrote to General Sumner that secret organizations were poisoning the minds of the natives against the United States government. From Santa Barbara reports came of nightly meetings of secessionists "having for their object the seizure of public property here and in Utah and to raise the standard of rebellion in California." United States Attorney Dimmick wrote to General Sumner that the secessionists in the south were getting more noisy and that every county officer was with them. From Napa they wrote that the secessionists were getting dangerous. Indeed Captain Davidson complained that his ears were "stuffed with all sorts of rumors and reports."[40]

---

[37] *Alta,* Aug. 25, 1861; *see also* Sept. 22, 1861. *Bulletin,* Aug. 26, 28, 30, 31, Sept. 2, 1861.

[38] At the town of El Monte, about fourteen miles from Los Angeles, an armed and mounted band of about sixty men paraded through the streets bearing a "deep red flag with a black bear painted on it" (*Alta,* June 6, 22, 1861; Sacramento *Union,* June 24, 1861; *Records of the Rebellion,* ser. 1, Vol. L, part 2, pp. 479–80).

[39] Quoted by the *Alta,* June 6, 1861.

[40] *Records of the Rebellion,* ser. 1, Vol. L, part 1, pp. 563–66, 622; part 2, pp. 707, 924–25.

In a petition to the War Department, dated August 28, 1861, a number of San Francisco merchants remonstrated against withdrawing the able-bodied men from California for service elsewhere, pointing out that California was in need of all its able-bodied men to fight against the secessionists at home. The petition stated that the majority of the state officers were undisguised secessionists; that three-eighths of the citizens of California were natives of the southern states, and "almost a unit in this crisis," all hating the Union and all well organized. It was stated that there were 16,000 Knights of the Golden Circle in California.[41]

Upon his arrival in 1861 General Sumner was convinced that there was some "deep scheming to draw California into the secession movement; in the first place as the 'Republic of the Pacific' expecting afterward to induce her to join the Southern Confederacy."[42] Likewise Colonel Evans at Visalia was convinced that there was a large number of secessionists in the southern counties who were well organized and armed, "ready at a moment's warning to take up their arms against the Government of the United States." He wrote that it was an everyday occurrence for them to ride through the streets and "hurrah for Jeff. Davis, and Stonewall Jackson; and often give groans for the Stars and Stripes"; that they were calling the soldiers "Lincoln's hirelings," who wear "Abe Lincoln's livery."[43] A number of fist fights between soldiers and secessionists occurred. General Wright, Sumner's successor, was less of an alarmist. He wrote to Washington that the rumors of secession organizations within California had upon investigation been found to be "highly exaggerated." He was confident that a sufficient mili-

---

41 *Ibid.*, part 1, pp. 589–91.

42 *Records of the Rebellion*, ser. 1, Vol. L, part 1, pp. 471–72. Sumner was ordered to California to relieve General Johnston, on March 22, 1861. He arrived in California on April 24, 1861, and assumed command on the following day.

43 *Records of the Rebellion*, ser. 1, Vol. L, part. 2, pp. 236–37.

tary force would avert all danger of disturbances from the secret organizations. He requested Governor Stanford to call out the militia of Napa and Solano counties to quell any disturbances that might occur at Napa.[44]

Undoubtedly the extent and strength of these secret societies had been considerably exaggerated, as was to be expected of an overheated war-mind at a time when even the most judicious people become credulous and ready to make a mountain out of a molehill. However, documents and indirect evidence seem to substantiate the belief of the existence of such organizations. From time to time the papers published so-called exposés of the purposes, oaths, signs, and signals of the Knights of the Golden Circle. Government Detective Gustav Brown reported that in the counties of San Luis Obispo and Los Angeles the Knights of the Golden Circle were divided into three grades, each with signs, grips, and passwords. Also that the members were armed and intended to commence a guerilla warfare in case of a draft in California.[45]

Provost Marshal Robert Robinson reported that the Knights of the Columbian Star numbered about twenty-four thousand, and that, together with the Knights of the Golden Circle and the men they could control, they numbered around fifty thousand. According to his report the obligation of the members was to "resist the enforcement of any and all unconstitutional laws by the administration." Each member was obliged to equip himself with a rifle, a revolver, bowie knife, and powder. C. L. Weller and ex-Governor Bigler were officers of the organization.[46]

Attitude of the military authorities.—The military authorities adopted vigorous precautionary measures. General Sumner ordered additional military forces for Los Angeles, Alcatraz

---

[44] *Records of the Rebellion,* ser. 1, Vol. L, part 2, pp. 210, 211; part 1, pp. 797, 1091.

[45] *Records of the Rebellion,* ser. 1, Vol. L, part 2, pp. 1018–19; *also* pp. 1037–38.

[46] *Records of the Rebellion,* ser. 1, Vol. L, part 2, pp. 938–41. How far these reports are reliable is difficult to ascertain.

Island, Benicia, and the presidio. He gave orders to his officers to "repress with a strong hand any organization which aimed to resist or impede the measures of the Government."[47]

His successor, General Wright, was more moderate. He believed in taking strict measures to suppress any disturbances but he did not believe in being unduly harsh. For instance, upon the arrival of the news of the assassination of President Lincoln, he ordered the officers to be prepared for any emergency; but when he was informed that a number of men had been arrested by individual members of the provost guard without any authority whatever, simply on the general principle that the arrested ones had been pointed out by some irresponsible person as sympathizers with the cause of the south, he strongly disapproved of such conduct.[48]

His lenient attitude was approved by those accused of disloyalty and by the majority of the Union men who had not been carried away by the war excitement. But the ultra loyalists accused him of catering to the secessionists. They petitioned the War Department to remove General Wright and they asked General McDowell, who succeeded General Wright, to institute a proper inquiry into the matter.[49] In his letter to the adjutant general at Washington General Wright claimed that his policy was

> fully endorsed by the sensible portion of the community . . . . Were I to be guided by the dictates of the radical press [he said] I should crowd my forts with men charged with disloyalty, keep this country in constant ferment . . . . These radicals seem to believe that it is my special duty to arrest every man or woman whose sentiments do not coincide exactly with the Government.[50]

---

[47] The southern element in California ridiculed Sumner's undue alarm. See *Weekly San Joaquin Republican*, Sept. 17, 1861.

[48] *Records of the Rebellion*, ser. 1, Vol. L, part 2, p. 1210.

[49] McDowell assumed command July 1, 1864. Wright was later transferred to the command of the department of Columbia. On the way to assume his command he was drowned in the wreck of the "Brother Jonathan," July 30, 1865.

[50] *Records of the Rebellion*, ser. 1, Vol. L, part 2, pp. 846–47.

Attitude of the state authorities.—The military authorities were well supported by the strong loyal element. Also the state authorities and the more influential part of the press approved of the war policy of the administration. Even Governor Downey, who as late as 1862 advocated that the United States should adopt a mere defensive policy, held that since the war was already an accomplished fact, all the states in the Union were equally committed to this policy.[51] He faithfully carried out all the provisions of the federal government. Governors Stanford and Low were unquestionably loyal. Each legislature passed a resolution indorsing the policy of the administration and pledging the support of California.[52]

California's contribution in men.—But California's contribution to the war was not confined to suppression of disloyalty within her own borders. She also contributed men and money to the army of the Union. The draft law was not extended to California,[53] yet, out of a population of about 400,000 souls California contributed, during the war period, over sixteen thousand men. The first requisition for troops made by Secretary of War Cameron upon the Governor of California was dated July 24, 1861. It called for a regiment of infantry and five companies

[51] California, *Sen. Jour.*, 1862, 49–54.

[52] California, *Statutes*, 1862, 603; 1863–1864, 546–48. There were of course a number of members of the legislature who secretly and even openly sympathized with the south.

[53] In reply to a resolution of the House of February 20, 1865, inquiring the reasons for the non-enforcement of the draft law in California, Secretary of War Stanton stated that it was thought to be inexpedient to withdraw the able-bodied men from the Pacific Coast, thus leaving the coast unprotected and exposed to attack (*Records of the Rebellion*, ser. 3, Vol. IV, 1201). Undoubtedly the distance of the state from the scenes of the war, and the heavy cost of transportation, were also important factors. Jno. Mason, acting assistant provost marshal general of California and Nevada, advised the Washington authorities not to extend the draft to California and Nevada, claiming that due to the nature of the population and settlement of the country it would be difficult to enforce such a law; it would require a large force to bring in all the deserters (*ibid.*, ser. 1, Vol. L, part 2, pp. 966–67).

of cavalry to guard the overland mail routes.[54] Enlistment went on rapidly and by September the organization was completed.

When the government at Washington was informed that the Confederate government was planning to despatch an army to seize New Mexico, Arizona, and probably penetrate California, it called upon Governor Downey to equip and organize at the earliest date possible four regiments of infantry and one regiment of cavalry to be placed at the disposal of General Sumner.[55] The loyal press, displeased with the slowness of enlistment, warned the young men of California that if they would not enlist the United States government would have to resort to drafting. But the policy of sending her volunteers to western Texas did not seem to find favor in California. A group of San Francisco business men protested to the Secretary of War against draining California of her fighting men when they were needed at home. Also General Sumner pointed out to the War Department that California was threatened by an active secessionist element.[56] The plan for the expedition was abandoned, but the troops called for were organized and "held ready for service on the Pacific Coast and elsewhere."

When a Confederate force of several thousand men under the command of General Sibley arrived in New Mexico about the middle of December, 1861, and captured Albuquerque and Santa Fé, the government revived the former plan. The "California Column" consisting of five companies of the first California cavalry, ten companies of the first California infantry, and a light battery of four brass fieldpieces together with the fifth California infantry, was despatched in April, 1862, under the command of Brigadier General of Volunteers Carleton. Hearing

---

54 *Records of the Rebellion*, ser. 1, Vol. L, part 1, 543; Orton, *Record of California Men in the War of the Rebellion*, 12. The requisition was made by telegram from Washington to the farthest point west, and thence by pony express to California.

55 Orton, *Record of California Men in the War of the Rebellion*, 12.

56 Orton, *Record of California Men in the War of the Rebellion*, 23–24, 27–28.

of the approach of the "California Column," General Sibley, who had already lost most of his supplies, evacuated New Mexico and retired beyond the Rio Grande. All the forts and towns in Arizona and New Mexico were reoccupied by the Union forces. The "California Column" also performed valuable services in quelling Indian disturbances on the frontier and in protecting the mail routes.[57]

A number of young Californians who were anxious to participate in the actual conflict on the eastern battlefields offered their services to the state of Massachusetts in return for the financing of the cost of organization and transportation. The proposition was accepted by Massachusetts and the company raised was known as the "California Hundred" or "A" company of the second Massachusetts cavalry regiment. Shortly after, a battalion of four companies was raised for Massachusetts under the same conditions as the first company. This became known as the "California Battalion."[58] The California "Hundred" and "Battalion" participated in over fifty engagements. On May 23, 1865, they attracted considerable attention in the grand review in Washington. Out of 400 officers and men mustered into the "Battalion" in California only 148 remained to be mustered out in the final discharge.[59]

California's contribution to the sanitary fund.—California also contributed $1,233,831.31 to the sanitary commission. The first movement in this direction began in 1862, in San Francisco, when it was decided to start a subscription fund for the relief of the wounded soldiers. A committee of thirteen, known as the committee of the soldiers' fund, was organized for canvassing the city. On September 19, 1862, the committee remitted a draft for $100,000 by telegraph to Dr. Bellows, president of the United States sanitary commission. A second draft for $100,000 was

[57] Orton, *Record of California Men in the War of the Rebellion*, 47, 64–67.

[58] *Ibid.*, 848–53.

[59] *Ibid.*

remitted on the first of October. The committee then distributed a circular throughout California, Oregon, Washington, and Nevada appealing for contributions. In 1864 President Bellows arrived, made several addresses, and was instrumental in organizing the California branch of the United States sanitary commission with Governor Low as president.

The devices used for raising money were manifold. Aside from regular monthly subscriptions, collections were made at public amusement places, at churches, schools, fairs, picnics, public elections, from sales at auction, and by various gifts. The first California draft came at a critical period in the life of the sanitary commission when its treasury was almost depleted. It "was the making and saving of the United States Sanitary Commission" says Stillé. California's contribution excited emulation on the part of other states. But in no part of the United States was the work of collecting money for the fund so systematically organized as in California.[60]

Summary.—The great majority of the people of California were loyal to the Union and might be relied on under all circumstances to keep order and sustain the federal government. Rhodes's statement that on the eve of the Civil War California "was in danger of joining the South,"[61] was unwarranted by the facts. There was at the beginning of the war, however, a strong sentiment in favor of an independent Pacific republic, but by the end of 1861 this movement was practically extinguished. The status of California was then definitely fixed. However, the strong southern element in California, particularly in the southern counties, was formidable enough to threaten the peace of the community.

---

60 Stillé, *History of the United States Sanitary Commission*, 233.

61 Rhodes, *History of the United States*, V, 255.

CHAPTER XI

ATTITUDE OF CALIFORNIA TO THE LEGAL TENDER NOTES DURING THE CIVIL WAR

Issue of the legal tender notes.—The State of California was loyal to the Union during the Civil War, yet in one respect her loyalty might be thought questionable; namely, her attitude toward the legal tender notes.

When the Civil War broke out the United States Treasury was empty and money could be borrowed only at very high rates of interest. The government resorted to the issuing of notes, declaring them to

> be receivable in payment of all taxes, internal duties, excises, debts and demands of every kind due to the United States, except duties on imports, and of all claims and demands against the United States, of every kind whatsoever, except for interest upon bonds and notes, which shall be paid in coin, and shall also be lawful money and legal tender in payment of all debts, public and private, within the United States, except duties on imports and interest as aforesaid.[1]

The purpose of making the notes legal tender was to insure their negotiability. At first there was considerable opposition to this radical measure. Its constitutionality and expediency was questioned but the plea of "absolute necessity" silenced opposition. Soon the people of the United States became reconciled to the measure and the notes even became popular, especially among the debtor and speculative classes. They were undoubtedly more desirable than the "wild cat" issues.

[1] United States, *Statutes at Large*, XII, 345.

Reception of the notes in California.—In California, however, the notes received a less friendly welcome. Opinion differed as to the constitutionality and expediency of their issue. Some argued that all previous attempts to issue paper money to supplant gold and silver terminated in "disgraceful failure." They prophesied that within a short time the notes would be depreciated and be worth little more than the value of the blank paper. Others questioned the expediency of making the notes legal tender, holding that in either case the same amount of notes would purchase the same amount of goods; the only difference would be that, with notes nominally at par, goods would be sold at a higher price.[2] The loyal press, on the whole, approved of the act and denounced the opponents of the notes as traitors and secessionists.

When the depreciated notes began to appear in increasing quantities the business people of the state became uneasy. The attitude of California toward the new paper currency became a disputed matter. Unlike the eastern states, where paper money was a medium of exchange even before the war, in California specie was the only recognized currency. Moreover, the constitution of the state prohibited the creation and circulation of paper money. It provided that:

> The Legislature shall have no power to pass any act granting any charter for banking purposes; but associations may be formed, under general laws, for the deposit of gold and silver, but no such association shall make, issue, or put in circulation any bill, check, ticket, certificate, promissory note, or other paper, or the paper of any bank, to circulate as money.
>
> The Legislature of this State shall prohibit, by law, any person or persons, association, company, or corporation, from exercising the privileges of banking, or creating paper to circulate as money.[3]

As a result of these prohibitions, and the fact that gold was the main staple commodity of the state, Californians had become

---

[2] Quoted in the Sacramento *Union*, July 25, 1862; *Bulletin*, Oct. 8, 1862.

[3] *California Constitution of 1849;* Browne, *Debates*, App., p. VI. These strict measures against paper money were due to the experiences with paper money during the panic of 1837 (Goodwin, *Establishment of State Government in California*, 175, 177–78).

accustomed to a metallic currency and attributed to this stable medium of exchange their prosperity at a time when eastern states suffered from depression. Hence the business community looked with suspicion upon the attempt to introduce an unstable fluctuating paper currency, fearing it would work unfavorably in their commercial transactions at home and abroad. The question arose whether the notes should be received at par, or at their actual value with gold as a standard. It was pointed out that all contracts in California were entered into on a specie basis and it would be impossible to have two separate currencies, varying in their value, and make them both legal tender. It was prophesied that banks would not receive the notes at par on deposit; that merchants would raise their prices high enough to cover the discount on the notes and the result would be speculation and a financial panic. To avoid these evil results the proponents of the metallic currency advocated treating "the treasury notes" in California "as merchandise."[4]

On the other hand, there were many in California who denied that the prosperity of the state was due to the gold currency. They argued that the acceptance of the notes as the currency of the state would enhance the value of real estate and would reduce the rates of interest by increasing the quantity of money in circulation. It was also pointed out that the notes were the only financial means with which the government could suppress the rebellion, hence those who refused to accept the notes at par struck a blow at the credit of the government and were no better than traitors.[5]

Legal tender notes and state taxes.—The question soon arose whether legal tender notes were receivable at par for state, county, and city taxes. The state revenue act provided that "taxes must be paid in legal coin of the United States. A tax

[4] *Alta,* July 30, 31, 1863; *Bulletin,* Jan. 25, June 19, July 25, 26, 28, 1862.

[5] Sacramento *Union,* April 4, 1862; *Bulletin,* July 23, Aug. 2, Sept. 22, Oct. 2, 1862; *Alta,* Aug. 6, 1862.

levied for a special purpose may be paid in such funds as may be directed.'' Many contended that it was the duty of California to receive the notes for taxes because it would be disloyal to refuse to do so upon the mere technicality that the state revenue law provided for the collection of taxes in coin. On the other hand, it was pointed out that the state assessments were made on a specie basis of valuation, hence if the taxes were paid in a currency worth from ten to twenty per cent less than specie, the state revenue would be curtailed considerably.[7]

The question soon reached the state courts. On July 28, 1862, a suit was brought in the twelfth district court by the taxpayer Perry against state collector Washburn to compel the latter to accept United States legal tender notes in payment of the tax due at his office. The court was asked to issue a mandamus directing the collector to receive the notes in payment of the tax and to issue a valid receipt for the taxes. The tax collector's reply was that the state law provided that taxes be collected in coin. The court decided the case in favor of the defendant.

The plaintiff then appealed to the state supreme court. The opinion of the court delivered by Chief Justice Field was that the act of Congress of February 25, 1862, had no reference to state taxes. The act of Congress, the court held, provided that the notes should be a legal tender in payment of all taxes, internal duties, and debts to the United States, but when it:

> . . . . refers to obligations other than those to the United States, it only uses the term ''debts''; the notes it declares shall be ''a legal tender in payment of all *debts*, public and private.'' Taxes are not debts within the meaning of this provision. A debt is a sum of money due by contract, express or implied. A tax is a charge upon persons or property to raise money for public purposes. It is not founded upon contract; it does not establish the relation of debtor and creditor between the tax payer and State.[8]

---

[6] California, *Political Code,* II, 52, section 3888.

[7] *Alta,* July 31, 1862; *Bulletin,* July 23, 1862.

[8] *Perry* v. *Washburn,* 20 California, 350. An act of March 12, 1880, declared Legal Tender Notes to be receivable at par in payment of all taxes due to the state, county, or municipality (California, *Statutes,* 1880, p. 8).

The highest court of the state thus ruled that the state was under no obligation to receive the government notes in payment of state taxes.

The state treasurer and the federal direct tax.—A controversy also arose in connection with the payment of the federal direct tax. In 1861 Congress passed an act levying a direct tax of $20,000,000 to be apportioned among the states of the Union according to their population. The act provided for the assessment, levying, and collecting of the taxes by the agents of the federal government. But any state which assumed the responsibility was to be allowed fifteen per cent discount on all amounts paid into the treasury prior to July 1, 1862, and a discount of ten per cent on the portion paid prior to October 1, 1862.[9]

California agreed to assume the responsibility of assessing and collecting her quota of the tax which amounted to $254,538.11⅔. Out of $70,932.56 collected by September 1, 1862, only $1,570 were in legal tender notes. But the state treasurer converted the gold coin into notes which he had purchased from a brokerage firm at 92⅘ cents on the dollar, and on September 28 he tendered $63,839.36 in notes to the United States Assistant Treasurer Cheesman, as a portion of the state's direct tax quota.[10] Cheesman telegraphed to Secretary Chase asking whether he should consent to accept notes from a state whose constitution, law, and custom recognized only a metallic currency. Secretary Chase's reply was to accept the notes. The state saved by this process of brokerage some $4,486.39.[11]

---

[9] United States, *Statutes at Large,* XII, 296.

[10] *Annual Report* of the State Treasurer for the year 1862. California, *Sen. and Assembly Jours.*, 1862, App., Doc. 2, pp. 23–24.

[11] *Annual Report* of the state treasurer for the year 1862. California *Sen. and Assembly Jours.,* 1862, App., Doc. 2, pp. 23–24; *Bulletin,* Oct. 2, 1862. Since the payment was made on October 8, 1862, Cheesman refused to recognize the claim of California to the ten per cent discount, in spite of the claim of Ashley that the payment was made on September 28, 1862, and that it was no fault of the state of California that Cheesman refused to accept the money. But the U. S. authorities refused to recognize the claim of California, and the amount of $709,326 remained upon the books of the Treasury as a debt against the state of California.

The action of the state treasurer was severely criticized in California as a petty speculation. Governor Stanford demanded that the treasurer explain by what authority gold placed in the federal direct tax fund had been converted into depreciated paper currency and the currency then tendered to the United States Treasurer.[12] But Ashley proceeded to exchange the gold coin remaining in the direct tax for legal tender notes, and tendered to Cheesman in greenbacks $183,060.10, the balance due to the government on account of the direct tax.[13] In a letter to Governor Stanford, Cheesman protested against the action of the state treasurer, claiming that the people had paid the taxes in coin, and the state treasurer who was merely the custodian of it was unauthorized to exchange the gold for the paper.[14] The loyal press condemned the conduct of the state treasurer. The legislature was called upon to take action.[15] A special committee in the assembly condemned Ashley's conduct as "wholly unauthorized by law."[16]

Ashley contended that the law of Congress intended the collection of the tax in government notes. All the other states had paid the tax in notes and if California were to pay in gold she would have contributed more than her quota by so much as gold exceeded the value of the notes in California. The money

---

[12] California, *Sen. Jour.*, 1863, 51–52.

[13] Correspondence in relation to the payment of California's quota of the direct tax (California, *Sen. and Assembly Jours.*, 1863, App., Doc. 15, p. 5).

[14] *Ibid.*, 5–7.

[15] Sacramento *Union*, Jan. 12, 13, 14, 20, 1863; *Bulletin*, Jan. 3, 9, 1863. *Also* the Sierra *Democrat*, Red Bluff *Beacon*, Shasta *Courier*, La Porte *Messenger*, and Nevada *Journal* condemned Ashley's conduct. Ashley was accused of pocketing the differences between the prices actually paid for the paper notes, and the actual selling price of the greenbacks on that day (Sacramento *Union*, Jan. 14, 1863).

[16] *Reports* of the Special Committee of the Assembly (California, *Sen. and Assembly Jours.*, 1863, App., Doc. 16; Sacramento *Union*, April 16, 1863). The Senate was, however, inclined to pass the matter over. To satisfy the consciences of the loyal men, the money saved by this transaction was appropriated to the commendable purpose of aiding the recruiting of officers and men.

saved by this transaction amounting to some $24,260 could be used to pay the creditors of the state, or the legislature could donate this money to the federal government. In that way the federal government would receive the benefit; but not so if the donation were made under the guise of taxation, for then the government would receive the gold in the same nominal value as paper money and would pay it out on the coast to the contractors who were already charging the government high prices.[17]

Now the state had a right to pay the direct tax in legal tender notes. But the strong sentiment against this course indicated that the majority of the people of California were averse to the use of greenbacks for public as well as for individual transactions. The board of supervisors of San Francisco voted to pay the interest on the city bonds in gold, although by paying in notes the city would have saved a large sum of money.[18]

Opposition to the legal tender notes.—The decision of the *Perry* v. *Washburn* case greatly encouraged the proponents of the gold currency. And when the notes continued to depreciate, the mercantile community of California began to cast about for ways and means to maintain a metallic currency. The press was full of editorials and letters discussing the matter.

> As the matter now stands [complained a San Francisco business man] the laboring class and the producers are the ones who suffer most—they who are least able to bear the burden—while the capitalist and the broker are greatly benefitted . . . . Our employes say they cannot receive them at par, for the reason they cannot use them at their boarding houses, butcher's and grocer's. We paid off with them on Saturday, and on Monday, twenty-five out of fifty men refused to go to work, unless we would promise to pay in gold coin. Now, we say something should be done to regulate this matter, and we hope the merchants and business men will call a meeting at an early day, and take such action as their wisdom and patriotism may suggest. For ourselves, we wish to sustain the Government, but would like the burden to fall equally upon all classes.[19]

---

[17] *Annual Report* of the State Treasurer for 1862 (California *Sen. and Assembly Jours.,* 1863, App., Doc. 2, pp. 23–29).

[18] Sacramento *Union,* Oct. 30, 1862.

[19] *Alta,* Sept. 17, 1862.

To protect themselves against loss, commission men and importers adopted the practice of inserting in every contract a clause providing for payment in gold coin or its equivalent.[20] The leading merchants of San Francisco then decided to adopt a circular agreement neither to receive nor to pay out notes at any but market value, taking gold as a standard. It was expected that the merchants of the interior would also sign this agreement. If any one should refuse to pay in gold, his name was to be entered in the black book, and in future dealings he would be compelled to pay for goods in gold in advance of delivery.[21]

The paper men denounced the policy of the San Francisco merchants as disloyal and treasonable. State Attorney General Pixley and Secretary of the Treasury Ashley held that the legal tender act was a war measure and that California must either accept the notes or separate from the government. The policy of the California merchants was stabbing the government's credit and was a new kind of treason.

> Why should not the notes and bonds of the United States of America pass among its own people at par [wrote Pixley]? Yet the merchants and bankers of San Francisco make merchandise of Government bills, refuse them in trade, reject them at their counters, dishonor them and take them at discount or drive them to the broker. The Chamber of Commerce has repudiated them by formal resolution. Yet the merchant pays his Eastern debts in them, remits gold to buy paper, buys in New York with greenbacks. . . . . Yet General Hooker and Col. Matheson, who are fighting our battles, and the five California regiments who are protecting the frontiers of California, or tramping the burning sands of Colorado at $13 per month; and the 9th regiment of Infantry, who garrison our forts; . . . . officers and men are all paid in Legal Tender notes, which when used to sustain themselves, their wives and families, are receivable at 10 per cent discount.[22]

---

[20] *Herald,* Oct. 23, 1862. Quoted in Sacramento *Union,* Oct. 27, 1862.

[21] *Bulletin,* Nov. 10, 1862.

[22] *Bulletin,* Sept. 29, 1862. Commenting upon this article the *Bulletin* said, "Mr. Pixley thinks everybody who refuses to accept Legal Tender Notes is a traitor, except himself and the other state officers who think they are entitled to payment in gold."

Exemption from the Legal Tender Act.—On February 12, 1863, a resolution was introduced in the assembly asking Congress to exempt California from the operation of the legal tender law on the ground that California was a gold-producing country and the state constitution recognized a metallic currency only. The legal tender law was therefore working a hardship on her without any "adequate benefit or advantage to the government of the United States." The proponents of this measure argued that Congress obtained the right to make paper money legal tender from the right of self-preservation, hence by the same power of necessity it could declare that this necessity existed on the Atlantic but not on the Pacific Coast.[23] The opposition questioned the constitutionality of such a measure, for under the Constitution the citizens of each state are entitled to the privileges of citizens of the several states. But were California exempted from the operation of the legal tender act, then her citizens would have to pay more government taxes than the citizens of the other states, where paper money was a legal currency. The resolution was rejected.[24]

The Specific Contract Act.—The scheme to protect themselves against the depreciated paper currency by means of an agreement or exemption having failed, the mercantile community began to look for a new plan. A bill was introduced in the assembly which recognized both specie and notes as lawful money, but it allowed people to enter into a contract in each transaction as to the kind of money in which they would pay their obligations. The court was to enforce such a contract. The champions of the measure argued that under this law a man would simply be held to perform his contract in good faith, whether it provided for payment in specie or in notes. Such an act would restore confidence in business circles as creditors

[23] California, *Assembly Jour.*, 1863, 208; the resolutions are printed in the *Bulletin*, Feb. 13, 1863; *Alta*, Feb. 15, 1863.

[24] California, *Assembly* Jour., 1863, 226–27.

would no longer fear the contingency of being paid with depreciated paper money.[25] The opposition questioned the constitutionality and expediency of the measure. Some held that it was an attempt to nullify an act of Congress. The bill, however, passed both houses with comfortable majorities.[26]

Opposition to the Specific Contract Act.—As time went on the soft currency forces gained strength. In his annual message of 1863, Governor Stanford, who had signed the specific contract bill, contended that the act was questionable from a patriotic as well as from an economic point of view, for by restricting the free circulation of the government's notes California was helping to weaken the effective prosecution of the war against the seceding states. Moreover, the prosperity of California was checked for want of capital, which was waiting at her doors to enter as soon as the state adopted the standard of value of paper money.[27]

Much was said about the high rates of interest in California:

> . . . . Why should money be worth two per cent per month in San Francisco and only seven per cent per annum in New York?
>
> Speak of this to an Eastern capitalist and the reply is "Yes, but my money will not pass there," and no consideration of future profits will avail to induce the immediate sacrifice in exchange. . . . . Importers and moneyed men generally see their present interest in maintaining our exceptional system.
>
> Importing goods has been about on a par with successful stock gambling, ... Of course, a full double profit is seldom made, but it is no less certain that the trader has the principal benefit of the premium on gold, a small share only falling to the consumer.[28]

---

[25] California, *Assembly Jour.*, 1863, 249; Sacramento *Union*, March 18, 1863; *Bulletin*, March 19, 1863.

[26] Sacramento *Union*, March 18, 1863; *Alta*, March 19, 1863; California, *Assembly Jour.*, 1863, 380.

[27] The proponents of a metallic currency criticized Governor Stanford for his stand against the Specific Contract Act. One of the strong defenders of this act was John Alexander Ferris. His opinions on this question were published in the local contemporary papers. *See* his *Financial Economy of the United States Illustrated* . . . . San Francisco, 1867.

[28] Sacramento *Union*, Dec. 19, 1863; California, *Sen. Jour.*, 1863–1864, 37–38.

A bill to repeal the Specific Contract Act was introduced in the senate of 1863–64 by Smith, of Butte, a mining district. The author of the bill contended that the Legal Tender Act was the supreme law of the land, and no state had a right to pass statutes discriminating against the government's notes. "The capitalists, the snug patriots," he said, "reject the notes with which the soldiers who fought the battles were paid."[29] Hartson, who was formerly one of the champions of the Specific Contract Act, was now convinced that the law not only impaired an act of Congress, but also operated for the benefit of bankers only. For the law applied only to contracts made in writing, hence the bankers were protected by it but not the poor man. Outside of San Francisco, he pointed out, debts were liquidated in government notes.[30]

The question was discussed extensively in the press, in the legislature, and at public meetings. The most influential part of the press was in favor of the Specific Contract Act. The hard currency men contended that the law created confidence in business; it was to the advantage of the California farmers to have a favorable bill of exchange in dealing with England and her colonies, the main markets for the California surplus produce. The repeal of the law would throw business into confusion; there would be a gold price and a greenback price for every article.[31] Governor Low pointed out the adverse effects on state finances of a change from gold to paper money.[32]

From the interior came petitions urging the repeal of the Specific Contract Law, while from the mercantile communities of San Francisco, Sacramento, and Marysville were sent remon-

29 Sacramento *Union,* Jan. 15, 1864; *Bulletin,* Jan. 15, 16, 1864.

30 Sacramento *Union,* Jan. 15, 1864.

31 *Bulletin,* Jan. 28, 29, 30, Feb. 6, 1864; *Alta,* Jan. 17, Feb. 7, 1864; Sacramento *Union,* Dec. 16, 24, 1863; Mariposa *Gazette,* Jan. 23, 1864.

32 California, *Sen. and Assembly Jours.,* 1863–1864, App. II, Doc. 8.

strances against the proposed repeal of the law.[33] On February 4, 1864, the manufacturers, mechanics, and workingmen of San Francisco held a mass meeting protesting against the proposed repeal of the Specific Contract Act. Immediately after the resolutions were adopted, United States Assistant Treasurer Cheesman stood up and asked the privilege to speak, but the audience drowned his voice with hisses, groans, and catcalls. Outside the hall Cheesman was jeered at and threatened violence by the mob.[34]

In the legislature San Francisco was denounced as a turbulent place governed by mobs. Cheesman was offered the use of the assembly chamber in order that he might express his views on the currency question. In his address Cheesman argued that the Legal Tender Law had been approved by the California members in Congress; that the government was liberal to California in expending millions of dollars for the army on the coast, and allowing free use of the mines. Hence it was not right to discriminate against the government notes. He said it might eventually result in rebellion.[35]

The advocates of paper currency telegraphed to Secretary Chase asking his opinion about the California Specific Contract Act. The Secretary replied: "I am clearly of opinion that the California gold law is against National policy, and I shall be much gratified to see California declare herself in favor of the

---

[33] A petition in favor of the repeal of the law came also from the soldiers of the United States army (California, *Sen. Jour.*, 1863–1864, 285). The San Francisco Trades' Union sent petitions against the repeal of the law (*Bulletin*, Jan. 30, Feb. 6, 10, 1864).

[34] *Bulletin*, Feb. 5, 1864; *Alta*, Feb. 5, 1864. One of the circulars announcing this meeting reads: "Mechanics and Workingmen to the rescue! A crisis has arrived!" The *Sonora American Flag*, Feb. 11, 1864, a bitter opponent of the Specific Contract Act, claimed that very few of the mechanics attended the meeting, though the rich contractors compelled their employees to attend. The meeting was attended largely by the "rowdies" and disloyalists.

[35] *Bulletin*, Feb. 10, 1864.

currency for the whole people, by its repeal.''[36] The paper currency men felt triumphant, but the hard currency men argued that the ''people of California can think for themselves and will not dance whenever Secretary Chase whistles.''[37] The act was finally defeated by a majority of 24 to 14. ''The announcement of the defeat of the bill,'' said the *Bulletin,* affected the people like a ''sweet sleep after a night of delirium.''

Constitutionality of the act.—The failure of the attempt to repeal the Specific Contract Act did not entirely discourage the ''paper'' men. They were determined to force the question upon public attention again. It was rumored that at the next state convention a resolution would be introduced to denounce the policy of an exclusive gold currency and to urge the governor to call an extra session of the legislature for the purpose of repealing the Specific Contract Act. At the local conventions the currency issue was uppermost.[38]

Again the old arguments in stock were brought up by both sides. The paper men made much of the arguments that the ''shylock law'' was unconstitutional, disloyal, and impracticable; that the hard times were due to the war between the two currencies and the want of capital to develop resources. The hard money men argued that gold was the standard of value among all the commercial people of the world; that paper money drove specie from the market; caused a rise in prices; excited speculation; created luxurious habits; operated disadvantageously on labor and on the farmer; that the Specific Contract Act was not unconstitutional and did not discriminate against the government notes; that it merely gave the people the right to choose between the two kinds of currency, and the fact that no con-

[36] The dispatches are printed in the California, *Assembly Jour.,* 1864, 323; *Sen. Jour.,* 1863–1864, 287; Sacramento *Union,* Feb. 10, 1864; Mariposa *Gazette,* Feb. 13, 1864.

[37] Sacramento *Union,* Feb. 10, 1864; *Bulletin,* Feb. 10, 1864.

[38] *Alta,* Aug. 1, 1864; Sacramento *Union,* July 28, 1864.

tracts of any importance had been made payable in paper money showed that the people desired to retain the gold currency.[39]

To settle the question of the constitutionality of the Specific Contract Act, people began to call for a decision of the state supreme court on this matter. It was not necessary to wait very long. During the July term of 1864, the supreme court decided two important cases involving the currency question. The first case was *Lick* v. *Faulkner,* which involved the constitutionality of the Legal Tender Law. The court sustained the constitutionality of the law as a means to carry on the war.[40] The second case, *Carpentier* v. *Atherton,* which involved the constitutionality of the Specific Contract Law, was of still greater interest to the people of Câlifornia. The facts of the case were these: In a contract made April 2, 1864, it was promised to pay $500, in United States gold coin. When the debt became due, the debtor tendered to his creditor $500 in government notes. The court ordered and adjudged that the defendant should pay his debt in gold coin as specified in the contract. The defendant appealed to the state supreme court. The counsel for the appellant argued against the constitutionality of the Specific Contract Law. He pointed out that the law creating the treasury notes provided that the notes should be a legal tender for all debts not specifically exempted in the act. But the state law provided for payment in a specific kind of money even for debts not excepted under the act of Congress. The effect of the state law was therefor to defeat the object of the law of Congress, hence it was invalid. Counsel for the defendant argued that the power of Congress to issue legal tender notes was not disputed, but there was nothing in the Legal Tender Act to indicate that it was the intention of Congress to substitute a paper for a gold currency. It simply recognized two kinds of lawful money, favoring gold.

---

39 *Annual Report* of the President of the San Francisco Chamber of Commerce, May 10, 1864; *Alta,* Aug. 2, 3, 4, 12, 1864; *Monitor Gazette,* March 4, Dec. 24, 1864.

40 *Lick* v. *Faulkner,* 25 California, 404–34.

The Specific Contract Act merely supplied a "remedy wanting at the common law, but entirely within the *spirit* of equity jurisdiction, in decreeing specific performance."[41]

The court decided that the Specific Contract Act was constitutional, and contracts made payable in a specific kind of money could not be performed in any other form.

> If one agrees generally to pay or deliver to another [the court held] a given number of dollars, he may perform his contract by the payment of the specified sum in any kind of dollars which are recognized as such and made a legal tender for the purpose by the law of the land; for by doing so he fulfils his engagement according to its letter; but if he contracts to pay his debt in a particular kind of money, his obligation cannot be discharged in accordance with his stipulation by payment in a different kind of money; and though by the unaided rules of the common law he could not be compelled to perform specifically that which he had promised, yet, in morals, his obligation to do so is in no degree diminished.[42]

The decision of the court was hailed jubilantly by the hard money men. They now called for the court to decide whether the Specific Contract Law was retroactive, that is, whether it applied to contracts made before the passage of the act. This question, too, the court decided in favor of the hard money men. In *Galland et al.* v. *Lewis et al.* and in *Ottis* v. *Haseltine,* the decision of the court was that "a contract for the payment of a sum of money in United States coin," entered into before the passage of the Specific Contract Act could only be "performed" by the payment of the kind of money specified."

> In all the cases where laws confessedly retrospective have been declared void [the court held] it has been upon the ground that such laws were in conflict with some vested right, secured either by some constitutional guarantee or protected by the principles of universal justice. But when an Act like the one now in question takes a contract as it finds it, and simply enforces a performance of it according to its terms, it is not liable to

[41] *Carpentier* v. *Atherton,* 25 California, 564–67.

[42] *Carpentier* v. *Atherton,* 25 California, 570. The opinion of the court was delivered by Justice Curry with the concurrence of his colleagues. Chief Justice Sanderson did not express any opinion, but since he was the author of the law, it is naturally to be presumed that he was satisfied with the decision.

objection because it may have a retroactive operation by way of relation to past events . . . . The Act of 1863, instead of being opposed to the principles of essential justice, is approved by them all.[43]

Persistency of the "paper men."—The Specific Contract Act, and the several court decisions, had virtually assured a gold currency for California. But the phantom of paper money was still hovering over the state. The paper men continued their steady complaint that the slack times and unemployment were due to the crusade against the nation's currency. As a result of this unfortunate policy, they argued, California was suffering from a financial depression not experienced by the other states. Because of the lack of capital, rates of interest were so high that farms could not be improved, mines could not be worked, and real estate was declining. Were the national currency adopted in California, capital would flow from the old states and men would seek investment, for they would no longer have to suffer a heavy discount on their paper money. Interest rates would then come down thus enabling people to borrow money to develop the natural resources of the state. They complained that the mercantile community of San Francisco was dictating to the entire coast a policy that was of interest only to the wealthy capitalists and merchants, who were making fabulous sums of money by shutting out eastern capital; by purchasing their goods in the east with depreciated greenbacks and selling in California for gold coin, while the business men and consumers of the interior were suffering hardship from this policy. It was pointed out that the business men of the interior were paying the San Francisco merchants with gold coin for goods which they were selling at home for depreciated notes. Hence, what California needed was a circulating medium with which all business throughout the state could be transacted on an equal basis.[44]

---

[43] *Galland et al.* v. *Lewis et al.*, 26 California, 46–50; *Ottis* v. *Haseltine*, 27 California, 80–84.

[44] *Monitor Gazette,* Aug. 5, 26, Oct. 28, Dec. 9, 1865; San Andreas *Register,* June 24, July 15, Oct. 28, 1865.

The national currency men attempted to introduce the question into the political campaigns. In the interior several county conventions passed resolutions favoring the repeal of the Specific Contract Act. To fortify their position they addressed a letter to Secretary of the Treasury McCulloch asking his opinion on the currency question in California, hoping that his views might have some influence on the policy of the state. McCulloch's reply was much to the satisfaction of the paper men. In his letter dated March 28, 1865, he said:

The decision of the Supreme Court of California, that United States notes could not be received for taxes, and the subsequent Act of the Legislature of the State, which seemed like an attempted nullification of the National authority making these notes lawful money, have undoubtedly done much mischief to the State, and not a little to the country generally . . . .

. . . . The Legal Tender acts were war measures; and California could not place herself, as she has done apparently, in opposition to these war measures, without indirectly assailing the national credit, and casting her influence in no small degree on the side of those who, with bloody hands, were attempting the dismemberment of the Union. . . . .

In regard to the wisdom of her policy in adhering to an exclusive metallic currency, as far as California herself is concerned, it may seem to be almost indelicate for me to express an opinion. When, by refusing to recognize the authority of Congress in making United States notes lawful money, she places herself in antagonism to the credit of the Government, every supporter of the Government, no matter where he may reside, has the right to criticize and to condemn her action, but her domestic policy, so far as it affects California alone, is a matter in which the citizens of other States have no direct interest. . . . . California would have been a much richer and more prosperous State if her circulation had been a mixed instead of an exclusively metallic one. . . . .

California needs a well regulated credit system; she needs a paper circulation to quicken enterprize and give impetus to business; she needs a lower rate of interest; she needs to be cured of the mania for an exclusive metallic currency.[45]

---

[45] The letter was published in the Washington *Chronicle* and in the San Francisco *Bulletin* of May 6, 1865. The New York *Post* of April 5 criticized McCulloch's letter, though it regretted that the ''California tribunals should have thought fit to take this course [referring to the decisions of the California Supreme Court on the currency question], for the reason that it occasions one of those unpleasant conflicts of jurisdiction between the State Governments and the Federal which it is important to avoid, and because it is so far an interference with the

While McCulloch's letter was a feather in the cap of the paper men, the hard money men resented the interference of the Secretary of the Treasury in the affairs of the state. They denied that California was languishing for want of a paper currency; they denied that the Specific Contract Law discriminated against the national currency. Not the law but the people discriminated in favor of gold. They denounced the politicians who were clamoring against the Specific Contract Act, while they were silent about the state law requiring the payment of taxes in coin. If it is disloyal to compel debtors to pay in gold, said the *Alta,* it is equally disloyal to compel taxpayers to pay in gold. If members of the legislature wish to favor greenbacks, let them receive greenbacks themselves. "Sauce for the goose must be sauce for the gander."[46]

The San Francisco Chamber of Commerce issued an address to the people of California combating the attempts of the paper men to create jealousy and alienation of feeling among the people of the interior toward the merchants of San Francisco.[47] On August 4, 1865, a mass meeting of workmen of San Francisco was held to protest against the politicians who were scheming to repeal the Specific Contract Act.[48] At the Democratic state convention of 1865, a resolution was adopted unanimously declaring

> that the whole history of California is a triumphant vindication of her state policy of a gold and silver circulating medium; and that any change in this respect would be disastrous in the extreme; that unwritten contracts for work, labor, and services should by law, in all cases, be enforced in gold and silver coin.[49]

The Union state convention adopted no resolution on the currency question, but it defeated by a large majority resolutions for the repeal of the Specific Contract Law, the establishment of a

fixed policy of the Government." Quoted in San Francisco *Bulletin,* May 9, 1865.

[46] *Alta,* July 8, Aug. 4, 15, 19, Sept. 22, Oct. 4, 1865.

[47] *Address of the San Francisco Chamber of Commerce,* Sept. 1865.

[48] *Alta,* Aug. 5, 1865.

[49] Davis, *Political Conventions in California,* 225.

national banking system in California, and the passage of a law providing for the collection of state revenue in government notes.[50]

The decision of the Nevada Supreme Court that the Nevada Specific Contract Act was in conflict with the law of Congress and therefore void,[51] created some excitement in the financial circles of Nevada and California. In Virginia City a meeting of bankers was held and a resolution was unanimously adopted declaring that no credit would be extended to persons who paid their debts, created under the Specific Contract Act, in paper currency. The leading merchants of Virginia City announced that they would continue to transact business on a gold and silver basis, and would blacklist any one who discharged debts with greenbacks.[52] Deploring the pernicious effect of the decision, the Sacramento *Union* pointed out that the merchants of California would be forced to restrict credit in Nevada and conduct business on a cash basis.[53]

Encouraged by the decision of the Nevada Supreme Court, the California paper men again made an effort to have the Specific Contract Act repealed, and a bill to this effect was introduced in the senate. On January 24, 1866, Senator Smith, of Butte, opened the discussion with a long and eloquent speech. He advocated the repeal of the act on the ground of loyalty to the general government and the welfare of the people of California. He asserted that the money-lenders and bankers were arrayed against the people who were commonly opposed to the act.[54] But none of the claims bore any weight with the gold

[50] *Ibid.*, 222.

[51] *Milliken* v. *Sloat*, 1–2 Nevada, 481–511. In a decision of two to one the court declared that "all such laws stand in direct and brazen antagonism to the policy of the nation." The Specific Contract Act of Nevada was passed January 4, 1865.

[52] Sacramento *Union*, Jan. 3, 22, 1866.

[53] Sacramento *Union*, Jan. 3, 22, 1866. A proposition was made to increase the number of judges to overrule the decision.

[54] Sacramento *Union*, Jan. 25, 1866, gives a phonographic report of the debate.

currency men. Chace, of San Francisco, held that the legal tender notes were not lawful money, because with the termination of the War of the Rebellion the exigency requiring the issue of such notes had ceased, and without such an exigency Congress had no power to retain such a law. Johnson, of El Dorado, and Pearce, of Sonora, held that the act of Congress creating the legal tender notes had always been unconstitutional. The bill was defeated, again blasting all hopes of the paper men.[55]

Summary and conclusion.—From these numerous expressions of public opinion it is seen that the majority of the people of California, at least the most influential part of the population which shaped public policy, was in favor of the gold standard, and steadfastly clung to it in spite of bitter opposition at home and advice from Washington.[56] And thus, while in the east gold was quoted at a premium, in California notes were bought

---

[55] Sacramento *Union*, Feb. 14, 16, 1866. In an article of Feb. 17, 1866, D. O. McCarthy, the editor of the San Francisco *American Flag*, asserted that seven senators received the sum of $12,800 each for voting against the repeal of the Specific Contract Act and that $24,000 was distributed in the lobby. A special committee was appointed in the senate to investigate the charge of bribery. McCarthy was summoned to the bar of the senate to answer questions concerning the charge he made, but he refused to answer any questions. He was then adjudged guilty of contempt of the senate and was imprisoned. *See* California, *Sen. and Assembly Jours.*, 1864–1865, App. II, 11. In 1868 a bill was introduced in the assembly to provide for the enforcement of ''verbal or parol contracts'' in gold currency. The sponsors of the bill pointed out the difficulty of making written contracts in certain transactions, with the result that the small merchants, doctors, lawyers, and farmers were frequently paid in depreciated currency. The proposition was voted down partly in fear lest it might endanger the Specific Contract Act to which the new bill was to be an amendment (Sacramento *Union*, March 16, 1868).

[56] In the eastern states the notes circulated at par, but in California notes were considered as merchandise, with gold as a standard; hence while in the east gold was at a premium, in California the notes were at a discount. But the value of the notes in exchange for gold was greater in California than in the east. For instance, when gold was quoted in New York at 143, at which rate the value of the notes was 69½ cents to the dollar, in California notes were accepted at 74 cents to the dollar (*Address of the San Francisco Chamber of Commerce*, Sept., 1865; *Alta*, March 10, 1863). For fluctuations in the price of gold, see the valuable appendixes in Mitchell, *History of Greenbacks.* The policy adopted in California was followed also in Oregon and Nevada.

at a discount. Whether the policy of adhering to a metallic currency, at a time when paper was the national currency, enhanced or retarded the economic development of California is a question open for discussion. It is certain that the prosperity of California during this period was due to a number of causes quite apart from the currency policy. Primarily it was the result of war conditions.[57]

There is much to be said in favor of the arguments on both sides of the controversy. Without the Specific Contract Act it would have been difficult for California to retain her gold currency. And this sound currency undoubtedly helped greatly to stabilize her economic life; for a currency that fluctuates in value is always destructive to commerce, especially in countries remote from the centers where the current value of money is determined. This was the case in California, since the fluctuations of the notes depended upon circumstances in the remote eastern markets, far from the sphere of California's observation.

The paper men were in error when they contended that the gold currency was responsible for the high rates of interest. Rates of interest are always high when the demand for capital is greater than the supply. In new communities where real estate is rapidly rising in value and the demand for capital to develop the national resources is greater than the surplus capital at hand, rates of interest are generally high.

As to the argument of the soft currency men—that the California monetary policy was detrimental to the interests of labor—it is a well established fact that the greatest sufferers from a depreciating currency are the men whose income is derived from salaries or wages. For with the continual deprecia-

[57] The Civil War brought to California a large influx of people many of whom settled there. In the east the war encouraged the establishment of manufacturing industries, and stimulated a considerable import and export trade with Europe and other parts of the world. Some of her export commodities were grain, wool, quicksilver, ores of copper, silver, and gold, and turpentine. The exporting trade for 1864 was estimated at about $10,000,000 in value, exclusive of treasury shipments (*Bulletin*, April 29, 1865).

tion of the currency, prices rise more rapidly than wages and the rise of wages is very seldom commensurate with the rise of the cost of living. Hence it was very much to the interest of the wage-workers in California to retain the gold currency. The trouble, however, was that there were two legal currencies of unequal value. In the absence of a specific contract a debtor could liquidate his obligation by the tender of depreciated treasury notes as well as specie. The big business men were of course well protected by the Specific Contract Act. Even in the absence of such a contract the interior merchant was obliged to pay in gold in order to keep his credit good. But the small business men and the wage-workers disposed of their goods and services usually without a written contract as to the specific kind of money to be paid, with the result that they were frequently forced to accept depreciated legal tender notes at par in full payment.

Undoubtedly the ones who benefited most from this currency policy were the bankers and big merchants, who pocketed handsome profits by buying their goods in the eastern markets with cheap paper money and selling them at home for gold coin. We must not, however, think that the merchants were the only ones who benefited from the difference in value of the two currencies. Comparing the current retail prices in the eastern markets with the San Francisco prices, we see that the consumer also was greatly benefited by this policy.[58]

The next question to be considered is: did the California monetary policy conflict with the national currency policy? In the case of *Lane* v. *Oregon*, decided in 1868, the Supreme Court of the United States held that greenbacks were not legal tender

[58] For instance, at the beginning of 1864, butter was sold in New York at 34½ cents a pound in paper. Adding to this the charges of insurance, freight, drayage, etc., the total cost of butter amounted in greenbacks to 46½ cents a pound. The same quality and quantity of butter was sold in California in gold at 31 cents a pound. See *Bulletin*, Feb. 6, 1864.

for state taxes.[59] In *Bronson* v. *Rodes,* decided by the United States Supreme Court during the same term, the court held that the notes were not legal tender in settlement of a contract specifically calling for payment of gold or silver coin.[60] According to these decisions the several acts of California involving the currency question were constitutional. At the same time it seems plain that the policy of California nullified, to a certain extent, a federal law. To be sure the circulation of the federal notes throughout the state was not actually prohibited. Their use, however, was practically banned by the state laws and public opinion, to the displeasure of the national government. As far as California was concerned, the law giving legal tender quality to treasury notes was of little effect.

---

[59] 7 *Wallace,* 71–81. The facts of the case were these: The legislature of Oregon passed a statute, some time after the issue of the Legal Tender Notes, that the state taxes should be paid in gold and silver coin. In 1864, the treasurer of Lane County tendered to the state treasurer the sum of $5,460.96 as state revenue for Lane County, in United States greenbacks. The state treasurer refused to accept the money. The court decided that the plaintiff was to recover from the defendant the sum claimed in specie. The state supreme court affirmed the judgment The case was brought to the United States Supreme Court. The decision of the court was as follows:

''To the existence of the States, themselves necessary to the existence of the United States, the power of taxation is indispensable. . . . There is nothing in the Constitution which contemplates or authorizes any direct abridgment of this power, by national legislation. . . . If, therefore, the condition of any State, in the judgment of its legislature, requires the collection of taxes in kind, ... or in gold and silver coin, it is not easy to see upon what principle the national legislature can interfere with the exercise, to that end, of this power, original in the States, and never as yet surrendered.''

The conclusion, therefore, was that Congress did not intend, by the general terms of the currency acts, to restrain the states from collecting taxes in coin; and that the action of Congress in making the notes legal tender for debts, ''has no reference to taxes imposed by State authority, but relates only to debts in the ordinary sense of the word, arising out of simple contracts or contracts by specialty, which include judgments and recognizances.''

[60] 7 *Wallace,* 254. The court said: ''Express contracts to pay coined dollars can only be satisfied by the payment of coined dollars. They are not '*debts*' which may be satisfied by the tender of United States notes.'' See also *Deuting* v. *Sears,* 11 Wallace, 879; *Trebilcock* v. *Wilson,* 12 Wallace, 687–700; *Hepburn* v. *Griswold,* 8 Wallace, 603–39; *Legal Tender Cases,* 12 Wallace, 457–681.

RETROSPECT

I have presented in this paper a study of the federal relations of California during her frontier era. In many respects California was a typical frontier community; for the problem of the American frontier was essentially one of civilization and Americanization: establishment of government; removal of obstructing agencies; concerting policies for the disposition and appropriation of natural resources; constructing adequate means of communication and transportation to connect the new communities with the centers of trade, industry, and population. It is a program that necessarily involves the paternalistic national government. Hence in studying the federal relations of California during the period chosen, we incidentally study in general outline the federal relations of the American frontier—of the far west as well as of the trans-Alleghany and trans-Mississippi frontiers. We find in California the characteristic needs and demands of the American frontier; we find the frontier attitude toward the federal government, the tendency to look upon the national government as a paternal institution whose duty it is to assist liberally in the development of the new country, and the tendency to emphasize strongly the rights of the people. In a word, we find the typical self-confident, self-assertive, "dissatisfied frontier."

In many other respects, however, California was unique. Most new communities develop gradually; California sprang at once to full stature. No other community was forced to grapple with so many difficult problems as was California. Only in a few other cases in United States history has civil government been ushered in with so much violent discussion. Louisiana, Missouri, and Illinois also had to face the question of foreign land titles, but nowhere was it so troublesome as in California. On account of her remoteness from the centers of trade and population, the problem of communication and transportation was more serious in California than in many other frontier communities. In some respects even the Indian question was more embarrassing in California than elsewhere. Hence the California frontier served as a laboratory for experimentation. Here the federal government first tried out the policy of concentrating the Indians on small military reservations of land. This policy was later extended to Oregon and Texas. The California mining code spread over the mining region along the Pacific Coast. The California policy of adhering to a metallic currency during the Civil War period was adopted in Oregon and Nevada.

The people in California had an exalted conception of the importance of their state whose gold, they claimed, saved the Atlantic states from bankruptcy. Indeed many a time they boastfully declared that the settlement of Americans in California marked an epoch in world history; that not only was California enriching the whole nation, but she was also destined to revolutionize the economic, social, and political life of the Pacific islands and Asia. These American settlers believed they were performing a great service to the nation when they tore themselves away from their native homes, relatives, and friends to go to the far west to colonize a new land and to establish there American institutions. Hence as a token of appreciation of their valuable services they expected liberal attention from the general government.

The paternalistic federal government was not heedless of the needs and demands of the young community on the Pacific Coast. Indeed it was extremely liberal: it lavished millions of dollars there; it gave to the young state a princely patrimony of some nine or ten millions of acres of good land; it allowed the free exploitation of the mineral lands without asking a dollar of revenue; it paid the heavy "war debts" of the state. Perhaps it was too liberal. But democratic federal governments are usually dilatory, especially when conflicting sectional interests are involved. While California tended to exaggerate her importance and her needs, the strict constructionist southern statesmen underestimated both. They denied that the California gold was enriching the nation more than was the cotton of the south. They claimed that California was exhausting the national treasury. ''We are shamefully neglected by the general government,'' was the usual complaint voiced by the California spokesmen; ''California wants too much'' was the common charge of the southern statesmen. ''Do not talk to us about a want of liberality to California,'' exclaimed Senator Toombs, of Georgia, ''we have expended untold millions of dollars for her to every single dollar that was ever spent on most of the southern states.''

With points of view at such variance, it could naturally be expected that the demands of California would not always be granted—at least not liberally and rapidly enough. This gave rise to complaints, protests, and even hints of secession. Just as in the case of the trans-Alleghany frontier, the people of California turned to dreams of independent existence whenever they believed that their rights were being neglected by the federal government. To be sure the country was more welded in the middle of the nineteenth century than it was when the trans-Alleghany frontier talked of separation. But the Pacific Coast, severed from the central government by a frontier of hostile Indians and by thousands of miles of desert and mountain barriers, was the most isolated of all the American frontier communities.

I have closed my study with the year 1869 because by that time practically all the problems which had caused considerable agitation throughout the early period of the existence of the state had been settled; and especially because the year 1869 witnessed the completion of the transcontinental railroad which bound the Atlantic and Pacific coasts with iron bars. California then lost the feeling of isolation; she ceased to be a mere outpost of civilization and became truly a part and parcel of the American Union. This great event, more than anything else, marks the close of the frontier era of California.

BIBLIOGRAPHY

The material for this study is found principally in the federal documents, the California state publications, and the contemporary California newspapers.

To the first class of source material belong: (1) the Congressional Globe and Appendixes, which contain the debates upon the various measures, resolutions, bills, and other valuable documents not found elsewhere; (2) the Serial Documents, which contain the messages of the Presidents, the annual reports of the Secretaries of War, Interior, Navy, and Treasury, the annual reports of the Postmasters General, and Commissioners of Indian Affairs, and General Land Office, committee reports, memorials, and occasionally the correspondence between the state and federal officials and among the federal officials themselves; (3) the Statutes at Large; (4) the Supreme Court reports.

To the second class of source material belong: (1) Browne's Debates in the Constitutional Convention of California in 1849; (2) the Journals and Appendixes of the California legislature which contain the proceedings of the legislature, reports of committees, messages of the governors, annual reports of the surveyor general, comptroller, treasurer, and superintendent of education; (3) the statutes; (4) the reports of the California supreme court.

The newspapers are valuable for editorial comments, accounts of public meetings, party conventions, and stenographic reports of some of the important debates in the legislature, which are to be found nowhere else. The San Francisco *Alta, Herald, Bulletin,* and the Sacramento *Union* have been used more extensively than any others, chiefly because they had a longer existence and were by far the most prominent papers throughout the state during the period under discussion. The newspaper files examined are preserved in the Bancroft Library and in the State Library at Sacramento.

Poole's *Descriptive Catalogue of Government Publications,* and Hasse's *Index of Economic Material in Documents of the State of California* are valuable guides to the federal and state documents, but they are inadequate for a study of this kind. The best method is to follow carefully the references and cross-references in the indexes of the individual publications, and examine every page of the more important documents. There are of course no indexes to the newspapers. The investigator must examine carefully each page, each column, each item.

A. PRIMARY SOURCES

I. Federal Documents

Congressional Globe and *Appendixes:* Containing the debates, proceedings of Congress, important State papers, and the laws of the United States. 29–40 Congress, Washington, 1847–1868.

Donaldson, Thomas. *The Public Domain. Its history, with statistics . . . .* Washington, 1881. (United States Public Land Commission, 1879–1880.) See Serial Number 1975.

Serial Number

108 18 Cong., 2 Sess., Sen. Ex. Doc. 7.

447 28 Cong.; 1 Sess., House Report 546. (Rhode Island Affairs, 1841–1842.)

497 29 Cong., 2 Sess., House Ex. Doc. 4. (Message and Department reports.)

499 29 Cong., 2 Sess., House Ex. Doc. 19. (Correspondence of military and naval officers and President's Message, Dec. 22, 1846.)

503 30 Cong., 1 Sess., Sen. Ex. Doc. 1. (Message and Department reports.)

507 30 Cong., 1 Sess., Sen. Ex. Doc. 33. (Court Martial of Fremont, 1847–1848.)

509 30 Cong., 1 Sess., Sen. Ex. Doc. 52. (Treaty of United States and Mexico and Proceedings of Senate thereon.)

521 30 Cong., 1 Sess., House Ex. Doc. 70. (New Mexico and California, Correspondence and Message of the President, July 24, 1848.)

537 30 Cong., 2 Sess., House Ex. Doc. 1. (Reports from California. With Message of December 5, 1848.)

550 31 Cong., 1 Sess., Sen. Ex. Doc. 1. (Message of the President, Dec. 3, 1849, and Department reports.)

561 31 Cong., 1 Sess., Sen. Ex. Doc. 52. (Correspondence of General Riley with Message of May 22, 1850.)

565 31 Cong., 1 Sess., Sen. Report 97. (Report of Committee on Post Office and Post Roads on mail service in California, April 4, 1850.)

569 31 Cong., 1 Sess., Sen. Ex. Doc. 1. (Message and Department reports.)

573 31 Cong., 1 Sess., House Ex. Doc. 17. (Message on California and Correspondence, 1850, 975 pp.)

577 31 Cong., 1 Sess., House Ex. Doc. 59. (Thomas B. King, *Report on California*, 1850, 32 pp.)

581 31 Cong., 1 Sess., House Misc., Doc. 44. (California Memorial of 1850.)

587 31 Cong., 2 Sess., Sen. Ex. Doc. 1. (Message and Department reports.)

589 31 Cong., 1 Sess., Sen. Ex. Doc. 18. (W. C. Jones, *Land Titles in California,* 1851.)

595 31 Cong., 2 Sess., House Ex. Doc. 1.

612 32 Cong., 1 Sess., Sen. Ex. Doc. 1. (Reports of the Secretaries of the Navy and Interior.)

614 32 Cong., 1 Sess., Sen. Ex. Doc. 26.

619 32 Cong., 1 Sess., Sen. Ex. Doc. 50. (Mail service for California. Reports of the Secretary of the Navy and Postmaster General, March 23, 1852.)

630 32 Cong., 1 Sess., Sen. Report 14. (Report of Committee on Naval Affairs on navy yard and depot in the bay of San Francisco, Jan. 6, 1852.)

631 32 Cong., 1 Sess., Sen. Report 267. (Report of Committee on Post Office and Post Roads on mail service, June 15, 1852.)

634 32 Cong., 1 Sess., House Ex. Doc. 2. (Indian and Military Affairs in California.)

635 32 Cong., 1 Sess., House Ex. Doc. 2. (Annual Report of Postmaster General, Nov. 29, 1851.)

688 33 Cong., Special Sess., Sen. Ex. Doc. 4. (Report of the Indian agents in California and various Correspondence, 405 pp.)

692 33 Cong., 1 Sess., Sen. Ex. Doc. 1. (Department reports.)

710 33 Cong., 1 Sess., House Ex. Doc. 1. (Message and report of the Secretary of the Interior.)

743 33 Cong., 1 Sess., House Report 168. (Report of the Committee of Ways and Means on civil fund.)

758 33 Cong., 2 Sess,, Sen. Ex. Doc. 78. (*Report of the Explorations and Surveys to ascertain the most practicable and economical route for a transcontinental railroad, 1853–1854.* 12 vols.)

778 33 Cong., 2 Sess., House Ex. Doc. 1 (Reports of the Secretaries of War and Navy, and on the Post Office.)

808 33 Cong., 1 Sess., House Report 1.

811 34 Cong., 1 Sess., Sen Ex. Doc. 1.

824 34 Cong., 1 Sess., Sen. Ex. Doc. 101. (Committee of Vigilance of 1856.)

870 34 Cong., 1 Sess., House Report 274. (Pacific Railroad and Telegraph. Report of the Select Committee, July 24, 1856.)

881 34 Cong., 3 Sess., Sen. Ex. Doc. 43. (Committee of Vigilance of 1856.)

942 35 Cong., 1 Sess., House Ex. Doc. 2. (Message. Reports of the Departments of State and Interior.)

944 35 Cong., 1 Sess., House Ex. Doc. 2. (Reports of the Navy and Interior.)

997 35 Cong., 2 Sess., House Ex. Docs. 1, 2.

1000 35 Cong., 2 Sess., House Ex. Doc. 2.

1025 36 Cong., 1 Sess., Sen. Ex. Doc. 2.

1031 36 Cong., 1 Sess., Sen. Ex. Doc. 26. (Letter of Postmaster General relating to the Butterfield overland route, March 22, 1860.)

1056 36 Cong., 1 Sess., House Doc. 84. (Expenditures on account of private land claims in California. Also Black's Report of May 22, 1860.)

1080 36 Cong., 2 Sess., Sen. Ex. Doc. 1. (Annual Report of Postmaster General Holt, Dec. 1, 1860.)

[1126½] 37 Cong., 2 Sess., House Ex. Doc. 1. (Abridgment of Message and of reports of the Departments, 1861–1862.)

1182 38 Cong., 1 Sess., House Ex. Doc. 1. (Report of the Secretary of the Interior.)

1220 38 Cong., 2 Sess., House Ex. Doc. 1. (Reports of the Department of the Interior and of the Post Office, 1864.)

1240 39 Cong., 1 Sess., Sen. Report 105. (Report of Committee on Mines and Mining on the mineral land bill of 1866.)

1248 39 Cong., 1 Sess., House Ex. Doc. 1.

1254 39 Cong., 1 Sess., House Ex. Doc. 1.

1272 39 Cong., 1 Sess., House Report 66. (Julian's report on the mineral lands, June 5, 1866.)

1289 39 Cong., 2 Sess., House Ex. Doc. 29. (J. R. Browne, *Report on the Mineral Lands in the West of the Rockies*, 1866.)

1326 40 Cong., 2 Sess., House Ex. Doc. 1.

1366 40 Cong., 3 Sess., House Ex. Doc. 1. (Report of the Secretary of the Interior.)

1414 41 Cong., 2 Sess., House Ex. Doc. 1. (Report of the Secretary of the Interior.)

1560 42 Cong., 3 Sess., House Ex. Doc. 1. (Report of the Secretary of the Interior.)

1975 46 Cong., 3 Sess., House Ex. Doc. 47, pt. 4. (Donaldson, *Public Domain*, 1881.)

6222 Report of the Department of the Interior for 1911.

United States. *Statutes at Large and Treaties of the United States of America*, I, II, V, IX–XVII, XXXIV. Boston and Washington, 1845–1907.

United States. *Treaties, Conventions, International Acts, Protocols, and Agreements between the United States of America and Other Powers, 1776–1909.* Compiled by William M. Malloy. Washington, 1910. 2 vols.

United States. *Treaties, 1850–1853. . . . . Message from the President of the United States, Communicating Eighteen Treaties made with Indians in California. . . . . 1851–1852.*

United States. Attorneys General. *Official Opinions,* IX. Washington. 18 vols.

United States. Presidents. *A Compilation of the Messages and Papers of the Presidents, 1789–1897.* By James D. Richardson. Washington, 1899. 10 vols.

United States. War Department. *The War of the Rebellion.* A compilation of the Official Records of the Union and Confederate Armies. Published under the direction of the . . . . Secretary of War. Washington, 1880–1901. 70 vols.

United States Supreme Court. *Reports.*

Fleming et al. v. *Page.* 9 Howard, 1850.

Cross et al. v. *Harrison.* 16 Howard, 1853.

Arguello et al. v. *United States.* 18 Howard, 1855.

United States v. *Johnson.* 1 Wallace, 1863.

United States v. *Moreno.* 1 Wallace, 1863.

United States v. *Yorba.* 1 Wallace, 1863.

Lane County v. *Oregon.* 7 Wallace, 1868.

Reynegan v. *Bolton.* 5 Otto, 1877.

Mining Company v. *Consolidated Mining Company.* XII Otto, 1880.

II. California State Documents

California. Adjutant General's Office. *Record of California Men in the War of the Rebellion, 1861 to 1867.* Revised and compiled by Brig. Gen. Richard H. Orton. . . . . Sacramento, State Office, 1890.

California. Constitutional Convention, 1849. *Report of the Debates in the Convention of California, on the Formation of the State Constitution, in September and October, 1849.* By J. Ross Browne. Washington, 1850.

California. *Political Code,* II. Sacramento, 1872.

California. *Statutes, 1849–1870.* San José, San Francisco, Sacramento, 1850–1870.

California Legislature. *Journals of the Assembly and Senate and Appendices to the Journals.* 1st to 20th sessions. San José, San Francisco, Sacramento, 1850–1874. The *Journals* of the assembly and senate were published separately but bound together for the first and second sessions, 1850, 1851. The *Appendices* were bound with the *Journals,* 1st–5th sessions, 1850–1854. From the 6th to the 12th sessions, 1855–1861, they were published separately. 1863 to date combined.

Speeches on Resolutions upon the State of the Union delivered in the senate and assembly at the twelfth session of the California legislature. 18 speeches. Sacramento, 1861.

California State Library Publications. *History of Political Conventions of California 1849–1892.* By Winfield J. Davis. Sacramento, 1893.

California Supreme Court. *Reports.*

The People v. *Naglee.* 1 California, 1850.

In the matter of Carter Perkins and Robert Perkins. 2 California, 1852.

Hicks v. *Bell.* 3 California, 1853.

Stoakes v. *Barret.* 5 California, 1855.

Billinger v. *Hall.* 7 California, 1857.

In the matter of Archy on habeas corpus. 9 California, 1858.

Doll v. *Meador.* 16 California, 1860.

Perry v. *Washburn.* 20 California, 1862.

Van Valkenburg v. *McCloud.* 21 California, 1863.

Terry v. *Megerle.* 24 California, 1864.

Ottis v. *Haseltine.* 27 California, 1864.

Galland et al. v. *Lewis et al.* 26 California, 1864.

Lich v. *Faulkner.* 25 California, 1864.

Carpentier v. *Atherton.* 25 California, 1864.

III. Newspapers

Alameda Gazette. 1856–1862; 1864–1866.

Grass Valley National. 1861.

Mariposa Gazette. 1863–1865.

Marysville Appeal. 1861.

Merced Morning Transcript. 1862.

Monitor Gazette. 1864–1866.

Monterey Californian. 1846–1847.

Nevada Journal. 1853–1861.

Nevada City Gazette. 1864–1866.

Nevada City Transcript. 1861–1862.

Niles' Register. Baltimore and Philadelphia. 1845–1849.

Placer Herald. 1852–1863.

Placer Times. Established in Sacramento April 28, 1849. Continued as *Daily Placer Times and Transcript* after June 16, 1851. Removed to San Francisco and published there until December 15, 1855.

Sacramento. Democratic State Journal, 1852–1854, 1855–1857; *Democratic Journal,* 1854–1856;

California Statesman. 1854–1855.

State Tribune. 1855–1856.

Sacramento Transcript. 1850–1851.

Sacramento Union. 1851–1869.

San Andreas Register. 1864–1866.

Los Angeles—

Los Angeles Semi-Weekly Southern News.

Los Angeles Star.

San Francisco—

Alta California. 1849–1870.

California Chronicle. 1854–1858.

California Star. 1847–1848.

California Courier. 1850–1852.

Evening Bulletin. 1855–1869.

Herald. 1850–1862.

Journal. 1852–1861.

Pacific News. 1849–1851.

Placer Times and Transcript. 1853–1855.

Whig. 1852.

Wide West. 1857–1858.

San José Tribune. 1861.

San Rafael—

Marin County Journal. 1861–1862.

Shasta Courier. 1864.

Sonoma County Democrat. 1862.

Stockton Argus. 1860–1861.

Stockton Weekly San Joaquin Republican. 1861.

Visalia Delta. 1864.

Visalia Sun. 1860.

IV. Contemporary Works

[Benton, Thomas Hart]. *Thirty Years' View: A History of the Working of the American Government for Thirty Years, from 1820 to 1850. . . . .* New York, 1854–1856. 2 vols.

Bidwell, John. *California, 1841–48.* 1877. MS in Bancroft Library.

Bryant, Edwin. *What I saw in California: Being the Journal of a Tour . . . . across the Continent . . . . and through California . . . . 1846, 1847. . . . .* New York, 1848.

Buchanan, James. The Works of James Buchanan, Comprising his Speeches, State Papers, and Private Correspondence. Collected and edited by John Bassett Moore. Philadelphia and London, 1908–1911. 12 vols.

Burnett, Peter H. *Recollections and Opinions of an Old Pioneer.* New York, 1880.

Contains valuable documents on the question of civil government.

California Miscellany. . . . . See Carmany, John H., and Cyrus W.

California Railroads. *A Collection of Pamphlets on Railroads from the Mississippi to the Pacific.* 10 vols.

Calhoun, John C. *Correspondence,* edited by J. Franklin Jameson. *In* American Historical Association, *Annual Report,* 1899, II. Washington, 1900.

[Carmany, John H., and Cyrus W.] *California Miscellany. Being a Repository of Reports, Pamphlets, etc.* San Francisco, 1860–66. 14 vols.

Coleman, Wm. T. *Vigilance Committee of 1856.* MS in Bancroft Library.

Colton, Rev. Walter. *Three Years in California.* New York, 1850.

Valuable for the early part of the American period.

Crosby, E. O. *Statements of Events of Calif[ornia] from 1851 to 1865.* 1878. MS in Bancroft Library.

Cutts, James Madison. *The Conquest of California and New Mexico. . . . .* Philadelphia, 1847.

Contains important documents.

Dana, Richard Henry. *Two Years Before the Mast.* New York, 1840.

Gives an interesting description of the hide trade.

Davis. *Sixty Years in California. . . . .* San Francisco, 1889.

Dempster, C. J. *Vigilance Committee [1877?].* MS in Bancroft Library.

Dillon, Sidney. "Historic Moment; Driving the Last Spike of the Union Pacific." *Scribner's Magazine,* 1892, No. 12, pp. 253–259.

Farnheim [Thomas Jefferson]. *Early Days of California. . . . .* Philadelphia, 1860.

Field, Stephen J. *Personal Reminiscences of Early Days in California.* . . . . Copyrighted, 1880.

Ferris, John Alexander. *The Financial Economy of the United States Illustrated, and Some of the Causes Which Retarded the Progress of California Demonstrated.* . . . . San Francisco, New York, 1867.

Fitch, George Hamlin. "How California Came into the Union," *Century Magazine,* XL, 775–792 (September, 1890).

Foote, Henry Stuart. *War of the Rebellion . . . . Consisting of Observations Upon the Causes, Course and Consequences of the Late Civil War in the United States.* New York, 1866.

Forbes, Alexander. *California: A History of Upper and Lower California.* . . . . London, 1839.

Frémont, John Charles. *Memoirs of My Life.* . . . . Vol. I. Chicago and New York, 1887.

Greeley, Horace. *The American Conflict: A History of the Great Rebellion in the United States of America, 1860–64.* . . . . Chicago, 1864–1867. 2 vols.

Recollections of a Busy Life. New York, 1868.

Gwin, Wm. M. *Memoirs on History of United States, Mexico, and California.* 1878. MS in Bancroft Library.

An interesting work by an eminent California politician.

Hayes. *Collection, Southern California, Local History, 1860–1863.* Vols. 19, 48, 50.

In Bancroft Library. Newspaper clippings, especially valuable for the rare Los Angeles newspapers.

[Ide, Simeon.] *Bibliographical Sketch of . . . . William B. Ide: With . . . . Account of One of the Largest Emigrating Companies . . . . and . . . . "The Virtual Conquest of California, in June, 1846, by the Bear Flag Party . . . ."* [Claremont, N. H., 1880].

Jefferson, Thomas. *The Writings of Thomas Jefferson.* Library edition. Edited by Andrew A. Lipscomb. Washington, 1903. 20 vols.

Used Vol. XIII.

Julian, George W. *Political Recollections, 1849 to 1872.* Chicago, 1884.

Kelly, George Fox. "Land Frauds of California. Startling Exposures. Government Officials Implicated. . . . . 1864." *In* "Pamphlets on California Lands," II, No. 10.

[Kemble, Edward C.] "The History of California Newspapers." *In* the Sacramento *Union,* December 25, 1858.

King, Thomas Butler. *California: The Wonder of the Age.* . . . . New York, 1850. Reprint of his *Report on California.* (See Serial number 577.)

Larkin, Thomas O. *Documents for the History of California, 1839–1856. Papers of Thomas O. Larkin, Consul of the United States in California before the Conquest.* Presented to the Bancroft Library, 1875.

Used Vols. II, III, IV.

Official Correspondence as United States Consul and Navy Agent, 1844–1849. MS. in Bancroft Library. 2 vols. in one.

Lieber, Francis (compiler). *California Scrap-Book, 1848–1849.*
Newspaper clippings. In the Bancroft Library.

Pamphlets on California Lands. 3 vols.
Vol. I contains some of the opinions of the United States Land Commissioners for California, and miscellaneous matter on the California lands.

Polk, James K. *The Diary of James K. Polk,* edited by Milo Milton Quaife. Chicago, 1910. 4 vols.

Robinson, Charles. *The Kansas Conflict.* New York, 1892.
Contains an interesting account of the Sacramento squatter riots of 1850.

Root, Frank Albert, and Connolley, William Elsey. *The Overland Stage to California. . . . .* Topeka, 1901.

Ryan, William Redmond. *Personal Adventures in Upper and Lower California, in 1848–1849. . . . .* London, 1850. 2 vols.

San Francisco Chamber of Commerce. Address: "Repeal of the Specific Contract Act, 1865."

Sherman, Edwin A. *The Life of the Late Rear Admiral John Drake Sloat. . . . .* Oakland, 1902.

Sherman, William T. *Memoirs. . . . .* New York, 1875. 2 vols.

State Register and Year Book of Facts: for the years 1857, 1859. San Francisco, 1857, 1859.

Stillé, Charles J. *History of the United States Sanitary Commission, being the General Report of the Work during the War of the Rebellion.* Philadelphia, 1866.

Stockton, Robert F. *A Sketch of the Life of Com. Robert F. Stockton, with an Appendix comprising his Correspondence With the Navy Department Respecting his Conquest of California. . . . .* New York, 1856.
Contains important documents.

Stuart, James F. *Land Titles in California.*
Open letter in addition to "Titles to Lands in the State of California." *In* "Pamphlets on California Lands," Nos. 14, 15.

Taylor, Bayard. *Eldorado, or Adventurers in the Path of Empire. . . .* New York, 1850. 2 vols.

Thompson, Wady. *Recollections of Mexico.* New York and London, 1847.

Tuthill, Franklin. *History of California.* San Francisco, 1866.

Webster, Daniel. *The Private Correspondence.* Edited by Fletcher Webster. Boston, 1903. 2 vols.

Wilkes, Charles. *Narrative of the United States Exploring Expeditions During the Years 1838, 1839, 1840, 1841, 1842.* Philadelphia, 1844. 5 vols. and Atlas.

Willey, Rev. Samuel H. "Recollections of General Halleck." *Overland Monthly,* IX, No. 1, July, 1872.

The Transition Period of California, from a Province of Mexico in 1846 to a State of the American Union in 1850. San Francisco, 1901.

Wilson, Henry. *History of the Rise and Fall of the Slave Power in America.* Boston, 1872–1884. 3 vols.

B. SECONDARY MATERIALS

Adams, Edgar H. *Private Gold Coinage in California, 1849–1855.* Brooklyn, New York, 1913.

Bancroft, Hubert Howe. *History of California.* San Francisco, 1884–1890. 7 vols.

Popular Tribunals. San Francisco, 1877. 2 vols.

Burgess, John W. *The Middle Period, 1817–1858.* New York, 1897. ("The American History Series," IV.)

Carter, Charles Frederick. *When Railroads Were New.* New York, 1910.

Chapman, Charles. *A History of California: the Spanish Period.* New York, 1921.

Cleland, Robert Glass. "The Early Sentiment for the Annexation of California: An Account of the Growth of American Interest in California. From 1835 to 1836." Austin [1915]. Reprinted from the *Southwestern Historical Quarterly,* XVIII, Nos. 1, 2, and 3.

Coy, Owen C. *The Settlement and Development of the Humboldt Bay Region.* 1918. MS Thesis (Ph.D.), University of California Library.

Dewey, David Rich. *A Financial History of the United States.* New York, 1918.

Duniway, Clyde A. "Slavery in California After 1848," American Historical Association, *Annual Report,* 1905, I, 243–248.

Earle, John Jewett. *The Sentiment of the People of California With Respect to the Civil War, 1861–1865.* 1904. MS thesis (M.A.), University of California.

Eldredge, Zoeth Skinner. *The Beginnings of San Francisco from . . . . 1774 to . . . . April 15, 1850.* San Francisco, 1912. 2 vols.

Eldredge, Zoeth Skinner (editor). *History of California.* New York, 1915. 5 vols.

Ellison, William Henry. "Indian Policy in California, 1846–1860." In *Mississippi Valley Historical Review,* IX, No. 1 (June, 1922).

The United States Indian Policy in California, 1846–1860. 1918. MS thesis (Ph.D.), University of California Library.

Fankhauser, William C. *A Financial History of California: Public Revenues, Debts, and Expenditures.* Berkeley, 1913. (University of California, *Publications in Economics,* III, No. 2.)

Fite, Emerson David. *The Presidential Campaign of 1860.* New York, 1911.

Garrison, George Pierce. *Westward Extension, 1841–1850.* New York, 1906. ("The American Nation," XVII.)

George, Henry. *Addresses. Our Land and Land Policy, National and State.* No. 7. San Francisco, 1871.

Goodwin, Cardinal. *Establishment of State Government in California, 1846–1850.* New York, 1914.

The Trans-Mississippi West (1803–1853). A History of Its Acquisition and Settlement. New York, 1922.

Hall, Fredric. *The History of San José and Surroundings. . . . .* San Francisco, 1871.

Hill, Joseph John. *American Fur Trade in the Far Southwest.* MS.

Hill, Robert Tudor. *The Public Domain and Democracy. . . . .* New York, 1910. (Columbia University, *Studies in History, Economics and Public Law,* XXXVIII, No. 1.)

Hittell, John Shertzer. *A History of the City of San Francisco and incidentally of the State of California.* San Francisco, 1878.

Hittell, Theodore H. *History of California.* San Francisco, 1885–1897. 4 vols.

Hunt, Rockwell Dennis. *Genesis of California's First Constitution, 1846–1849.* Baltimore, 1895. (John's Hopkins University, *Studies in Historical and Political Science,* XIII, No. 8.)

Legal Status of California, 1846–1849. American Academy of Political and Social Science, *Annals,* XII, 387–408 (November, 1898).

Johnston, Alexander. *American Political History, 1763–1876,* edited and supplemented by James Albert Woodburn. New York, 1912. 2 vols.

Kuykendall, Ralph Simpson. *History of Early California Journalism.* 1918. MS thesis (M.A.), University of California Library.

Lindley, Curtis Holbrook. *A Treatise on the American Law Relating to Mines and Mineral Lands Within the Public Land States and Territories Governing the Acquisition and Enjoyment of Mining Rights in Lands of the Public Domain.* San Francisco, 1903. 2 vols.

McCormac, Eugene Irving. *James K. Polk. A Political Biography.* University of California Press, Berkeley, 1922.

Meigs, William Montgomery. *The Life of John Caldwell Calhoun . . . .* New York, 1917. 2 vols.

The Life of Thomas Hart Benton. Philadelphia and London, 1904.

Mitchell, Wesley C. *History of Greenbacks.* Chicago, 1913.

Morrow, William W. *Spanish and Mexican Private Land Grants.* San Francisco, Los Angeles, 1923. A pamphlet of 27 pages.

Moses, Bernard. *Establishment of Municipal Government in San Francisco.* Baltimore, 1889. (John's Hopkins University, *Studies in Historical and Political Science,* VII, Nos. 2–3.)

"Legal Tender Notes in California," *Quarterly Journal of Economics,* VII (1892–1893), 1–25.

Neff, Andrew L. *Mormon Migration to Utah.* MS thesis (Ph.D.), University of California Library.

Orfield, Matthias N. *Federal Land Grants to the States with Special Reference to Minnesota. . . . . Bulletin* of the University of Minnesota. Minneapolis, 1915.

Paxson, Fredrick Logan. *The Last American Frontier.* New York, 1911.

Rhodes, James Ford. *History of the United States, from the Compromise of 1850, to the Final Restoration of Home Rule at the South in 1877.* New York, London, 1909–1919. 8 vols.

Richman, Irving Berdine. *California under Spain and Mexico, 1535–1847.* Boston, 1911.

Royce, Josiah. *California, from the Conquest in 1846 to the Second Vigilance Committee in San Francisco. . . . .* Boston, 1886 ("American Commonwealths.")

"The Squatter Riot of '50 in Sacramento," *Overland Monthly,* ser. 2, VI, 225–246 (September, 1885).

Sabin, Edwin Legrand. *Building the Pacific Railway; the Construction Story of America's first iron thoroughfare between the Missouri River and California. . . . .* Philadelphia and London, 1919.

Schuckers, J. W. *The Life and Public Services of Salmon Portland Chase.* New York, 1874.

Schurz, Carl. *Life of Henry Clay.* Boston and New York, 1887, 2 vols.

Shinn, Charles Howard. *Mining Camps: A Study in American Frontier Government.* New York, 1885.

Stanwood, Edward. *A History of Presidential Elections.* Ed. 4; Boston and New York, 1892.

Stephenson, George M. *The Political History of the Public Lands from 1840 to 1862. From Pre-emption to Homestead.* Boston, 1917.

Thomas, David Yancey. *A History of Military Government in Newly Acquired Territory of the United States.* New York, 1904. (Columbia University, *Studies in History, Economics, and Public Law,* XX, No. 2.)

Thwaites, Reuben Gold (editor). *Early Western Travels, 1748–1846. A Series of Annotated Reprints of some of the best and rarest contemporary volumes of travel . . . .* Cleveland, 1904–1907. 32 vols. Used Vol. XVIII.

Wagstaff, A. E. (compiler and editor. *Life of David S. Terry . . . . .* San Francisco, 1892.

Wright, Benjamin. *Banking in California.* San Francisco, 1910.

Yale, Gregory. *Legal Titles to Mining Claims and Water Rights in California, under the Mining Law of Congress, of July, 1866.* San Francisco, 1867.

Young, John P. *Journalism in California. Pacific Coast and Exposition Biographies.* San Francisco, 1915

INDEX